BARTH'S THEOLOGY OF INTERPRETATION

Through his single-minded insistence on the priority of the Bible in the life of the church, Karl Barth (1886-1968) decisively shaped the course of twentieth-century Christian theology. Drawing on both familiar texts and recently published archival material, *Barth's Theology of Interpretation* sheds new light on Barth's account of just what it is that scripture gives and requires. In tracing the movement of Barth's earlier thinking about scriptural reading, the book also raises important questions regarding the ways in which Barth can continue to influence contemporary discussions about the theological interpretation of scripture.

Barth Studies

Series Editors

John Webster, Professor of Theology, University of Aberdeen, UK
George Hunsinger, Director of the Center for Barth Studies,
Princeton University, USA
Hans-Anton Drewes, Director of the Karl Barth Archive, Basel, Switzerland

The work of Barth is central to the history of modern western theology and remains a major voice in contemporary constructive theology. His writings have been the subject of intensive scrutiny and re-evaluation over the past two decades, notably on the part of English-language Barth scholars who have often been at the forefront of fresh interpretation and creative appropriation of his theology. Study of Barth, both by graduate students and by established scholars, is a significant enterprise; literature on him and conferences devoted to his work abound; the Karl Barth Archive in Switzerland and the Center for Barth Studies at Princeton give institutional profile to these interests. Barth's work is also considered by many to be a significant resource for the intellectual life of the churches.

Drawing from the wide pool of Barth scholarship, and including translations of Barth's works, this series aims to function as a means by which writing on Barth, of the highest scholarly calibre, can find publication. The series builds upon and furthers the interest in Barth's work in the theological academy and the church.

Barth's Theology of Interpretation

DONALD WOOD
King's College, Aberdeen UK

ASHGATE

Published by
Ashgate Publishing Limited
Gower House
Croft Road
Aldershot
Hampshire GU11 3HR
England

Ashgate Publishing Company
Suite 420
101 Cherry Street
Burlington, VT 05401-4405
USA

Ashgate website: http://www.ashgate.com

British Library Cataloguing in Publication Data
Wood, Donald, 1969-
    Barth's theology of interpretation. - (Barth studies)
    1. Barth, Karl, 1886-1968 2. Bible - Hermeneutics
    I.Title
    220.6'092

Library of Congress Cataloging-in-Publication Data
Wood, Donald, 1969-
    Barth's theology of interpretation / Donald Wood.
        p. cm. -- (Barth studies)
    Includes bibliographical references and index.
    ISBN: 978-0-7546-5457-5 (hardcover) 1. Barth, Karl, 1886-1968. 2. Bible-
    -Hermeneutics. I. Title.

    BS476.W655 2007
    220.6092--dc22

                                                                    2006035622

ISBN: 978-0-7546-5457-5

Printed and bound in Great Britain by MPG Books Ltd, Bodmin, Cornwall.

Contents

Acknowledgements

This book is a slightly revised version of a doctoral thesis submitted to the University of Oxford in 2004. My thanks first to John Webster, who supervised the thesis with characteristic patience, grace, and care. Thanks also to Ray Anderson, Paul Fiddes, Rob Price, Alan Torrance, and John Yocum—all of whom in one capacity or another read and helpfully commented on some aspect of the argument developed here. No doubt each in his own way could wish I had done many things otherwise, and readers are asked—ὃ γέγραφα, γέγραφα—not to charge my errors to their accounts.

Dr. Hans-Anton Drewes of the Karl Barth-Archiv in Basel, Switzerland, kindly provided access to and valuable advice about the archive's collection of unpublished material, and the Karl Barth *Nachlasskomission* granted leave to refer to some of that material here. A portion of the argument developed in Chapter One first appeared in 'Ich sah mit Staunen: Reflections on the Theological Substance of Barth's Early Hermeneutics', *Scottish Journal of Theology* 58 (2005), pp. 184–98. I am grateful to its publishers for permission to set it in a larger context.

Awards from Regent's Park College and the Faculty of Theology at Oxford University helped fund earlier stages of the research. Later, an award from the College of Arts and Social Sciences at the University of Aberdeen underwrote a short research visit to Basel. Less formal, but no less valuable, support was provided by many others. I am especially aware of the unwavering commitment of my parents, whose encouragement at every step sustained this project from beginning to end.

Finally, I am privileged to dedicate this to my wife, Marieke, in gratitude and love.

Abbreviations

B-R	*Karl Barth-Martin Rade: Ein Briefwechsel*
B-Th	*Karl Barth-Eduard Thurneysen: Briefwechsel*
CD	Barth, *Church Dogmatics*
Christliche Dogmatik	Barth, *Die christliche Dogmatik im Entwurf*
ET	English translation
KD	Barth, *Die kirchliche Dogmatik*
PT	Barth, *Die protestantische Theologie im 19. Jahrhundert*
Römerbrief 1919	Barth, *Der Römerbrief (Erste Fassung) 1919*
Römerbrief 1922	Barth, *Der Römerbrief 1922*
UCR I	Barth, *Unterricht in der christlichen Religion. Prolegomena*
UCR II	Barth, *Unterricht in der christlichen Religion. Die Lehre von Gott/Die Lehre vom Menschen 1924/1925*
UCR III	Barth, *Unterricht in der christlichen Religion. Die Lehre von der Versöhnung/Die Lehre von der Erlösung 1925/1926*
WG	Barth, *Das Wort Gottes und die Theologie*

Introduction

'Listen to my last piece of advice: exegesis, exegesis and yet more exegesis! Keep to the Word, to the scripture that has been given to us.'[1] Thus Karl Barth in February 1935, taking leave of his students from the University of Bonn, after he was dismissed from his academic post for showing only qualified support for the National Socialist government.

It is a revealing statement, neatly distilling a set of convictions entirely characteristic of Barth's theology: the radical precedence of God's self-giving and the genuine consequence of meaningful human action; the differentiated identity of God's Word and the scripture it engenders; and the ordered freedom of Christian existence under the Word. More closely, it illuminates a particular vision of Christian theology as a joyful and confident listening to the scriptures in which God wills to be heard and obeyed. For Barth, Christian theology is not finally an exercise in self-justifying intellectual construction nor another instance, more or less effective, of some general cultural reflexivity. It is, rather, as a function of the Christian church, a specific mode of creaturely responsibility, a venture taking shape within a given location and discharging a given duty. The central terms of its self-description are drawn from Christian confession: God, revelation, scripture, church, proclamation. Christian theology serves the church's proclamation of the gospel, and it does so in the first instance by continually drawing the church's attention to scripture's authoritative witness to God's self-revelation in Jesus Christ. Just so it is free—both to recognize the urgency of serious theological work in face of the internal and external troubles that in various forms always press in upon the church, and to rejoice in the recognition that God has relieved the church of the burden of securing its own existence and integrity in the world.

It says something important about the larger trajectory of more recent Christian theology in the West that so many of us still find it so difficult to account for Barth's advice, much less to follow it. That is not to say it has simply gone unheeded: Barth is widely credited with reordering modern discussions about the sources and norms of theological argument; for better or worse, we no longer appeal to the sustaining value of religious experience or to the cultural progression of the gospel as freely as earlier generations. More positively, one of the most remarkable features of current theological discussion is an increasingly widespread

---

[1] Karl Barth, *Das Evangelium in der Gegenwart*, Theologische Existenz heute 25 (München, 1935), p. 17, quoted with a helpful account of the context in Eberhard Busch, *Karl Barth. His life from letters and autobiographical texts*, trans. John Bowden (Philadelphia, 1976), pp. 255–9.

interest in the theological interpretation of scripture among biblical scholars and Christian theologians alike. And this shared interest—which raises a number of fundamental questions about the authority of the scriptural texts, the relationship of the academy to the church, and the constitution of the theological curriculum—in its own way reflects Barth's continuing influence.

Nevertheless it remains true that many of us find Barth's advice at best impracticable and at worst profoundly unsettling. Within the academy, we continue to worry about transgressing the institutional boundaries between theological subdisciplines—and about our competence to meaningfully try. More closely, there are real concerns about the intellectual authenticity and cultural responsibility of the sort of theological deference to scripture Barth seems to be advocating, and a corresponding sense that the real motivations behind and abiding value of his work must surely lie elsewhere.

My own sense is that reading Barth well means, among other things, taking him seriously at just this point. Whatever else we want to say about him, in other words, we need to acknowledge the force of Eduard Thurneysen's well-known judgment that Barth 'is and remains a student and teacher of holy scripture. Whoever would understand him otherwise will not understand him'.[2] Further, I want to suggest, we need to see Barth not only as an astonishingly confident and creative reader of scripture, but as a theologian who thought deeply about what it means to read well the classical texts of the Christian tradition.

This conviction about the scriptural orientation of Barth's thinking comes to expression here in a study of what is generally called 'Barth's hermeneutics'. Reduced to its simplest terms, it is an account of some of the ways in which Barth described the act of scriptural interpretation as a responsibility and privilege of the Christian church. It is not intended as a simple recommendation of Barth's theology of interpretation, nor as a comprehensive critical treatment of the many theological-hermeneutical issues raised in it. Rather, it offers a more straightforwardly analytical account of this material in the hope that readers—whatever decisions they finally make about the integrity and adequacy of Barth's claims—may find such an account an aid to their own constructive work.

This is, in other words, a project of modest proportion and aspiration: I have simply tried to understand something of what Barth had to say about the nature of the scriptural text, the identity of its readers, and the relationship between them. I have done so by tracing certain characteristic themes and patterns of argument through a series of representative texts from the two decades following Barth's first public break with some of his earlier theological convictions. And I have generally concentrated my attention on Barth's more explicitly hermeneutical moments—those places where he takes up directly the question of how we ought to

---

[2] E. Thurneysen, 'Karl Barths Theologie der Frühzeit', in *Antwort. Festschrift Karl Barth* (Zürich, 1956), pp. 831–64 (832).

conceive of the church's interpretative freedoms and responsibilities before holy scripture.

In calling this a study of 'Barth's theology of interpretation', I hope to stress from the start that it is an account of Barth's *theology*. It is an obvious point, but perhaps still important as a reminder that we will do well not to move too quickly past Barth's own irreducibly theological language to more general talk of texts and traditions and conditions of understanding. Accounts of 'Barth's hermeneutics' have sometimes run aground at just this point: By treating the properly doctrinal material in Barth simply as a modulation within a broader hermeneutical discussion, they risk obscuring the real distinctiveness and coherence of Barth's position—as well as the real challenge that his theology of interpretation puts to us. For Barth, terms such as 'church' and 'prayer' and 'forgiveness of sins' matter hermeneutically, not least because they do not fit neatly within standard accounts of readerly competence and privilege. And so I have from time to time highlighted ways in which reading Barth can help us reconsider a whole series of assumptions still widespread in more recent discussions of theological hermeneutics: that holy scripture is simply one more compelling example of an authoritative religious text, the church simply one reading community among others, the proclamation of the gospel one more instance of the actualization of textual meaning, and so on. The problem here is not the use of the term 'hermeneutics' itself, but with its theologically problematic accretions, which often go unrecognized.

On Barth's own account, any such discussion of the church's reading has its own dangers: Like all forms of communal self-reflection, it can easily decline into self-justification. And even the most healthy hermeneutical debate can prove a distraction from the more urgent and fruitful business of actually reading scripture. It was exegesis, and not hermeneutics, to which Barth called his students. But a recognition of 'the logical and material priority of biblical exegesis over hermeneutics'[3] in Barth should not prevent us from recognizing that Barth did have a good deal to say about what scripture is and how it ought to be read, and from reading this material with care.

There are, of course, any number of ways of reading this material in Barth, many of which have been pursued to good effect.[4] My own approach is guided by a sense that Barth's hermeneutical proposals have sometimes suffered from an inattentiveness to their specifically theological character and their function within

---

[3] Paul McGlasson, *Jesus and Judas: Biblical Exegesis in Barth*, American Academy of Religion Academy Series 72 (Atlanta, 1991), p. 2.

[4] Among the most recent full-length studies, see especially Helmut Kirschstein, *Der souveräne Gott und die heilige Schrift. Einführung in die Biblische Hermeneutik Karl Barths* (Aachen, 1998); Richard E. Burnett, *Karl Barth's Theological Exegesis. The Hermeneutical Principles of the Römerbrief Period* (Tübingen, 2001); Benoît Bourgine, *L'Herméneutique Théologique de Karl Barth. Exégèse et dogmatique dans le quatrième volume de la* Kirchliche Dogmatik (Leuven, 2003).

Barth's own work. There is a widespread tendency towards the comparative in the secondary literature (Barth and Schleiermacher, Barth and Gadamer, Barth and the historical-critical method, etc.), a movement which if made too quickly can serve to flatten out the theological contours of Barth's work. However illuminating it may be to place Barth in relation to broader developments in interpretative theory (and not only those with which he was more or less directly involved), I would argue that much of what makes Barth's hermeneutics so interesting can best be brought to light by attending to connections internal to his own work. Concretely: If what initially catches one's attention in reading Barth's hermeneutical reflections is the sheer confidence with which he appeals to specifically Christian doctrines to negotiate issues arising from specifically churchly—but just so genuinely and exemplarily human—reading practices, what keeps one's attention is his actual deployment of these doctrinal resources both in addressing familiar questions and framing new ones. Partly this speaks to Barth's style; he was if nothing else an original thinker, in the sense that many of his ideas strike one as at once entirely fresh and totally characteristic. But it also indicates a direction in which theological hermeneutics can fruitfully engage Barth as it carries out its ongoing work.

The constructive aspect of the following discussion, then, can perhaps be most easily comprehended in the suggestion, not that contemporary theological hermeneutics can or should simply parrot Barth's distinctive voice, but that it can continue to learn from him how central Christian doctrines (of the trinity, the incarnation and resurrection, justification, the church, and so on) can shed new light on the questions of textuality and history, context and meaning, communicative authority and interpretative freedom with which we remain so occupied. In the course of the discussion I have tried to indicate some of the ways in which this may be the case, but as my main interest is in the preliminary work of simply attending to what Barth had to say, I have not tried to work out these implications systematically.

By way of general orientation, a few words about the scope and shape of the argument developed in this book: It limits itself to texts that some readers will consider representative of 'the early Barth'. I am not convinced that such constructs are uniformly helpful—periodization has perhaps become too prominent a feature of some recent Barth scholarship. But I am happy for readers to entertain such qualifications in their own minds as they read what follows. At least it will help avoid some misunderstandings if readers are clear that I have limited the scope of the argument to a set of writings beginning with the 1917 lecture 'The New World in the Bible' and ending with the first volume of the *Church Dogmatics*. How far such a limitation is possible or justified is a question to which only the discussion as a whole can provide an answer. Here we can simply register that whatever initial historical-genetic commitments it involves are fairly minimal, centered on the basic claim that 'The New World' lecture advertises a beginning of sorts, publicly introducing a new understanding of and posture towards the Bible while announcing a substantial shift in Barth's attitude towards his liberal Protestant heritage. The survey of some representative texts from 1917 through 1924 in Chapter One provides further details.

This survey traces, first, the effects of Barth's decision to describe the relationship between the biblical text and its contemporary readers in terms drawn from the Bible itself. By understanding the act of scriptural reading in the light of scriptural accounts of God's free disposition of his servants, Barth is able to speak of the text in active terms, as a creaturely reality taken up as an instrument of God's rule, and to that extent as a text possessing a freedom and authority corresponding to God's own. Barth can also stress that the act of scriptural interpretation has a thoroughly self-involving character determined by the object of interpretation. And he can begin to describe what he perceives to be a basic inattentiveness to the text in standard historical-critical readings of the Bible in specifically theological terms, as a reflex of a desire to distance oneself from the announcement of God's comprehensive rule with which scripture claims its readers.

This understanding of the problematic of scriptural interpretation is then traced through a reading of the first two editions of the commentary on Romans. The condensed and polemically focused hermeneutical statements of the famous prefaces to the commentary are read in view of Barth's exegesis of Romans 4, which (especially in the first edition) is materially and stylistically closely related to 'The New World' lecture. This section explores the hermeneutical significance of Barth's christological understanding of the unity of history, arguing that, for Barth, the Pauline emphasis on the uniqueness and comprehensiveness of God's act in Christ provides the basis on which we can speak of a unity in history that renders the differences between times and cultures as of real but only secondary importance. This is the theological basis of Barth's controversial claim that the task of biblical interpretation involves going beyond a recognition and exploration of the historical and cultural distance between the biblical text and the contemporary interpreter to a responsible restatement of the text's subject matter.

With his first academic appointment, Barth began a series of exegetical, historical, and doctrinal studies leading up to his dogmatics lectures of 1924–25, and the latter half of Chapter One provides a focused overview of some of this material. A reading of Barth's lectures on Calvin, the Reformed confessions, and Schleiermacher highlights the importance of Barth's increasing identification with the Reformed tradition and his growing confidence in deploying the resources of this tradition—especially the Protestant scripture principle—in articulating the hermeneutical instincts outlined in earlier lectures and commentaries. And a high-level introduction to the Göttingen dogmatics lectures stresses the importance of Barth's decision to develop a doctrine of scripture in trinitarian terms.

Chapter Two is dedicated to a reading of Barth's lectures on modern Protestant theology. The historiographical material in these lectures helps illuminate Barth's claim that the hermeneutics he derives from scripture is generally applicable. And the first part of this chapter seeks to demonstrate this point by unpacking Barth's description of the task of writing a history of theology as an act of responsibility, humility, and faith—along the way noting that a stronger ecclesiological emphasis accompanies Barth's continuing stress on the methodological implications of the doctrine of justification. This section also reintroduces the question of Barth's relationship to general trends in nineteenth- and twentieth-century hermeneutical theory, comparing Barth's claims regarding the distinctiveness of *Geschichtswissenschaft* with Dilthey's and Bultmann's. And here, once again, the theological specificity of Barth's claims is highlighted.

A reading of these historical lectures also provides occasion to explore the familiar question of how we might best locate Barth's theology of interpretation vis-à-vis some defining convictions of modern hermeneutical theory. So in the second part of Chapter Two, I take up the suggestion that modern general hermeneutics can be understood as one of the ways in which modernity has sought to contain the social consequences of violent conflict over the interpretation of authoritative texts. And I attempt to show that the significance of Barth's alternative account of the grounds and limits of interpretative pluralism, open dialogue, and hermeneutical self-regulation remain largely unappreciated.

Together, the sketch of Barth's early postliberal development and the exposition of his historiographical commitments provide an orientation to the reading of the prolegomena to the *Church Dogmatics* offered in Chapters Three and Four.

The exposition of this material begins with the straightforward suggestion that Barth's doctrine of the Word of God is best read as an extended restatement of the Protestant scripture principle—one that Barth believed necessary in order to clarify the distinctiveness of his dogmatic project in the face of liberal Protestant and Roman Catholic alternatives, and which he believed required a broad dogmatic context involving an extended development of a trinitarian doctrine of revelation. It then proceeds to address two overlapping sets of issues.

The first involves asking how Barth describes the necessity, character, and limits of the church's interpretative work. On Barth's account, scriptural interpretation is grounded theologically in a description of God's hiddenness in revelation, which opens up time and space for the church to live with and from scripture in the world. The life of the reading church is described above all as a life of obedience, in which the church acts freely and authoritatively under the graciously free and authoritative Word of God in scripture. And the church's recognition of the limits of its interpretative work come to expression in the doctrines of election and scripture and above all in prayer.

The second set of issues has to do with the polemical thrust and ecumenical scope of Barth's prolegomena. Throughout the doctrine of the Word of God, Barth sharply distinguishes his own endorsement of the Protestant scripture principle and the doctrine of revelation it involves from liberal Protestant and Roman Catholic doctrines of being. In order to capture this aspect of Barth's argument, the exposition picks up the standard objection that the scripture principle is self-referentially incoherent and attempts to clarify Barth's response to it. In general terms, I argue that, while Barth recognized the force of the objection, he was able to develop a consistent set of responses to it while pressing the counterclaim that only on the basis of the scripture principle (understood as theological practice—as unswerving loyalty to scripture) is it possible to speak theologically of the church as the obedient community of Jesus Christ.

Two final points: First, I have gratefully referred to and cited the standard English translations of Barth where available. And although the quality of these translations varies, I have generally stayed close to them. But the translations here are finally based on my own reading of the original texts and are my responsibility. Where it seemed the best way to preserve a nuance or resonance, I have simply transcribed the German, either in place of or to supplement the English translation.

Second, most of the English translations cited here pre-date contemporary inclusive language sensibilities. For the most part, I have not tried to rework them. More generally, I have used both masculine and feminine pronouns generically; in neither case is any exclusion implied. Nor is the occasional use of the first-person in restating Barth's argument intended to imply an uncritical acceptance of the claim at issue or to put off those who do not share Barth's theological convictions. It simply seemed the most economical way to underline the point that on Barth's own terms theology cannot be done from the sidelines.

Chapter 1

Discoveries and Developments

This chapter surveys Barth's reflections on biblical interpretation from 1917, when he delivered the Leutwil address on 'Die neue Welt in der Bibel', up through 1924 and the prolegomena of the *Göttingen Dogmatics*. It does not pretend to provide a complete account of the early development of Barth's hermeneutics, still less of his theology as a whole. Rather, it is a survey in which the choice of texts and the mode of their exposition strictly serves the goal of providing an orientation to the theology of interpretation developed in the first volume of the *Church Dogmatics*.

The chronological and material limitations of the survey follow from this aim: Texts that may be of decisive importance in a genetic treatment of Barth's theology as a whole will not be considered here, while other texts not always discussed in works with broader genetic interests feature prominently. Similarly, while I have tried to give some sense of the progression of Barth's thinking, I have generally preferred extended conceptual paraphrase to close circumstantial description of the texts that do pass under review.

But it may be that precisely as a self-consciously partial and tendentious survey the reading developed here can incidentally contribute to the broader debate over Barth's theological development. Within its self-appointed limitations, it can highlight a significant continuity in Barth's theology during this period—namely, Barth's intense engagement with scripture, an engagement that issued both in material theological decisions and in methodological reflections on the interpretation of the Bible. Without pursuing a more comprehensive historical study, it would be too much to say precisely how Barth's reading of scripture relates to the other factors that influenced the development of his thinking during this period. But on the basis of the following exposition one may well suggest that a balanced account of that development must give due consideration to Barth's sustained engagement with the Bible, and further observe that such consideration has not always been extended in treatments of this theme.

That is to say, we need to be aware of what Helmut Kirschstein has called a widespread 'relativization of biblical hermeneutics'—a factoring out of the complex of scriptural appeal and interpretative reflection—in some prominent strands of Barth interpretation. Kirschstein is especially interested in the socialist and historicist readings of Barth most closely associated with F.-W. Marquardt and

Trutz Rendtorff.[1] But we can easily detect a corresponding move in much recent Anglo-American work on the 'postmodern Barth', with its own tendency to decline Barth's theological interests into instances of some more general cultural and philosophical resonance (the candidates range from Weimar expressionism to poststructuralist philosophy).[2] Such attempts to align Barth's theology with more fashionable trends in contemporary intellectual culture can be enormously suggestive, and they have served to generate interest in Barth where it might not otherwise be expected. But one suspects that in much talk of the 'postmodern Barth' the adjective is of far more interest than the noun. In any case, one can sometimes observe in studies with strong comparative interests a certain impatience with some of the particularities of Barth's theology, not least his exegetical determinations and the accounts of scriptural authority that attend them.

That said, the marginalization of the scriptural impulse in Barth may well prove more influential where it is less programmatic. We might think here, for example, of Bruce McCormack's widely regarded 1995 study of Barth's early intellectual development,[3] in which McCormack carefully tracks Barth's movement away from the idealist trajectory of nineteenth-century liberalism towards a nuanced theological realism. The result is a fluent account of Barth's theological maturation, but one in which some important aspects of Barth's own self-definition remain largely unexplored. Others have stressed the need to accord a higher profile to Barth's historical and ethical material from the 1920s, and with them to Barth's discovery and articulation of a distinctively Reformed theology.[4] For our own purposes, it is especially important to observe how scriptural reading and commentary tend to remain peripheral in McCormack's account. Thus, for example, Barth's early sermons are mined for traces of movement in his theological convictions, but there is no real reflection on the significance of the fact that they are *sermons*, finally inexplicable without reference to the particular forms of scriptural engagement they entail. Again, the exegetical lectures from Göttingen and Münster play no significant role; nor do important early lectures such as 'The New World in the Bible' and 'Biblical Questions, Insights, and Vistas'. And, perhaps most obviously, McCormack's reading of Barth's *Römerbrief* seems to suggest that the form of the book is relatively unimportant for an understanding of its intention. Concretely, McCormack fails to address at any

---

[1]   See Kirschstein, *Der souveräne Gott*, pp. 8–23.

[2]   See, among many others, Richard H. Roberts, 'Barth and the Eschatology of Weimar: A Theology on its Way?', in *A Theology on its Way? Essays on Karl Barth* (Edinburgh, 1991), pp. 169–99; Isolde Andrews, *Deconstructing Barth: A Study of the Complementary Methods in Karl Barth and Jacques Derrida* (Frankfurt a/M, 1996); Graham Ward, *Barth, Derrida and the Language of Theology* (Cambridge, 1997).

[3]   Bruce L. McCormack, *Karl Barth's Critically Realistic Dialectical Theology. Its Genesis and Development 1909–1936* (Oxford, 1995).

[4]   See esp. John Webster, 'Barth's earlier theology: some unfinished tasks', in *Barth's Earlier Theology. Four Studies* (London, 2005), pp. 1–14.

length the interpretative questions raised by Barth's claim that his *Römerbrief* was in fact a commentary—a genuine exercise in biblical exegesis.

'The purpose of this book', Barth wrote in his 1932 preface to Hoskyns' English translation of the sixth edition of the *Römerbrief*:

> neither was nor is to delight or to annoy its readers by setting out a New Theology. The purpose was and is to direct them to Holy Scripture, to the Epistle of Paul to the Romans, in order that, whether they be delighted or annoyed, whether they are 'accepted' or 'rejected', they may at least be brought face to face with the subject-matter of the Scriptures.[5]

And much earlier, on reading a draft of Brunner's review of the first edition, the subtitle of which spoke of Barth's theological 'program', Barth responded:

> 'A program?' Is it really? [Paul's] Romans itself certainly isn't. And my book at least doesn't want to be one. But by that you mean to say it is the blueprint of a new theology? Then the story of the suffering of Romans can start afresh.[6]

In the light of these and similar statements from Barth, McCormack's assertion that the first *Römerbrief* was 'the writing of a new theology in the form of a biblical commentary'[7] at least requires quite careful qualification. And much the same could be said of McCormack's survey of the influences on Barth's decision to essentially rewrite the *Römerbrief* for the second edition, a survey that ignores Barth's claim (made in response to Jülicher's critique of the first edition) that a fundamental impetus behind the revision was a more extensive and intensive study of the Pauline letters:

> Some reference must ... be made here to the circumstances which have led to an advance and to a change of front. First, and most important: the continued study of Paul himself. My manner of working has enabled me to deal only with portions of the rest of the Pauline literature, but each fresh piece of work has brought with it new light upon the Epistle to the Romans.[8]

---

[5] Barth, *Romans*, p. x; cf. p. ix: 'My sole aim was to interpret Scripture.'

[6] Barth to Brunner, 18 December 1918, in *Karl Barth–Emil Brunner Briefwechsel 1916–1966*, ed. Eberhard Busch et. al. (Zürich, 2000), p. 40.

[7] McCormack, *Dialectical Theology*, p. 138; cf. p. 182: 'The first edition of *Romans* represented Barth's first major effort at an explication of his new theology.'

[8] See McCormack, *Dialectical Theology*, p. 216–40; cf. *Römerbrief 1922*, p. vii (ET 3), in view of Adolf Jülicher's complaint that 'the other letters of the apostle appear in this commentary on Romans even more seldom than in any other of which I know. But is a Paul really to be understood completely by *one* of his letters, as an Augustine perhaps by the conclusion of his *Confessions*?' ('A Modern Interpreter of Paul', in *The Beginnings of Dialectical Theology*, ed. James M. Robinson, trans. Keith R. Crimm (Richmond, 1968), pp. 72–81 (74)). The effects of McCormack's orientation appear, for example, in his claim (pp.

None of this calls into question the genuine significance of McCormack's achievement. But it may serve to remind us that as we continue to work towards a rounded account of Barth's earlier theology, we need also to view Barth as a reader, and more specifically as a reader of scripture. 'It is no coincidence, but of the most profound *material* necessity, that [the time immediately following Barth's break from liberalism] is a determinedly *exegetical* period, [and that] the first documents of this theological and theological-historical revision are interpretations of *scripture*'.[9] And although our interest here is not simply in tracking Barth's early exegetical work or the ways in which his reading of scripture influenced his developing theology, we will attempt at every point to keep the scriptural orientation of his work in view.

'The New World in the Bible'

'The New World in the Bible' contains Barth's only sustained public reflection on biblical interpretation between the start of the war and the publication of the first *Römerbrief*.[10] This alone is enough to secure its importance for any treatment of Barth's early hermeneutics. But it also serves as a useful point of departure for such a treatment in that it brings to expression several central elements of Barth's larger intellectual and spiritual movement away from liberal Protestantism. And to best grasp the significance of the lecture and to clarify its relationship to the *Römerbrief*, we begin with a slightly closer look at the circumstances of its composition.

The lecture was given as the last in a series of three talks delivered in Eduard Thurneysen's church in Leutwil on 4–6 February 1917.[11] Thurneysen originally

---

231–2) that 'the discovery of Overbeck's posthumously published writings must be seen as the decisive impetus leading to the elaboration of [Barth's] new model of eschatology' in the second *Römerbrief*. But Kirschstein (*Der souveräne Gott*, pp. 91–2) seems more nearly correct in arguing that one must see Barth's work on 1 Corinthians 15—work that had occupied Barth for a year before his discovery of Overbeck—as 'the "key" to a radicalized understanding of Paul' in this text.

[9] Ingrid Spieckermann, *Gotteserkenntnis. Ein Beitrag zur Grundfrage der neuen Theologie Karl Barths* (Munich, 1985), p. 77.

[10] Kirschstein, *Der souveräne Gott*, p. 40.

[11] See *B-Th I*, p. 170, n.1: The lecture was delivered on Tuesday, 6 February 1917 (not, it should be noted, in 'Autumn 1916', as indicated in Karl Barth and Eduard Thurneysen, *Suchet Gott, so werdet ihr leben!* (Bern, 1917)). The lecture was omitted from the second edition of *Suchet Gott* (Munich, 1928) after its inclusion in Karl Barth, *Das Wort Gottes und die Theologie* (Munich, 1924), pp. 18–32, to which subsequent references refer. The standard English translation is still 'The Strange New World Within the Bible', in Karl Barth, *The Word of God and the Word of Man*, trans. Douglas Horton (London, 1928), pp. 28–50.

planned for Emil Brunner to deliver this closing address, but Brunner was uncomfortable with the assigned theme and instead opened the series on Sunday evening with a talk on 'God's Word in the Bible'. Thurneysen wrote to Barth on 17 January outlining the situation and extending the invitation to speak, confirming the date and topic nine days later, on 26 January.[12]

Barth replied that same day, admitting that he had thus far only some few ideas about the lecture and did not yet know how it was going to come together. What ideas he did have came from his ongoing work in Romans, where he had reached Chapter 4 and was struggling with Paul's appropriation of the language of faith, reckoning, and righteousness from the Abraham narrative of Genesis 15.[13]

On one level, the close structural and material relation between the lecture and Barth's comments on Romans 4 in the first *Römerbrief* may be viewed merely as a function of the situation outlined in the correspondence: He had a lecture to give on short notice and a notebook full of exegetical material from which to draw. Therefore he simply wrote up his most recent reflections and presented them in his lecture. No doubt there is much to be said for this view; throughout his career Barth often reused material, though this reuse was rarely mere repetition. But it is also possible to see this relationship in a broader and more significant light.

In the first place, one can argue that Barth's criticisms in the lecture of certain prevailing trends in biblical interpretation arise from his own discovery of the capacity of the Bible to astonish someone who, as a pastor, published theologian, and recipient of a considerable theological education, could be excused for thinking himself familiar with the scriptural texts. That is to say, Barth's hermeneutical questions arose in large part from his own engagement with the Bible itself; to that extent at least, the critical impulse of the lecture is (if largely implicitly) autobiographical. According to Barth's well-known self-assessment, the scriptural engagement that gave rise to these questions began in earnest in the summer of 1916, soon after Thurneysen suggested to Barth that in the light of the problems with the tradition of German liberal Protestantism (so evident since the outbreak of the war) on the one hand, and with religious socialism (as their meeting with Christoph Blumhardt had helped to reveal) on the other, a 'wholly other' theological foundation for preaching and pastoral care was required.[14] At this time Barth had turned in no small desperation to the Bible, especially to Paul's

---

[12] *B-Th I*, pp. 170, 173. Thurneysen's report on the impression made by each lecture in the series can be found in his letter of 20 February 1917 (*B-Th I*, p. 175).

[13] *B-Th I*, p. 174.

[14] See Barth, 'Concluding Unscientific Postscript on Schleiermacher', trans. George Hunsinger, in Karl Barth, *The Theology of Schleiermacher. Lectures at Göttingen, Winter Semester of 1923/24*, ed. Dietrich Ritschl, trans. Geoffrey W. Bromiley (Grand Rapids, 1982), pp. 261–79 (264); cf. Eberhard Busch, *Karl Barth. His life from letters and autobiographical texts*, trans. John Bowden (Philadelphia, 1976) p. 97.

letter to the Romans, searching for a way forward. And what he found there astonished him.

> During the work it was often as though I had caught a breath from afar, from Asia Minor or Corinth, something primaeval, from the ancient East, indefinably sunny, wild, original, that somehow is hidden behind these sentences. Paul—what a man he must have been and what men also those for whom he could so sketch and hint at these pithy sayings in a few muddled fragments!... And then *behind* Paul: what realities those must have been that could excite the man in such a way![15]

And as Barth read this text, as it were, for the first time—at the very least with a new attentiveness and 'joy of discovery'[16]—he also became aware that fundamental questions needed to be raised about mainstream biblical interpretation. Or in Barth's rather more colorful language, continuing the quotation from above: 'What a lot of far-fetched stuff we compile about his remarks, when perhaps ninety-nine percent of their real content escapes us!'

It is at least possible to read 'The New World in the Bible' along the lines Barth here suggests—as a movement from recognition to criticism, from the 'a breath from afar' to 'what a lot of far-fetched stuff'. And one can further argue that it is already the case at this stage that, as Paul McGlasson has claimed regarding the *Church Dogmatics*, 'the [hermeneutical] problems that are handled are generated by the intramural concerns of Barth's theological explication'.[17]

On this reading, this is part of the significance of the structure of the lecture: Barth begins by posing the question, 'What is there within the Bible?' And he immediately sharpens the question by providing a selective—one might say an almost impressionistic—survey of the contents of the Bible. There is, at first glance, apart from the crucial christological concentration of the survey, no obvious significance to Barth's selection of biblical passages or to the manner of their retelling. Certainly one notes with interest various hermeneutical assumptions in his narration; regarding the differentiated unity of the Bible as the 'chorus of prophets and apostles', for example—a move which makes it possible for Barth meaningfully to ask about the contents of the Bible as such. And one might reflect upon the importance of the fact that Barth is speaking here in a church as a pastor, and so may assume the viability of his question in a way that would not necessarily be possible in another institutional context. But these observations, though important in their own right, do not go far towards explaining the coherence of the lecture, specifically how this particular retelling of the contents of the Bible generates the hermeneutical concerns that Barth goes on to address in his remarks. One way of approaching the point at issue is suggested by the inverted commas

---

[15] Barth to Thurneysen, 27 September 1917 (*B-Th I*, p. 236; cf. Busch, *Karl Barth*, pp. 98–9).

[16] *Römerbrief 1919*, p. 4.

[17] Paul McGlasson, *Jesus and Judas: Biblical Exegesis in Barth* (Atlanta, 1991), p. 2.

that mark the terms 'angel of the Lord', 'servants of God', and, above all, 'the Lord' in Barth's narration of selected episodes from the Old Testament.[18] The problematic in these stories is precisely the identity of this God who chooses, calls, and directs his servants apparently without regard for their own willingness, ability, or worthiness to accept this choice and follow this direction. This problematic is only deepened by the observation that the God-directed history of Israel leads to the man Jesus Christ, who speaks with this same 'compelling power' and whose life finds an 'echo' in the church. Whatever else it says, the Bible speaks of *God*, and that is, in a very real sense, the problem. For, Barth implies, as the Bible speaks of the lordship of this God, it enjoys a particular objectivity of its own. It is taken up in God's exercise of his authority. And thus the reader of scripture is confronted by the Bible in an event that corresponds to the divine-human confrontations of which the Bible speaks.

This theological construal of the problematic of biblical interpretation has two immediate effects. First, it allows Barth to speak of the text in active terms. The Bible is not the passive object of interpretative scrutiny, still less the simple product of the act of interpretation. It stands over against the interpreter, giving answers to questions as it wills. If, as Barth says, 'we shall always find in it as much as we seek and no more',[19] that is not because he believes that the text basically is a concretion of the reader's interpretative interests. Rather it is because he thinks the text patient of our inquiry, much as God waited 40 years while Moses was 'living among the sheep, doing penance for an over-hasty act'[20] before he called him and commissioned him and assured him of his continuing presence. And because this patience of the Bible corresponds to the patience of the God of whom it speaks, it similarly moves towards the point at which it speaks, commanding attention for its own message and inviting the reader to respond appropriately: 'There is a spirit in the Bible that allows us to stop awhile and play among secondary things as is our wont—but presently it begins to press us on; and however we may object that we are only weak, imperfect, and most average folk, it presses us on to the main thing, whether we will or no.'[21] Patience, unlike vulnerability, is an inherently teleological notion. In its own time, the Bible authoritatively announces the existence of 'a new world, the world of God'.[22] The existence of the new world does not depend upon the possibilities inherent in this world; it is genuinely new, at once limiting the old world and superseding that limitation. Correspondingly, 'the holy scriptures', which announce to us this new world of God, 'will interpret themselves in spite of all our human limitations'.[23]

---

[18] Barth, 'Die neue Welt', pp. 18–19 (ET 29–30).

[19] Barth, 'Die neue Welt', p. 20 (ET 32).

[20] Barth, 'Die neue Welt', p. 18 (ET 28).

[21] Barth, 'Die neue Welt', p. 22 (ET 34).

[22] Barth, 'Die neue Welt', p. 21 (ET 34).

[23] Barth, 'Die neue Welt', p. 22 (ET 34).

This activity of the Bible—and this is the second point to be noted—evokes a very specific response from the reader. The Bible, Barth claims, judges us as we read it, giving us first the answers we deserve by giving to us what we seek in it and no more, and then by giving us the one answer that we do not and could never deserve—'the last highest answer' which is the new world of God. And this act of scripture in bringing us before God makes biblical interpretation a venture of the most serious sort. In announcing the coming of the new world of God, the Bible issues a summons for the reader to acknowledge this world and take her place in it. This is why Barth can say that 'we read the Bible rightly … when we read it in faith'; that is, when we accept the invitation issued by the Bible as an 'expression of *grace*', in so doing recognizing our unworthiness and looking beyond it to the summons of God.[24]

Though it is not thoroughly developed here, we can quickly recognize this as a comprehensively theological assessment of the identity of the reader of scripture and her relationship to the text. But it is important to note that as a theological assessment, it at once overlaps and is distinct from other, more familiar hermeneutical models. To take an obvious example, Barth clearly thinks interpretation is fundamentally self-involving; there is no room here for a hermeneutic in which maintaining a judicious distance from the text is regarded as a necessary condition for responsible interpretation. That said, his interest is not in promoting a general theory of personal knowledge as opposed to one that prizes detached objective knowledge. He is, rather, interested in how a sinful, unworthy reader may approach this text as it speaks of this God, or, perhaps better, as this God speaks through this text. The parallel situation, as Barth sees it, is Moses' encounter with God in the burning bush.[25]

One must keep this theological specificity in mind when evaluating Barth's criticisms of historical, moral, and religious readings of the Bible. Each critique begins with a point of agreement: There is, no doubt, history, morality, and religion in the Bible. But those who read the Bible fundamentally as a historical, ethical, or religious text will, if they attend to what this text actually says, quickly find it unsatisfactory. The Bible does not answer the historian's questions about why the history it records happened as it did; or, rather, it answers these questions in a way that the historian *qua* historian cannot meaningfully assimilate, by speaking of God as the Lord—the active subject—of this history. Similarly, on a close inspection the Bible offers remarkably little moral guidance for 'the good, efficient, industrious, publicly educated, average citizen of Switzerland'.[26] And while the Bible does contain direction for the religious life, fundamentally 'it is not the right human thoughts about God which form the contents of the Bible, but the right

---

[24] Barth, 'Die neue Welt', p. 22 (ET 34).
[25] Cf. Barth, 'Die neue Welt', p. 20 (ET 32).
[26] Barth, 'Die neue Welt', p. 24 (ET 38).

divine thoughts about humanity'.[27] Each of these flawed hermeneutical strategies—and this is where the peculiarly theological nature of the critique comes to the fore—are not simply instances of problematic political and institutional arrangements, though Barth does not deny that they are such. They represent, more deeply, the culpable refusal to listen in scripture to the command and invitation of the God who brings about a new world in the midst of the old. According to Barth, 'the Bible, if we read it carefully, makes straight for the point where one must decide to accept or to reject the sovereignty of God. This is the new world within the Bible.... One can only believe—can only hold the ground whither he has been led. Or not believe. There is no third way'.[28] The attempts to read the Bible merely historically, morally, or religiously are attempts to manufacture such a third way, attempts to 'seek our way out' of this situation in which we are placed as readers by the Bible. And as such they are, in reality, instances of unbelief.

Barth's conviction that the new world of God is not continuous with the old world and thus that it could not be appropriated as part of a larger cultural project provided him with a critical tool of scope and power. 'The New World' lecture is early evidence of this: Barth is able to construct a fundamental critique of a range of hermeneutical strategies by exposing them as commonly implicated in unbelief and just so critically inattentive to the text. There are, of course, real dangers here. Appeals to transcendence often serve to sanctify the worst forms of cultural criticism, and 'Die neue Welt' could be read a case in point. On this reading, Barth's language of the new world of God is merely utopian: Barth is adopting an unassailable conceptual standpoint from which he can deconstruct prevailing religious practices and theological assumptions—as it were overlooking the old world and unsettling its inhabitants with dispatches from abroad.

The reading offered here is more positive, suggesting that Barth's pathology of the modern church and its scriptural reading tends towards genuine theological affirmation. It also makes an important claim about the relationship between this lecture and Barth's later, more developed reflections on scriptural reading. The point is perhaps most easily made by asking, in view of Barth's later work, what is missing from this lecture.

In the first place, the lecture lacks any extended appeal to the scriptural and traditional doctrinal resources that could help order Barth's claims regarding the new world of God and its relationship to the old world of merely human possibilities, and which would simultaneously help avoid the appearance of special pleading. Barth's self-involving language and self-deprecating humor (as when he says of Jesus, 'His words cause alarm, for he speaks with authority and not as we theologians'[29]) go some way towards defusing the criticism that his picture of bourgeois culture generally and liberal Protestant theology in particular is

---

[27] Barth, 'Die neue Welt', p. 28 (ET 43).

[28] Barth, 'Die neue Welt', p. 26 (ET 41).

[29] Barth, 'Die neue Welt', p. 19 (ET 30).

tendentious and self-serving. But this rhetorical strategy cannot bear much weight without properly theological support. What is required, in short, is a fuller account of the identity of the God who requires and enables us to speak of and for him in and against the world, so that we cannot rest content merely reflecting on the conditions of our historical consciousness, moral deliberation, and religious experience. 'The New Word in the Bible' is an enormously suggestive first step towards such an account: Here we find Barth reflecting on the fact that the Bible records the history of a choosing, commissioning God and the people who are chosen and commissioned to speak and act as his servants. And we find him stressing the distance between those who so speak and so act in faith and those, including himself, who can at best 'stammer, hint at, and make promises about' the new world in the Bible because of their unbelief.[30] Crucially, we find him appealing to prayer as a genuine human possibility—'Lord I believe; help thou mine unbelief'—and speaking of God as the one who is to be known and named as Father, Son, and Spirit. But Barth does not develop these points in relation to the hermeneutical questions he has posed in any significant detail. This development begins in earnest when Barth takes up his academic appointment at Göttingen and is especially evident in his dogmatics lectures there and, above all, in the *Church Dogmatics*. That is to say, the rough sketch of scriptural reading in 'The New World' lecture and Barth's confident restatement of the scripture principle within a trinitarian doctrine of revelation in the first volume of the *Church Dogmatics* are two points on a single theological trajectory.

Much the same could be said with reference to Barth's statements about the history of modern biblical interpretation. For example, Barth traces modern attempts to read the Bible as a 'sourcebook for godly living' back to an inversion of revelation and religion characteristic of Schleiermacher. And he claims 'our grandfathers, after all, were right … when they would not allow facts to be turned upside down for them'.[31] Again, Barth claims that modern historicist approaches to scripture represent an extended failure to recognize that the Bible, while containing history, is not fundamentally a book that yields its message to historical-critical inquiry: 'Some men have felt compelled to seek grounds and explanations where there were none, and what has resulted from that procedure is a history in itself— an unhappy history into which I will not enter at this time.'[32] Both claims are entirely characteristic of Barth, and both are entirely undeveloped here. But both open up lines of historical-theological enquiry which Barth hints at more forcefully in the famous *Römerbrief* prefaces and which begins to develop at length in the historical and dogmatic lectures in Göttingen.

Again, these two points are not raised as criticisms of this lecture (which is, after all, a programmatic speech that does not pretend to comprehensiveness) so

---

[30] Barth, 'Die neue Welt', p. 31 (ET 48).
[31] Barth, 'Die neue Welt', p. 28 (ET 44).
[32] Barth, 'Die neue Welt', pp. 23–4 (ET 36).

much as observations about the way this first important public statement on biblical interpretation opens up to Barth's later reflections on the doctrinal and historical location of scriptural reading. Amidst the very real changes in emphasis and style over the two decades that separate the delivery of this lecture and the publication of *Church Dogmatics* I/2, we can discern real continuities, not least in the fact that the hermeneutical questions that Barth attempts to address arise from his desire to reflect upon the relationship of reader and text in terms suggested by scripture itself.

The Romans Commentary

> I remember exactly what I felt when in 1920 I opened [Barth's] Epistle to the Romans which had recently been published... [T]he author poured dogmatics over the epistle. It was a dogmatic that was strange to us. But that was not the worst; why should not someone write an uncommon dogmatic. Possibly this one did the fundamental conception of the epistle more justice than any other dogmatics. But that it claimed to be a commentary, that it occasionally took the liberty of giving a translation that the text did not permit, that ideas were interpreted into the text which the Apostle could not possibly have had in this context, that over and over again the book claimed to be an exposition of the epistle, whereas it was really only the author's own dogmatic concept—all this was offensive. That was against everything we had been brought up to. I read twenty pages, I read forty pages, I read sixty pages—but after that I shut the book, resolved never to open it again.[33]

Barth's commentary on Paul's letter to the church in Rome is on any reckoning a classic of twentieth-century theology. The publication of the first edition in 1919 is widely seen as a turning point in the history of modern Protestant thought, signaling 'the dawn of a new epoch'[34]—a transition away from nineteenth-century theologies of culture towards a theology of crisis that finds perhaps its most famous expression in the second, largely rewritten edition of Barth's *Römerbrief*. In both editions, the book also proved enormously controversial, in part for its material content—'it was a dogmatic that was strange to us'—but especially for its claim that it is a serious restatement of Paul's gospel, a genuine exegesis of Paul's letter to the Romans.[35] In short, the reception of the book was and is often

---

[33] O. Dibelius, 'Karl Barth: a Birthday Tribute', *The Listener*, 17 May 1956, pp. 639–40.

[34] The phrase is from Jörg Lauster, *Prinzip und Methode. Die Transformation des protestantischen Schriftprinzips durch die historische Kritik von Schleiermacher bis zur Gegenwart* (Tübingen, 2004), p. 258. Note Lauster himself thinks such imagery misleading; Barth is, on his account, much more a product of the nineteenth century than is often recognized.

[35] On the early hermeneutical debates generated by the *Römerbrief*, see Burnett, *Karl Barth's Theological Exegesis*; more generally on its reception, Cornelius van der Kooi,

dominated by hermeneutical questions provoked by the distinctiveness of Barth's approach to the text vis-à-vis standard modes of historical-critical exegesis. Thus to Otto Dibelius, reflecting on his first reading of the book in a tribute written on the occasion of Barth's seventieth birthday, the book was 'offensive' above all because it 'claimed to be an exposition of the epistle' when it clearly was nothing more than free, if worthy, theologizing.

From the perspective of later generations, the book certainly justifies its early reputation: In both editions, it is a difficult and provocative text. And naturally it has given rise to a wide-ranging secondary literature, in which questions about the relationship between the two editions (and so about the continuity of Barth's developing theology) occupy center stage. The two editions are in many ways very different indeed: The tone of the second is more urgent, its descriptions of the relationship between God and the world more vividly oppositional. But for our purposes, an analysis of these differences and of the developmental questions that attend them can recede into the background. Rather, while discussing each edition in turn, we will assume a very real continuity of intention between the two editions, and focus more closely on the hermeneutical claims pressed in the methodological prefaces to the book, trying to clarify, if not resolve, the questions they raise.

The *1919* Römerbrief

We have seen in 'The New World in the Bible' Barth presenting his initial reflections on the objectivity of scripture and suggesting in passing that this objectivity has not been respected by modern historical, moral, and psychological readings of the text. A number of themes familiar from 'The New World' recur in Barth's foreword to the first edition of the *Römerbrief*: Interpretation is a self-involving act, so that understanding Romans means taking 'a positive, active position alongside Paul instead of one of the passive detachment of an observer'.[36] Again, the text is patient of our preliminary inquiries, so that Barth can say 'the Letter to the Romans itself is also waiting'.[37] But the particular burden of this first *Romans* foreword is to situate Barth's own interpretative concerns vis-à-vis historical-critical readings of the text.

> Paul spoke to his contemporaries as a child of his age. But much more important than this truth is the other, that he speaks as a prophet and apostle of the Kingdom of God to all men in all ages. The differences between then and now, there and here, must be considered. But the differences have *no* significance for what really matters. The historical-critical method of biblical research has its place; it points to a preparation for

---

'Karl Barths zweiter Römerbrief und seine Wirkungen', in *Karl Barth in Deutschland* (1921–1935), ed. M. Beintker, C. Link, and M. Trowitsch (Zürich, 2005), pp. 57–75.

[36] *Römerbrief 1919*, p. 3.

[37] *Römerbrief 1919*, p. 3.

understanding that is never superfluous. But if I had to choose between it and the old doctrine of inspiration, I would resolutely choose the latter. It has a greater, deeper, more important place because it points directly to the task of understanding, without which all preparation is worthless. I am happy that I do not have to choose between the two. But all my attention has been directed towards seeing through the historical into the spirit of the Bible, which is the eternal Spirit.[38]

This obviously is a condensed and contentious statement—quite deliberately so, when one compares the preface as it was published to the several much longer and in many ways more revealing rough drafts Barth wrote immediately after finishing the commentary.[39] But taken at face value several of its most important claims are clear enough. Barth agrees with the concern of historical-critical exegesis to recognize the historical distance between Paul and the contemporary interpreter, but he refuses to accept that the recognition of such distance precludes the recognition of an even more fundamental unity binding the modern reader to the ancient writer. Or, put another way, historical-critical interpretation orients its investigation towards the recognition and characterization of the difference between the context in which Paul thought and wrote and the contexts in which he is later read. And while Barth is happy to accept that historical distance does involve contextual difference, and that this difference may legitimately be parsed in any number of ways, he insists it is a difference circumscribed by a more fundamental similarity. The language of the kingdom of God and the eternal Spirit serves to ground his point theologically: Because the kingdom of God stands over against every actual or ideal culture, the differences between cultures must be viewed as merely relative; the fundamental distinction between God and humanity involves the affirmation of a fundamental human solidarity (that is to say, Barth's famous tautology 'God is God' has an anthropological counterpoint: 'and humanity is humanity'). Therefore, Paul, 'as a prophet and apostle of the Kingdom of God' necessarily bears a message that applies 'to all men in all ages'. Similarly, if the eternal Spirit stands over against history (which is not to say that it is unrelated to history, but only that it cannot be assimilated into or made a predicate of history), then the nearer or farther historical distances that are bound up with cultural differences are to be viewed as relative distances within one history. Therefore a serious conversation between the wisdom of the past and that of the present is possible and, indeed, inevitable when those in the present begin to grapple with the genuinely serious questions of life. For these really serious questions arise continually in history, and those who seek answers to them here and now find themselves in the company of those who did so in the past. The implicit critique is that the posture of the historical critic—what Barth calls 'the passive detachment of an observer'—signals a failure to recognize this solidarity

---

[38] *Römerbrief 1919*, p. 3.

[39] See *Römerbrief 1919*, pp. 581–602; see the English translations in Burnett, *Barth's Theological Exegesis*, pp. 277–92.

and so a failure to understand the author of the text as one who was dealing with precisely these serious questions. Historical-critical exegesis rests content with the description of distance and difference. In contrast, Barth describes the goal of biblical interpretation—'the task of understanding' that goes beyond the preparatory work of historical-critical investigation—as 'seeing *through* the historical into the spirit of the Bible, which is the eternal Spirit'.

In seeking to understand more fully the basis and force of these hermeneutical statements regarding the validity but definite limitation of historical-critical interpretation, we return to Barth's claim that his reaction (or, as he would soon say, 'rage'[40]) against modern liberal Protestant theology and its hermeneutical commitments was a reflex of his reading of scripture. As we observed in reading 'The New World', the recognition of this movement from exegesis to hermeneutical reflection and critique allows us to see that Barth's hermeneutical proposals possess a theological specificity that prevents them from being understood in abstraction from their exegetical concomitants. So here we will attempt to unpack Barth's programmatic prefatory remarks about the unity of history, the self-involving character of serious historical inquiry, and the failure of historical-critical biblical studies at just this point by turning to the body of the commentary itself—specifically to Barth's treatment of Romans 4.1–8.[41]

Barth's reading of Romans 4 comprises four sections, each of which analyzes a set of concepts that at once speak to the theme of the chapter (and, more widely, of the book as a whole) and to the contemporary theological culture against which Barth is reacting. Thus the first section, 'God and the Hero' (4.1–8) explores Paul's

---

[40] See Barth's letter to Paul Wernle of 24 October 1919 (*Römerbrief 1919*, p. 638–46 (639)), in which Barth responded to Wernle's charge that he showed an unjustifiable contempt for late-nineteenth-century attempts to articulate a theology of the kingdom of God and the Spirit: '"Contempt" is not the right word for what I feel towards the "theology of the [18]90s." If you had said "rage", you would have come closer to the mark.' Barth's evolving attitude towards what he perceives as the indifference of liberal theology to Paul's basic concerns—initial puzzlement giving way to anger—is reflected in the difference in tone between the first and second editions of *Romans*.

[41] In one sense, then, we are simply attempting to relate Barth's hermeneutics to his exegesis. But it should be noted that this is not the same project as that undertaken by, *inter alia*, McGlasson, *Jesus and Judas*; Mary Kathleen Cunningham, *What is Theological Exegesis? Interpretation and Use of Scripture in Barth's Doctrine of Election* (Valley Forge, 1995); and John E. Colwell, 'Perspectives on Judas: Barth's Implicit Hermeneutic', in *Interpreting the Bible. Historical and theological studies in honour of David F. Wright*, ed. A.N.S. Lane (Leicester, 1997), pp. 163–79—viz., the attempt to deduce through a close reading of selected exegetical passages the interpretative assumptions, aims, and methods that inform Barth's exegesis, and in some cases to compare these with his explicit hermeneutical pronouncements. It is simply an attempt to bring out the fact that an emphasis on the theological specificity of Barth's hermeneutics follows from a recognition of Barth's insistence that the Bible speaks for itself.

reading of the Abraham narrative of Genesis 15 in conversation with the modern interest in outstanding figures of religious and cultural history characteristic of 'die Persönlichkeitskultur und das Seelenchristentum'.[42] The concepts treated in the following sections—'Faith and Religion' (4.9–12), 'Righteousness and Morality' (4.13–22), and 'History' (4.23–5)—as well as the mode of argumentation Barth employs in analyzing them, are familiar from 'The New World in the Bible'. But here the analysis is more detailed, and the connection between Barth's exegesis and his hermeneutical claims is clearer.

Barth introduces his exegesis of 4.1–8 by picking up the claim made in the previous chapters that the revelation of God in Christ at a single point in history illumines all history, allowing it to be seen as a coherent if inwardly differentiated whole whose movement and meaning is determined by God. 'While the work of God becomes apparent in Christ, it also reveals itself as the hidden unity of all history. The light of the day of God shines forward and backward.'[43] History as such is, therefore, a relational—and specifically a christological—concept, its unity established by the appearance of the kingdom of God in Christ. Correspondingly:

> historical individuals are a unified whole [*eine solidarische Einheit*], a family in one and the same house. They are, admittedly, gradated and differentiated as forerunners, contemporaries, and descendants of the Messiah, according to their special relationship to the great course of prophecy, fulfillment, and completion. But (what is more important than this variation!) they are bound together through their commonality—that in the Messiah the kingdom of God has come near them.[44]

In his freedom, God has come near in Christ. And in so doing, through this single event in time, he has bound all humans at all times to himself and just so to each other. In other words, the unity of history and of all people in history is a claim ingredient in the Christian gospel. 'We *can* take part in Christ, and therefore we can also understand history.'[45] And if the solidarity of all humanity and the unity of history is grounded christologically, it also follows that it is to be explicated soteriologically. All history is the history of God's *saving* work, the history of his patience with and creative renewal of *sinful* humanity.

The problematic in Romans 4.1–8 is whether Abraham, the 'Gottgeliebten und Glaubensmann der Vorzeit', is excepted; whether he stands as a dominant figure of religious history before Christ in a fundamentally different situation than do those who come after Christ. Undoubtedly, Barth admits, the Bible nowhere prevents us from recognizing that Abraham is in fact a figure from another time and place; it is both a proper description of religious history and a proper theological claim to call Abraham 'our forefather according to the flesh'. The Bible 'never denies that

---

[42] *Römerbrief 1919*, p. 117.
[43] *Römerbrief 1919*, p. 106.
[44] *Römerbrief 1919*, p. 106.
[45] *Römerbrief 1919*, p. 144.

"historical" developments and shifts have *also* taken place; it *also* offers material for *Religionsgeschichte*.[46] But the historical significance of Abraham as an outstanding religious personality is not the theme of the biblical account. Rather, the central concept of the biblical account of Abraham is *Erklärung*—his faith was *reckoned* to him righteousness, a reckoning that is 'God's free, sovereign, new act—as free, sovereign, and new as the divine "Let there be!" on the first day of creation'.[47]

> And just this free, effective memory of God that fructifies in the faith of Abraham distinguishes this faith from all immanent, historical, and psychological conditions which can be praised as 'significant' in him or others. Otherwise Abraham *was* indeed 'significant' in his 'works', as hero, as self-sufficient man, as a man head and shoulders above the rest.[48] But if the Bible would see his greatness in *that*, his faith would not be based on a divine 'reckoning'. The Bible would then speak (in tones we know only too well from almost any biography) of a righteousness won, conquered—as wages earned or booty triumphantly carried away. God appears then not as the Creator and Lord, but as the obliged party and debtor of the 'significant' man, as one inwardly bound to the productions of various individuals, indeed dependent upon them as the chief referee and prize-distributor. Now this indeed is how the individualistic idealists would have it. But in any case the Bible does not speak in this sense, does not speak of earnings and wages, but places all the weight on the creative 'reckoning' of God. It knows only *one* greatness, that of the coming kingship of God, and a greatness of *Abraham's* only insofar as *he* also, *he* already, has been allowed to stand under this divine lordship. That is why it does not portray Abraham as 'worker' (although he was that!), but as 'the one who did not work'; not as hero (although he was that!), but as a member of sinning, suffering humanity; not as 'the friend of God' and 'wonderful soul' (although he was that!) but simply as a believer, as one for whom God is too strong. And therefore it records Abraham's righteousness exclusively as the work of grace, as the free event of a divine creative thought, and God himself as the one who in his own unfettered power puts the wicked one right and calls a new world into being out of nothing.[49]

So precisely as a 'member of sinning and suffering humanity' Abraham stands in the same situation as we do, and we stand alongside him.[50] From this

---

[46] *Römerbrief 1919*, p. 107.

[47] *Römerbrief 1919*, p. 113.

[48] Literally, 'als Mensch, der alles Volk um Haupteslänge überragte', an allusion to 1 Sam. 10.23.

[49] *Römerbrief 1919*, p. 113–14.

[50] It is worth noting the relative lack of language about the church in Barth's account at this point. Hermeneutically, this sets him at some remove from those theologies which describe the contemporaneity of the biblical text largely in terms of the church's reading strategy, perhaps grounding a specifically churchly reading of the text by appealing to 'the authority of interpretative communities' (on which see Stanley Fish, *Is There a Text in This Class?* (Cambridge, MA and London, 1980)) or similar notions. For Barth, the reader of scripture is not contemporary with Abraham because, for example, he belongs to a

soteriological and christological construal of the unity of history and humanity—which is itself a reflex of the recognition of the comprehensiveness of God's act in Christ—it is a short step to Barth's hermeneutical claim that any attempt to view Abraham merely historically represents a *willful* failure to understand the text, a failure born out of the reader's desire to exempt himself along with Abraham from the humanity bound together in sin by the judgment of God in Christ.

> Instead of reckoning with *God* over against humanity, he *reckons* with God in the name of humanity. That is the presupposition under which he looks at *Geschichte* and writes *Historie*. He searches for the real or supposed high points of history so that by means of the great and small heroes which he finds there he might protect himself against the realism of the curse and salvation and against the universalism of judgment and grace as they arise from the invasion of revelation. For now there is only the question whether the Bible, whose contents he also refers to, shares this presupposition or whether precisely in the Bible the heroes of the past are not portrayed in the light of the divine new creation in Christ.[51]

From all this it is clear that Barth's reaction against historical-critical interpretation has less to do with exegetical mechanics than it does with substantive spiritual-theological questions regarding the freedom of God in his dealings with his creation, the inescapability of God's act in Christ, and so on.[52] And both Barth's positions on these questions and his willingness to deploy the language of sinful rebellion against those who take up a fundamentally different theological standpoint (language from which, importantly, he does not exempt

---

community which 'see[s] past and present and future linked by a "this is that" and "then is now" vision, a trope of mystical identity binding the story now to the story then, and the story then and now to God's future yet to come' (James McClendon, *Doctrine: Systematic Theology, Volume II* (Nashville, 1994), p. 45; more generally on McClendon's 'baptist vision', see his *Ethics: Systematic Theology, Volume I* (Nashville, 1986), pp. 31–4; and Nancey Murphy, 'Textual Relativism, Philosophy of Language, and the baptist Vision', in *Theology without Foundations: Religious Practice and the Future of Theological Truth*, ed. Stanley Hauerwas, Nancey Murphy, and Mark Nation (Nashville, 1994), pp. 245–70).

[51] *Römerbrief 1919*, p. 108; cf. p. 109: If Abraham is indeed justified by his works, 'then one may find what one seeks in history: the legitimation of the individual self-consciousness over against God.' But the question remains whether in the Bible's portrayal of history one really does find 'a riddling with holes of the general rule' set down in Romans 3.20: 'aus dem vom Gesetz gemeinten Handeln keine Gerechtigkeit kommt für Alles, was Fleisch heißt'.

[52] On a larger scale, see the slightly more qualified claim of Hans Frei, 'The Doctrine of Revelation in the Thought of Karl Barth, 1909–1922' (unpublished doctoral thesis, Yale University, 1956), pp. 125–6: 'Barth's enduring concern during the period after the break with Liberalism was not simply that of method—although it was this also, and often primarily—but that of finding *the clue* to proper theological method, a proper understanding of the relation of God to man within a proper *doctrine of God*.'

himself) correspond to his basic conviction that he has in fact heard the apostle Paul speak to these questions and that Paul can so speak again. For Barth, Paul does in fact announce that God has shut us all up in sin so that he might show mercy to us all; therefore understanding Paul means seeing that distinctions in time and place are merely secondary; seeing that we are, through a divine act over which we have no control, placed in a specific situation which we cannot escape; and seeing, therefore, that we cannot truly distance ourselves from Paul, but must take up a position alongside him in the recognition of the realism and universalism of God's act in Christ. When Barth complains of the 'cold-bloodedness' of modern historical enquiry and sharply distinguishes between the historical-critical method and the doctrine of inspiration, this is the underlying theological concern.

On the other hand, Barth does not feel compelled simply to choose between this spiritual-theological construal of scriptural interpretation and the historical-critical method. And this practical interpretative freedom again corresponds to Barth's christological view of history. History, as established and revealed in Christ, is complex. This is the case in two complementary senses. First, because the unity of history is established by the revelation of God in Christ at one specific point in time, history comprises the times of prophecy, fulfillment, and completion. But as Barth's reading of Romans 4.1–8 makes clear, these stages in history cohere: they are all parts of one history, so that Abraham too can only hope in the coming of the kingdom of God in Christ. Second, the invasion of history by revelation, and so the justification of the individual and the world, is a *hidden* act of divine judgment. For both these reasons, faith must, as it were, see stereoscopically.[53] Abraham is both sinner and justified; both an ancient figure of more or less historical significance and one in whose descendants all the nations of the earth will be blessed, one whose God is not the God of the dead but of the living; both our forefather according to the flesh and our contemporary in faith. The historical distinctions and public characteristics with which historical-critical exegesis has to do are not to be overlooked by a theological exegesis precisely because human beings are justified by grace through faith—*simul justus et peccator*.

The 1922 Römerbrief

The preface to the 1922 *Römerbrief* is in one sense simply an extended account of Barth's motives in revising the book so heavily for its second edition.[54] And here

---

[53] Cf. Barth's citation in the preface to the third edition (*Römerbrief 1922*, pp. xxiii (ET 19–20)) of Calvin's remark on Hebrews 11.1: 'Faith is ... the evidence of things not seen. But evidence means that things emerge into appearance, and is applicable only to what appears to our senses. In the realm of faith the two apparent opposites—evidence and things not seen—struggle with one another and are united. It is precisely the hidden things, inaccessible to our sensible perception, that are displayed by the Spirit of God.'

[54] *Römerbrief 1922*, esp. pp. vii–viii (ET 3–4).

as elsewhere, much of the secondary literature revolves around the question of whether Barth's description of these motives can be taken at face value. Once again, we will largely pass by this question, and simply continue to draw out some of the theological commitments involved in Barth's hermeneutical claims. And once again we will illustrate the issues under consideration by looking at the preface in the light of Barth's exegetical moves in the first verses of Romans 4.

We can begin by noting the changes in the outline of this chapter in the second edition. Barth titles the chapter 'The Voice of History', emending the first edition's 'The Voice of the Bible'. And the significantly different section headings and slightly different division of the text signal a move away from the typology of moral, religious, and historical approaches to the text that informed the structure of both 'The New World in the Bible' and the first *Römerbrief*. Here the chapter proceeds as follows: 'Faith is Miracle' (3.31–4.8); Faith is Beginning (4.9–12); Faith is Creation (4.13–17a); and 'Concerning the Value of History' (4.17b–25).

That said, the substance of the argument which we identified as so hermeneutically significant in the first *Römerbrief* is clearly recognizable in the second. Specifically, the unity of history is established theologically. The world 'is one whole, embraced and borne by the mercy of God'.[55] This pronouncement of the universal mercy of God 'is the content of the gospel (1.1, 16), proclaimed in fear and trembling, but under the pressure of an inescapable necessity'.[56] The righteousness of God that grounds the existence of the world 'is particularly visible when the world stands under judgment, under the No',[57] and Barth can claim that 'genuine fellowship is grounded ... upon what people lack. We recognize we are brothers when we recognize we are sinners'.[58] But 'we can no longer hear the No under which we stand apart from the divine Yes from which it proceeds'.[59]

God's righteousness is revealed 'through his faithfulness in Jesus Christ'. The faithfulness of God is that divine persistence by virtue of which he again and again provides, at many scattered points in history, possibilities, opportunities, and witnesses to the knowledge of his righteousness. Jesus of Nazareth is the one among these many other points in which they can all be perceived in their coherent meaning as a line, as the true central theme of history [*der eigentliche rote Faden der Geschichte*]. Christ is the content of this perception: the righteousness of God himself.[60]

The recognition of the unity of humanity is, again, inseparable from the recognition, on the one hand, of the sheer difference of God and humanity (and therefore the unity of all people in their distinction from God), and, on the other

---

[55] *Römerbrief 1922*, p. 107 (ET 132).
[56] *Römerbrief 1922*, p. 69 (ET 94).
[57] *Römerbrief 1922*, p. 70 (ET 95).
[58] *Römerbrief 1922*, p. 75 (ET 101).
[59] *Römerbrief 1922*, p. 69 (ET 94–5).
[60] *Römerbrief 1922*, p. 70 (ET 96).

hand, the genuine uniqueness of each individual person. All this is visible in Jesus as he appears to faith, as one accepts the verdict of the one, true God. 'Only our faith makes sense of history.'[61]

> The coordinates of eternal truth are set in Jesus, on the one hand holding together individual human beings, who normally move away from one another, and on the other hand holding apart human beings and God, who normally want to merge into one another. God is known and honored and loved in the light of this crisis. And in both cases what the usual religious language of separation and association really intends is restored in Jesus. The farthest *separation between God and humanity* is their real unity. Because time and eternity, human righteousness and the righteousness of God, here and beyond, are unambiguously torn apart in Jesus, in him they are also comprehended in God, just as unambiguously united. All 'law', all human being and having and doing, the whole course of this world and its inevitability, are an indication, a parable, a possibility, an expectation—and to this extent always also a lack, an inadequacy, a void, a yearning. But as this is recognized as such there shines above it the faithfulness of God, who acquits as he condemns, gives life as he kills, who says Yes when nothing but his 'No' is to be heard. In Jesus, God is *known* to be the *unknown* God. But this crisis also reveals the closest *association between human beings*—and with it nothing other than the real peculiarity, the real historical and personal particularity, the real *advantage* (3.1) of every individual person. The special possibilities of each individual are not destroyed but are realized in relation to their real content: the impossible. The personality of each individual is not excluded but is grounded through the great disquiet of the 'not yet' and the 'no longer'. The universal claim of faith is precisely the creative word that calls the individual out of the chaos of isolation.[62]

The problematic of Romans 4.1–8 is, again, whether the story of Abraham supports or undermines the claim of the comprehensiveness (or, in language more characteristic of the second *Römerbrief*, the 'complete otherness'[63]) of God's act in Christ. Or, put otherwise, whether the story of Abraham is merely negated by the gospel or is in fact revealed as truly significant as it bears witness to the resurrection of Christ.

> We choose as the paradigm for the thesis that faith is the meaning of the law as remote and classic a figure from the sphere of the law as possible. One cannot say we have made our task easier by this selection, for the historical location of Abraham's life is so wholly different from ours that we cannot take our place beside him on the same historical and psychological plane. If the revelation of God in Jesus simply dissolves the

---

[61] Stephen H. Webb, *Re-Figuring Theology. The Rhetoric of Karl Barth* (Albany, 1991), p. 77. One would perhaps do better to say faith *receives* the sense in history; while Webb can rightly say 'the unity of history is understood only through an interpretive act', we must be clear that for Barth such acts are not constitutive of that unity, which is grounded in the ways and works of God and which faith can only acknowledge as given.

[62] *Römerbrief 1922*, pp. 88–9 (ET 114).

[63] See, e.g., *Römerbrief 1922*, p. 90 (ET 115).

law and does not fulfill it; if it is merely some innovation or reaction in the series of phenomena that constitute the biblical (or extrabiblical) history of religion and not the transcendent meaning and substance of that entire history; if it is no more than a time next to other times, a history next to other histories, a religion among other religions, then its merely relative and incidental and particular character ought to become apparent when contrasted with so remote a time, history, and religion as Abraham's.... And also, when it is contrasted with his classical stature, his undoubted importance, caliber, and worth—our forefather according to the flesh who is the best of all in the world of flesh—a mere relative negation, sublimation, and dissolution of human being and having and doing, a mere phantom resurrection, a merely skeptical criticism, a mere fleshly opposition, its emptiness and questionableness will become evident to all.... Jesus would not be the Christ if figures like Abraham, Jeremiah, Socrates, Grünewald, Luther, Kierkegaard, Dostoevsky remained historically distant and were not rather in him understood in their essential unity, contemporaneity, and solidarity; if their positions were merely dissolved by the negation he proclaimed and were not at the same time established.... Jesus proves to be the Christ in this: that his light is none other than the light of the Old Testament and of the whole history of religion and of truth, the miracle of Christmas to which the whole *Adventswelt* of nature and history, creatures seen and unseen, looks as for the fulfillment of its waiting.[64]

And, again, the desire to see Abraham otherwise than in Christ, otherwise than as one justified only by faith, proceeds from a desire to exempt oneself from the judgment of God on all humanity.

If we were to find that God does in fact declare the visible 'works' of Abraham to be righteous, we should be faced by human being and having and doing, which, since they are already justified, clearly require no future justification, and that thus in direct contradiction to what we have already established [in 3.20, 27–31] is no longer exposed to the divine disturbing and questioning of the whole course of human life. The voice of history then proclaims Abraham's fame; it points him out as a 'significant man', a hero and personality. Then at this point, in Abraham's 'works', the righteousness of God becomes identical with human righteousness. And if at this point, why not at many others? The crisis of all humanity is then no longer unavoidable; the way through death to life is no longer inexorably necessary, nor the paradox of faith encountered in Jesus. Were there even at only one point in history a divine-humanity or human-divinity, that as such was directly visible and who was permitted to 'boast' in humanity (why would he not, if he really was that?)—then there would obviously be another, easier road to God than the way of death set before us in Jesus. And who would not prefer to choose this easier way?[65]

In the preface to the second *Römerbrief*, Barth characterizes the difference between 'understanding' and what passes for understanding and explanation in historical-critical inquiry in various ways—as a lack of hermeneutical self-

---

[64] *Römerbrief 1922*, p. 92–3 (ET 117–18).
[65] *Römerbrief 1922*, pp. 93–4 (ET 118).

awareness ('I cannot helping asking what *Verstehen* and *Erklaren* really mean, [and] whether Lietzmann, for example, has ever seriously put this question to himself'[66]); a 'lack of any tenacious determination to understand and interpret', so that 'the whole procedure assuredly achieves no more than a point of departure for genuine exegesis';[67] an ecclesiologically irresponsible investment in the politics of academic interpretation ('Do they not see that their students' future in the church truly represents not merely a practical question but a question of the highest material concern?'[68]). But in the light of the commentary proper, we can see all these specific polemics bound to an overarching indictment—that of a self-assertion of modern interests over Paul's, a literary and hermeneutical failure that reflects an attempt to escape the comprehensiveness of Paul's gospel.

On this reading, the *Romans* prefaces are not finally to be read as independent hermeneutical statements; rather, they are more immediately introductions to this particular commentary, and so introductions to a concrete theological description of the context in which biblical reading is to take place, and a corresponding description of that reading as a spiritual and ethical act. That this specific theological description gives rise to a generally applicable hermeneutic[69] is at one level simply another reflection of the comprehensiveness of the theological claims Barth finds in Romans. For while it is true that Barth embraces what one might call a general hermeneutic of trust,[70] the basic optimism and patience with authors and texts that are the ethical concomitants of such a hermeneutic are grounded by Barth in peculiarly theological ways: most immediately by his (rather sparse) appeal to the doctrine of inspiration,[71] but also, as we have seen, in his language of human solidarity in sin and in the forgiveness of sins.

---

[66] *Römerbrief 1922*, p. xii (ET 8–9).

[67] *Römerbrief 1922*, p. xi (ET 8). Whether this determination gives way sooner (Wernle) or later (Bultmann), whether it gives way to 'the cultured conscience of modern Protestantism' or to orthodoxy is of strictly secondary importance for Barth (see pp. xi, xv, xiv–xxii (ET 8, 11–12, 16–19)).

[68] *Römerbrief 1922*, p. xii (ET 9).

[69] 'I have, moreover, no desire to conceal the fact that my "biblicist" method—whose formula simply pronounces "consider well!" [*Besinn dich!*]—would apply also to the study of Lao-Tse and of Goethe, if it were my job to interpret Lao-Tse or Goethe; and on the other hand that I would have trouble applying it to some other biblical texts. The whole notion of "biblicism"—if it can be proven against me—may be taken to mean just this: that I have presupposed the Bible to be a good book, and that it is worthwhile taking its thoughts at least as seriously as one's own' (*Römerbrief 1922*, pp. xv–xvi (12)).

[70] See the discussion in Burnett, *Barth's Theological Exegesis*, pp. 192–8.

[71] The fact that Barth apparently had Calvin's doctrine of inspiration in mind here, and that Barth explicated Calvin's doctrine in largely ethical terms—as a call to adopt a fundamentally receptive (if also active and fairly flexible) posture towards scripture—does not undermine the fact that he does still appeal to the *doctrine* of inspiration, despite the fact that this appeal was predictably widely misunderstood. See further Barth, *Die Theologie*

Of course Barth was not alone in construing the ethical obligations placed upon a reader of historical texts, including the Bible, in biblical or theological terms. Jülicher, for example, when urging upon Barth the abiding importance of the nineteenth-century scientific exegetes, speaks of the duty to love one's neighbor as oneself, and asks how one who 'in holy egoism thinks only of his own problems and chides the dead, who can no longer answer him' can expect that a historical artifact such as the letter to the Romans should become alive to him.[72] The peculiarity of Barth's position is his characteristic movement from the specific claim that God speaks to sinners in the Bible to more general considerations regarding the importance of patient engagement with the tradition and contemporary theology as well as other texts past and present. At the decisive junctures, Barth characteristically refers to the forgiveness of sins and to prayer, arguing that in the gracious event in which God speaks through human agents, he at once finds a hearing for his own word and thereby establishes in history the hope that humans can in fact understand one another. This hermeneutical movement, in which a basic interpretative posture can be read off the miraculous encounter with God which is coincident with God's speaking and the forgiveness of sins, is largely undeveloped in the second *Römerbrief*. But Barth's later, more clear (and more self-consciously Reformed) exposition can properly be read as a development of, not a radical departure from, the theology of revelation in *Romans*.

> God stands before the human soul as 'either-or'; there is thus a human acceptance or rejection, affirmation or denial, waking or sleeping, apprehension or misapprehension vis-à-vis God. But ... as certainly as humanity has no organ by which to perceive the miracle, as certainly as all human experience and understanding stop precisely where— in God—it begins, there is for us always only the rejection, denial, sleeping-through, and misapprehension of God, the not-seeing of the invisible and the not-comprehending of what is incomprehensible. In so far as on the human side experience and understanding come to an affirmation and understanding of God, so far as our mental activity receives its direction and determination from God, taking the form of faith, the impossible, the miracle, the paradox has occurred.[73]

Again, because faith recognizes God's unique greatness—that in his own free initiative God reckons his creatures righteous—'it can calmly and with a certain sad humor rejoice in all genuine human greatness, in all confident belief, in all

---

Calvins 1922, ed. Hans Scholl (Zürich, 1993), pp. 522–3; ET *The Theology of John Calvin*, trans. Geoffrey W. Bromiley (Grand Rapids, 1995), p. 391. Barth provides a much more nuanced, and less ethicist, account of Calvin's doctrine of inspiration in Barth, *Die Theologie der reformierten Bekenntnisschriften*, ed. Eberhard Busch (Zürich, 1998), pp. 94– 100 (ET *The Theology of the Reformed Confessions*, trans. Darrell L. Guder and Judith J. Guder (Louisville and London, 2002), pp. 58–63).

[72] Jülicher, 'A Modern Interpreter of Paul', p. 81.

[73] *Römerbrief 1922*, p. 96 (ET 120–1).

heroism, in all refinement of soul, and in every human achievement in history'. And conversely, 'it can also with the same calm and with a certain smile of forgiveness mourn over all that equally genuine human death in sin, over atheism, heathenism, and degenerate depravity'.[74]

The broader practical interpretative consequences of all this are illustrated in an exchange between Barth and Martin Rade at the end of 1918. When Rade wrote to Barth claiming that those who were neutral towards the German war effort were not able to appreciate the depths at which the Germans experienced the problem of God in the war, Barth's reply acknowledged that the distinctiveness of the German and Swiss positions on the war may indeed entail misunderstandings—in theology no less than elsewhere. But he urged Rade not to allow this to happen, not least in Rade's reading of Barth's *Römerbrief* (a copy of which was just then being sent to Rade's journal *Christliche Welt* for review). And in so doing he reminded Rade of their common situation and common task: 'It would certainly be good if you would no longer fail to hear us simply because we were the neutral ones. Our concern [*Sache*] is *your* concern, just as your concern—without the 'war experience'—is *our* concern.' But again, that all this is true can finally only be described in a specifically spiritual and theological way, so that Barth concludes his letter: 'How much preoccupies you in this Christmas and New Year's season! Not a day goes by without our thoughts turning towards Germany in anxious attention. How must it be if one is standing in the middle of these events. But above all—for us and for you—is the view of God's coming kingdom, which appears where it finds readiness.'[75]

Discovering the Reformed Tradition

By the time the second edition of *Romans* was published in January 1922, Barth had moved 'von der Kanzel zum Katheder',[76] accepting a rather surprising invitation to assume the newly created honorary chair of Reformed theology at Göttingen.[77] Barth's difficulties in this period—as a Swiss in a German university, as a Reformed theologian on an officially Lutheran faculty, and so on—are well documented. Admittedly one of the stranger stories from the time—that after Barth's arrival in Göttingen the customary salutation at formal academic gatherings was amended to 'Magnifizenz, Spectabilitäten, Herren Professoren—

---

[74] *Römerbrief 1922*, p. 98 (ET 123).

[75] See *B–R*, pp. 143, 145–6.

[76] Cf. Karl Kupisch, *Karl Barth in Selbstzeugnissen und Bilddokumenten* (Stuttgart/Kiel, 1996), p. 28.

[77] See Busch, *Karl Barth*, pp. 123.

Herr *Pfarrer*'—may well be apocryphal.[78] But, as Eberhard Busch points out, it serves as a perfectly valid introduction to Barth in Göttingen. For as Barth engaged for the first time in professional academic theological work, he continued to orient his thought from the standpoint of the preacher's pulpit, so that he could (much to Harnack's dismay) state simply that 'the task of theology is at one with the task of preaching'[79] and in his earliest constructive dogmatics lectures identify preaching as the starting-point and goal of dogmatics.[80] In short, Barth the *Universitätslehrer* was in the first instance a teacher of the *church*.[81] Just how this is so is the subtext of the following remarks, in which we will continue our survey of Barth's more overt reflections on biblical interpretation through the historical and dogmatic lectures and occasional writings from his time in Göttingen.

The outlines of this period are straightforward: Barth began lecturing in Göttingen in the autumn of 1921 and stayed there through the summer semester of 1925, after which he took up a position as Professor of Dogmatics and New Testament Exegesis in the Protestant faculty of theology in Münster.[82] His academic work was for the first five semesters focused on classical texts and figures of the Reformed tradition (the Heidelberg Catechism and the Reformed confessions; Calvin, Zwingli, and Schleiermacher) and a series of New Testament texts (Ephesians, James, 1 Corinthians, and 1 John, with lectures on Hebrews planned but abandoned). It must be said that Barth was not the most disciplined lecturer, and this combined with the fact that he was learning the material on the fly, often staying only a few hours ahead of his students, means on the one hand that his lectures are full of fresh insights and on the other that they are full of gaps. For our purposes it is especially worth noting that in the Calvin lectures Barth promises a treatment of Calvin's commentary on Romans but actually delivers what is essentially a sketch of what Barth himself gleaned from Calvin in the way of broad hermeneutical principles. And in the Schleiermacher lectures, Barth, having again fallen behind schedule, abandons his treatment of the *Hermeneutics* perhaps a third of the way through, after only a single lecture.

In his sixth semester in Göttingen, Barth began a lecture cycle on Christian dogmatics that, together with lectures on Philippians, Colossians, and the Sermon on the Mount, occupied him throughout his final three semesters in Göttingen and his first term in Münster. The prolegomena of these dogmatics lectures represents something of a watershed in Barth's hermeneutical reflections: Here for the first

---

[78] See Eberhard Busch, *Die Anfänge des Theologen Karl Barth in seinen Gottinger Jahren*, Göttinger Universitätsreden 83 (Göttingen, 1987), p. 8.

[79] H. Martin Rumscheidt, *Revelation and Theology. An analysis of the Barth-Harnack correspondence of 1923* (Cambridge, 1972), p. 32.

[80] Barth, *UCR I*, p. 28 (ET 23).

[81] Busch, *Die Anfänge*, p. 13. See further Wolfgang Greive, *Die Kirche als Ort der Warheit. Das Verständnis der Kirche in der Theologie Karl Barths* (Göttingen, 1991).

[82] On this and the following chronological sketch, see Busch, *Karl Barth*, pp. 128–64.

time he attempts to shape a theology of scriptural interpretation within a larger dogmatic structure, deploying the resources of a trinitarian doctrine of revelation to describe interpretation as a venture of the preaching church in which it anticipates the judgment of God on its speaking by continually attending to scripture, reflecting on its own past and present reiteration of scripture's theme, and above all invoking God's grace as it does so. And although Barth systematically reworked and refined this prolegomenal material twice during the following decade (once in the aborted *Christliche Dogmatik* of 1927 and again in the first volume of the *Church Dogmatics*), his dogmatic presentation of the task of scriptural interpretation as an act of obedience and prayer did not undergo any further fundamental change in outline or substance. So in this section, a brief treatment of this dogmatic material will feature as the capstone of a thematic sketch of Barth's historical work in Göttingen. The exegetical lectures from the period will not, for want of space, receive independent treatment.

We begin with the simplest of observations: In Göttingen, Barth became both by calling and inclination a Reformed theologian. Barth, it seems, was never entirely sure why he was called to the Göttingen chair, although he later speculated that it had something to do with the fact that his first Romans commentary appeared to certain leaders of the Reformed church in Germany as the work of someone who wanted to take scripture seriously.[83] In any case, upon immersing himself in the sources, he quickly and increasingly sympathized with distinctively Reformed theology, and reported that after some initial hesitation he was able to pursue his appointed task 'with delight and with a good conscience'.[84]

We can immediately proceed to draw out the hermeneutical significance of Barth's early identification with the Reformed tradition in two ways: First, by attending to the centrality of the ethical question and the scripture principle in Barth's portrayal of classical Reformed theology; and second, by tracing the ways in which Barth's historical exposition and polemic deployment of the Reformed doctrines of revelation, scripture, church, and election open up to the constructive doctrinal work on scripture in his first dogmatics lectures. The first point, explored here largely in terms of Barth's Calvin lectures, incidentally raises the issue of Barth's historiography, which will be explored further in the next chapter; the second revolves around the lectures on the Reformed confessions and includes some reference to the Schleiermacher lectures. No claim is being made that this somewhat artificial if convenient procedure is the only or even the best way to approach these texts. It will, however, allow us to give some sense of the overall shape of these lectures while highlighting their continuity with Barth's earlier and later hermeneutical concerns.

---

[83] Busch, *Karl Barth*, p. 123.
[84] Busch, *Karl Barth*, p. 129.

Ethics and the Scripture Principle

The centrality of ethics in Barth's understanding of the Reformed tradition is immediately evident in the instructive if rough-hewn description of the relationship between Reformation and medieval theology with which Barth begins his 1922 Calvin lectures. The lectures open with a familiar statement on the relativity of all things historical, now invoked with reference to Reformation studies: God's eschatological kingdom limits history precisely as it establishes it. Because there exists an absolute distinction between God and us, eternity and time, God's new world and the old of merely human possibilities, the relative distinctions within history—including the distinction between the Reformation and medieval Catholicism—must never be absolutized. 'Calvin and Sadolet', Barth remarks, 'were pieces on *the same* chessboard'.[85]

> For the absolute is not directly visible on this world's stage. The great light in the reflection of which we see the reformers and their thoughts move is not itself a phenomenon; it does not become one thing among others. And what we *see* in the reformers, the reflection in which they stand, is only relatively and not absolutely different from what we see around them, in their predecessors and successors. It is *a* new [element], *an* other; but not *the* new, *the* other. It is at every point in continuity with what came before and what came after. *The* new is not a thing that we can *establish* in the reformers, and *the* old is not something that we can *establish* in the scholastics and mystics preceding them.[86]

Nevertheless, Barth will insist that the Reformation really is a (relatively) new thing on the horizontal plane of history precisely as it reflects the transcendent movement of the kingdom of God. On this historical plane the Reformation is a theology of the cross in contrast (but always also in continuity) with the medieval theology of glory and its 'more weary and resigned' modern counterpart;[87] it is a restless, quarrelsome church and theology in contrast (but not total contrast) to the confident, harmonious theology of the monastery and the Gothic cathedral. It is 'the eruption of a crisis that secretly ran though all the Middle Ages',[88] a crisis

---

[85] Barth, *Die Theologie Calvins*, p. 21 (ET 17).

[86] Barth, *Die Theologie Calvins*, pp. 19–20 (ET 16–17).

[87] See Barth, *Die Theologie Calvins*, pp. 87–8 (ET 65–6): 'The enthusiasm of pressing on to the immediate that once created the Gothic vault has changed into the enthusiasm for the concrete, for what has come into being, for what can be measured and controlled.... In modernity we simply have the Middle Ages now become clever and also weary.... In principle the distinction in both cases is from the *Reformation* insight, from *Plato* and *Paul*, and therefore from the medieval trends that point back to Plato and Paul and forward to the Reformation. The Reformation and all that is part of it in the Middle Ages and in modernity are both antimodern and antimedieval.'

[88] Barth, *Die Theologie Calvins*, p. 66 (ET 50).

more or less directly apparent in monasticism, Augustinianism, nominalism, and mysticism. It also stands in intimate historical connection with the Renaissance and its rediscovery of the intellectual and cultural ideals of antiquity. And the Reformation for its part gives rise to the complex of advances and anxieties which we, for lack of a better word, call 'modernity'.

Barth's description of the historical continuities and contrasts between the Middle Ages, the Reformation, and modernity is interwoven with spiritual-theological judgments that posit a real correspondence between time and eternity (or between what Barth, significantly modifying Calvin's use of the terms, calls sacred and secular history[89]). To pick up the metaphor from the quotation above, there is a 'reflection'—a genuine connection and correspondence—between the rule of God and the movement of creation under this rule. And one might say that Barth's central preoccupation in the Calvin lectures is the way Calvin understood this connection, described it theologically (and just so ethically), and embodied it in his concrete historical circumstances. Note by way of example Barth's summary of a 1537 memorandum on church order to the Genevan city council, which according to Barth 'in the critical portions' is Calvin's work.[90]

> It is a fact that in remarkable and instructive tension with the spiritual and even otherworldly character of Calvin's Christianity his community in its original conception is so expressly a *eucharistic community*, and also, as we have seen, that the *state*, by means of the confession made by the supreme authority and the sum of its citizens, should confess its identity with this community, and should thus show itself to be a Christian state, a legitimate power that God has instituted not only in his wrath but also in his grace. The parallels to what we find in Roman Catholicism are obvious.... But it should be pointed out again and again that in contrast to this strongly developed element of visibility in Calvin's concept of the church the thought of predestination offers very sharply an element of invisibility, so that there can be no real equation with the concept of medieval Catholicism. Let us recall at this point that in Calvin the *potestas ecclesiastica* comes under the heading of Christian liberty and has a place only there. The church is not for Calvin a saving institution, seriously though he takes it. It is the visible fellowship of believers. But in its proper place and with every necessary caveat we *do* have to take it *seriously* as such. In the eucharist there is no corporeal [*dingliche*] presence of God, no direct miracle, but in it we have the presence of the *promise* of God, the *symbol* and *sign* of the miracle, and where people find themselves in the fellowship of those who expect this, who look beyond the visible, there is the community of Christ on earth, and again it is to be taken *seriously* as such. Finally, even church discipline is not a way to God that is necessary for salvation. God's judgment remains sovereign over both those who are inside and those who are shut out. It is a *vinculum humanitatis*, a measure by which the community may keep its witness pure. And who permits us, Calvin thinks, not to use this visible measure, knowing its relativity? What we have here is the force and breadth of Calvin's genius that are almost beyond our comprehension—

---

[89] Barth, *Die Theologie Calvins*, pp. 1–3, 20 (ET 1–2, 17).
[90] Barth, *Die Theologie Calvins*, p. 357 (ET 265).

a clear vision of the this-worldly element on the one side and the otherworldly element on the other, but with an equal appeal to both as complementary to one another. In considering the church order for Geneva with its eerie concreteness, we must pay more attention than formerly to the transcendent, eschatological, and theocentric motifs in his theology, not being content merely to shake our heads at [those apparently extreme social consequences of Calvin's view that the state and church cooperate in enforcing the visible purity of the eucharistic community].[91]

The distinctive contribution of Reformed theology over against both Roman Catholicism and Lutheranism is, for Barth, the maintaining of this peculiarly theological tension of 'the this-worldly element on the one side and the otherworldly element on the other, *but with an equal appeal to both as complementary*'. The Reformed insight begins with the Lutheran recognition of the mercy of God to radically sinful human beings,[92] but in the French humanist Calvin takes up with a native seriousness unfamiliar to Luther the Renaissance

---

[91] Barth, *Die Theologie Calvins*, pp. 362–3 (ET 268–9). If we follow the train of thought in this quotation we recognize a movement evident already in 'The New World' and the *Römerbrief*: A close reading of the text (here, a recognition of a tension between Calvin's orientation towards a point beyond history, evident not least in his doctrine of election, and his interest in the ethical and religious purity of the church) gives rise to a theological formulation of the theme of the text (here, a formula that can articulate the ordered tension between sovereign divine action and responsible human action without dissolving it). This formulation is intended as an account of Calvin's thought; it is in this sense a genuinely historical reading grounded on the assumption that Calvin thought and acted coherently. But as a theological formulation it is not content explaining the tension in Calvin's thinking merely as the residue of incommensurable intellectual or social influences (Calvin's Lutheranism and his humanism, for example). Instead it presses on towards a point at which the historical description clearly includes a contemporary significance: Calvin was wrestling in Geneva in 1537 with the same tension between the divine and the creaturely that occupies all serious thinking and that motivates all serious action. Barth then concludes by suggesting almost in passing that modern readings of Calvin have missed this one truly significant point (only here the modern critics are seen shaking their heads rather than, as elsewhere, shrugging their shoulders (cf. *Römerbrief 1919*, pp. 594–5: 'Es ist mir eines der größten Rätsel geworden, wie kaltblütig wir heute im Großen Ganzen an Paulus vorübergehen. Wir haben ihn "historisch" erforscht, wir haben uns einige Schlagwörter aus seiner Werkstatt angeeignet, wir haben gerade über seine entscheidenden Gedanken mit leisem Mitleid die Achseln gezuckt und gehen gerade in unsern entscheidenden Gedanken die Wege, vor denen er am Stärksten gewarnt hat'). Substitute Paul for Calvin and modern biblical criticism for modern Reformation historiography and the parallel is complete. And whereas in our account of 'The New World' and the *Römerbrief* we argued that Barth's hermeneutical commitments could be read as exponents of exegetical-theological commitments, so here Barth's historiographical claims similarly are bound up with his conception of God's sovereignty in history.

[92] See Barth, *Die Theologie Calvins*, pp. 56–7 (ET 43).

question (which is also the medieval and modern question) of purposeful human action.[93]

Understanding Calvin the Reformer as a historical figure involves, on Barth's account, the attempt 'to see the inner and outer connections and the place of intersection on the historical and principial line'; 'a consideration from eternal and temporal angles at the same time' in which 'the necessity imposed by that double context' is seen and presented.[94] It involves the courage to grasp the unity of the old and new rather than the attempt to veil their difference.[95] And in the end, Barth can say of the particular object of this lecture series: 'I finally view the whole of this extraordinarily self-contained and complete and heroically successful life as a tragedy, as I do all else in history.'[96] But he is free to characterize even Calvin thus precisely because the tragedy of history is recognized in the hope of its redemption. 'If we are not afraid to see the *questionability* under which *all* stand, then we are in a position to see, too, that all after their manner and on their level stand at least under the *possibility* of *justification*.'[97]

In pursuing this rigorously dialectical description of the character of genuine human action before God, Barth is articulating what he understands as an authentic Reformed ethics in obvious if implicit contrast to what he perceives as Schleiermacher's 'imposing belief in culture and progress', in which 'the highest conceivable thing in this world is the commencement within it of the world to come'.[98] But we might also refer at just this point to Barth's famous correspondence with Harnack, whose 'Fifteen Questions to Despisers of Scientific

---

[93] Barth, *Die Theologie Calvins*, pp. 89–92 (ET 64–7); cf. pp. 109–10 (ET 81–2): '"Iustus *ex fide* vivit!" says Luther. Yes, indeed, says Calvin, and he says exactly the same thing, but he makes it a major instead of a minor third and says, "Justus ex fide *vivit!*" The third possibility, that of saying one word, seems at all times to have been for theology a squaring of the circle, an impossible possibility that God has reserved strictly for himself alone to proclaim. I at least know of *no* theologian, not even those of the Bible, who succeeded in doing what Luther and Calvin failed to do and speaking this word. The things we know are simply pointers to the fact that Christ *is* this Word, the Logos, pointers that are not themselves *the* Word, but *a* word, tilting sometimes more to the one side and sometimes more to the other.' On the significance of the Calvin lectures for an appraisal of Barth's early ethics, see John Webster, '"Life from the Third Dimension": Human Action in Barth's Early Ethics', in *Barth's Moral Theology. Human Action in Barth's Thought* (Grand Rapids, 1998), pp. 11–39 (esp. pp. 31–4).

[94] Barth, *Die Theologie Calvins* pp. 174–5 (ET 131).

[95] Barth, *Die Theologie Calvins*, p. 426 (ET 314).

[96] Barth, *Die Theologie Calvins*, p. 175 (ET 132).

[97] Barth, *Die Theologie Calvins* p. 341 (ET 252–3).

[98] Barth, *Die Theologie Schleiermachers. Vorlesung Göttingen Wintersemester 1923/24*, ed. Dietrich Ritschl (Zürich, 1978), pp. 140, 228 (ET *The Theology of Schleiermacher*, pp. 75, 126); cf. p. 65 (ET 32): 'Schleiermacher's basic orientation is *ethical*; there may be seen here his *Reformed* origin and schooling, though I would ask you here, too, to distinguish between school and scholar.'

Theology' appeared in January 1923, not long after Barth concluded his Calvin lectures. 'It is the secret of life in general', Barth had told his students, 'to know what Calvin knew, to look beyond to what is incorruptible, and then to live and *act* in the world of the corruptible precisely with this higher reference'.[99] Harnack was constitutionally unable to grasp how one could in good conscience make this parabolic movement normative for the ethical life, how one could 'remain forever between door and hinge', giving 'autonomous standing to what are transition points in Christian experience', namely those occasional crises in which the unbridgeable gap between the holy God and sinful humanity becomes clear.[100] For Harnack, this disparity between God and the world, when elevated to a permanent status and urged in such unrelenting terms, necessarily involves an ethically (Question 5), culturally (Questions 6 and 7), and religiously (Questions 10 through 14) irresponsible devaluation of the world. Perhaps the most telling question, precisely because it most clearly represents the degree to which Harnack saw in Barth's position a direct challenge to the very specific attainments of modern German culture, is this: 'If Goethe's pantheism, Kant's conception of God or related points of view are merely opposites of real statements about God, how can it be avoided that these statements are given over to barbarism?'[101] Of course Barth can respond quite simply to this line of argument (summed up in the charge that he is a Marcionite, severing 'every link between faith and the human'[102]) by referring Harnack back to his recognition of a genuine if irreversibly ordered correspondence between God's kingdom and world history:

> I would rather say that the human is the relative, the testimony, the parable and thus not the absolute itself on some pinnacles or heights of development as one would certainly conclude from your statements. In view of this the historically and psychologically discernible, that which we know in ourselves and others as 'faith', would be a witness to and a symptom of that action and miracle of God on us.[103]

In this instance Barth's metaphors have changed (the language of 'reflection' giving way to the language of 'parable', 'testimony', and 'witness'), but the intention we observed in the Calvin lectures of maintaining a real correspondence between time and eternity, between God's kingdom and world history, remains.

The hermeneutical significance of all this becomes clear when we recognize that Barth sees an internal relationship between the distinctive ethical impulse of Calvinism and the Reformed expression of the Protestant scripture principle. The

---

[99] Barth, *Die Theologie Calvins*, p. 398 (ET 293).

[100] See Rumscheidt, *Revelation and Theology*, p. 30.

[101] Rumscheidt, *Revelation and Theology*, p. 30. See further G. Wayne Glick, *The Reality of Christianity. A Study of Adolf von Harnack as Historian and Theologian* (New York, 1967), p. 227.

[102] Rumscheidt, *Revelation and Theology*, p. 37.

[103] Rumscheidt, *Revelation and Theology*, p. 48.

latter is, as it were, the formal correlate of the material concern at the heart of the Reformed church, and is to be explicated in connection with it.

> If the *Reformed* effort is ventured, then the special importance of holy scripture arises out of the quest for a *norm* by which to regulate the relations, the quest for a *rule* of faith and life, of knowledge and action. This becomes the primary and vital question. The relation to *time* to which this concern is linked makes it essential that there be a temporal *form* and *order* for us. The real relation is certainly to eternity, but since this is now related to time, form and order are required.[104]

On Barth's reading, the Reformed understanding of scripture as a concrete, publicly identifiable set of texts of axiomatic authority stands in clear contrast to the Roman Catholic determination of the normative shape of the gospel as transmitted in the tradition and the corresponding authority of the teaching office of the church.[105] But in the strongly Lutheran atmosphere of Göttingen, Barth was less concerned to draw out this familiar distinction than to press home the point that the Reformed scripture principle represents a sharp contrast to the Lutheran tendency to prioritize the gospel content of scripture over its canonical form. Thus during the Calvin lectures, as part of a series of largely undeveloped theses on this theme, Barth argues that 'scripture did not play quite the same part in Reformed Protestantism as in Lutheran. Its dignity here was one of principle as it never was in Lutheranism, no matter how highly the latter regarded it'.[106]

More importantly for our purposes, in addition to these very broadly drawn contrasts, Barth offers in his lectures on the Reformed confessions an important theological exposition of the scripture principle and of its hermeneutical consequences. In the broadest terms, the recognition that scripture enjoys

---

[104] Barth, *Die Theologie Calvins*, pp. 523–4 (ET 387).

[105] Cf. Barth, *Bekenntnisschriften*, p. 68 (ET 41–2).

[106] Barth, *Die Theologie Calvins*, p. 522 (ET 386). This point is developed at length at the beginning of Barth's lectures on the Reformed confessions: See Barth, *Bekenntnisschriften*, pp. 7–11 (ET 5–7), where Barth suggests that in Lutheran theology there is only a quantitative difference between scripture and the church's symbols, invested as these are in establishing and maintaining the confessional unity of the church across time and space. In contrast, the Reformed church's confessions (*not* 'symbols') aspire to be nothing other than better or worse indications of the Word which the confessing church has heard in scripture, occasional and provisional if sincere explications of the faith rooted in historical contingencies and self-consciously distinct from the revelation of God in scripture (p. 34). In short, for the Reformed church, 'Schrift bleibt Schrift, einzigartig, inkommensurabel, außerhalb der Reihe' (p. 33; cf. pp. 63–5, 74, 80). And see Barth's treatment of Christian vocation, including his brief remarks on how the difference between Lutheran and Reformed approaches to union with Christ are reflected in their conceptions of scripture in *UCR III*, pp. 245–53.

axiomatic authority[107] (that it is canonical) in the Reformed church and so is truly normative for the historical life (and especially the proclamation) of the church corresponds, according to Barth, to the Reformed confession of the sovereignty of God in his revelation; and in turn the true freedom of the church, including its freedom of exposition and proclamation, is exercised appropriately only when exercised under the authority of the scriptural text.

Scripture, Revelation, Election, Church

'The church acknowledges the rule of its proclamation in the Word of God alone and finds the Word of God in holy scripture alone.'[108] Positively, this means that the church (whose activity Barth characteristically centers on the proclamation of the Word[109]) really does exist in relation to the Word of God. Proclamation can and should depend upon, be grounded in, and direct itself towards this Word. But one must also keep in mind the very definite limitation implied in this thesis. Proclamation is not itself the Word of God; it is a human word grounded in, dependent upon, and directed towards the Word. And as such it is a human word which finds its measure and justification outside itself in the Word which it serves. 'According to the Reformed view, there exists no continuity between the Word of God and the faith which lives upon it. The Word of God is always something *other* than that which we, obedient to this rule, believe, confess, and proclaim.'[110] That is to say, there is no continuity between the Word of God and the life of the church except that which is established by the rule of the Word; it belongs to the authority of the Word to call the church into being, and any other attempt to describe the correspondence of the church and Word is groundless. Faith and its expressions are not interchangeable with the Word of God, but exist in a very specific sphere, subordinate to and dependent wholly upon the Word. And further, the absolute

---

[107] On Barth's use of the term 'axiom' in this connection, see *Bekenntnisschriften*, pp. 68, 104 (ET 42, 65); 'Reformierte Lehre, ihr Wesen und ihre Aufgabe', in *WG*, pp. 179–212 (195) (ET 'The Doctrinal Task of the Reformed Churches', pp. 218–71 (244)); *UCR I*, p. 271 (ET 222); cf. Barth, 'The First Commandment as an Axiom of Theology' in *The Way of Theology in Karl Barth: Essays and Comments*, ed. H. Martin Rumscheidt (Allison Park, 1986), pp. 63–78.

[108] Barth, *Bekenntnisschriften*, p. 67 (ET 41).

[109] Cf. Barth, *Bekenntnisschriften*, p. 86 (ET 53): 'Preaching is, according to the Reformed view, the central function of the church. One may risk the thesis: It is the real Reformed sacrament.' The eucharist, on Barth's account, accompanies preaching as a 'meaningful gesture' which serves to elucidate the content of the sermon. Just how this is so is developed more fully in Barth's dogmatics lectures.

[110] Barth, *Bekenntnisschriften*, p. 74 (ET 45). Cf. p. 64 (ET 38–9): '*Faith* confesses. But it does not confess itself, but what is *written*. In the Reformed church, faith is entirely *testificatio*, indication. The object itself is and remains something other, a second thing, something confronting us.'

distinction between the Word of God and the human word of the church is represented in the relative yet nevertheless concrete distinction between the human text of the Bible and all other texts: 'To the Reformers the *isolated* normativity of the Bible is important exactly as the image—as the only permitted and bidden image earthly image!—of the isolated authority of God.'[111]

The key term here—and it will be central to Barth's massively extended treatment of the scripture principle in the first volume of the *Church Dogmatics*—is 'witness'. Scripture exerts a unique authority in the church because as a human word it bears witness to the historically localized revelation of God in Jesus Christ. According to classical Reformed theology, the truth of God is not a general truth of time and eternity, God and humanity in relation. Rather the truth of God is the incarnate Word, and just so the authentic witness to this truth is the specific human word of the prophets and apostles, 'the witness of the Old and New Testaments of this Jesus Christ'.[112] Thus, according to Barth's reading of the *Institutes*, while Calvin entertains the *possibility* that God can be known through nature apart from 'the biblical revelation', it remains for Calvin only a possibility, a mere hypothesis. We actually know God only when we attend to his Word, 'where we find the works of God considered according to the rule of eternal truth'. And the limitation involved here is not least a spiritual one: We are dependent upon God's Word *as sinners*. We are not simply blind to the way of God in the world; we willfully distort what we perceive there. 'That is the Calvinist *step* of knowledge from the merely hypothetical *possibility* to the exclusive *reality* of revelation: The gulf of the fall and of grace lies between Here and There.'[113]

So Reformed theology holds in tension the possibility that a general knowledge of God can be gained by attention to things in the world and the claim that these things can actually speak to us of God only as we hear the Word by which all things are created. In this theology, the particularity of God's gracious revelation to sinful humanity finds its correlate in the unique authority of scripture and in the epistemological principle that 'God is not known mediately, but only *immediately*—only through God'.

> Exactly *by virtue of* its offensiveness, the scripture principle is the expression of this immediacy, of the simple facticity, of the paradox of revelation. The offense [*Ärgernis*] of revelation is inevitable and *necessary* in a world which lies in wickedness [*Argen*; cf.

---

[111]   Barth, *Bekenntnisschriften*, p. 80 (ET 49).

[112]   Barth, *Bekenntnisschriften*, p. 76 (ET 46).

[113]   Barth, *Bekenntnisschriften*, p. 77 (ET 47). In the background lies a formal parallel drawn by Barth between Reformed theology and 'the severe, critical older Platonism'. In both cases, the indissoluble relationship between the transcendent and the mundane is at the same time an 'uncrossable polar region which once for all *distinguishes* the Here from the There' (p. 75). But Reformed theology places scripture in the place of the Platonic regulative idea, and specifies this polar region as the fall from grace overcome (only) by grace.

1 Jn. 5.19]. It was the knowledge of the kindness of God towards the fallen world which in Reformed theology *burst* the Platonic scheme at this decisive point. One must now see [both sides of the Reformed idea of the knowledge of God]: how here the Reformed thought-world is wholly and consciously grounded on an element which finally is foreign and superior to the world and humanity. For the Reformers, a concept of superiority, majesty, and freedom lay in the term 'God' that was wholly foreign to their medieval predecessors, but which Lutheranism (perhaps even Luther himself) did not feel in this sharpness, or in any case had not shown to its best advantage in this sharpness or expressiveness. But under this concept, which characterized the whole theology of the Reformers, stood also God's revelation and the *witness* of God's revelation. For them, the isolation of God's revelation follows from the isolation of God. *Revelation* is not this and that, not all and everything, but this fixed, incomparable One. And so also the legitimate witness of revelation cannot be any human word concerning God one likes, but this fixed human word from God, the word of the prophets and apostles who are appointed and equipped by God to speak it—the word of scripture.[114]

Correspondingly, the *reading* of the Bible as the prophetic and apostolic witness to God's grace towards sinful humanity, a reading inescapably performed by just these same sinners, must be an act of humility, gratitude, and prayer. In this connection Barth recommends the advice of the Synod of Bern to church ministers: Above all, the reader should pray, emptying and preparing the heart, that he 'might better grasp and remember the mind and counsel of God, which lies hidden in the letters' of the scriptural text. 'Otherwise, one is wont to read holy scripture irreverently, as a worldly history, exercising the reason alone.' Such reading issues in 'conceited, fleshly wisdom' rather than the Word of God on which the church depends. The prayerful reader, on the other hand, submits himself to the text precisely so that he might thereby hear God speak in it—hear God speak, in the first instance, to him alone: The reader must approach the text 'with a naked and devoted heart' [*mit bloßem und ergebenen Gemüt*], seeking simply to receive from God, paying no attention what he will say to others on the basis of his reading.[115]

We must remember that this is an explication of a church confession: The distinction here between hearing the text and speaking from it is not made in the interests of abstracting the text from a concrete social setting or of identifying its meaning as something unrelated to its use (arguably a move not uncommon in modern academic biblical studies).[116] Nor, on the other hand, is it to abstract the individual reader from the church, or in any case to prioritize the relationship between the individual and God at the expense of the ecclesial and broader social identity of the reader. In these lectures, Barth more than once displays all the usual

---

[114] Barth, *Bekenntnisschriften*, p. 79 (ET 48–9).

[115] Barth, *Bekenntnisschriften*, p. 84 (ET 52).

[116] Cf. Charles M. Wood, *The Formation of Christian Understanding: An Essay in Theological Hermeneutics* (Philadelphia, 1981), p. 16, who claims that the origins of modern historical-critical exegesis coincide with the posing of an unprecedented question: 'What is it to understand a text, apart from any specific employment of it?'

Reformed suspicion of the individualistic spiritual immediacy of the *Schwärmer*.[117] Barth's approval of this confessional distinction between hearing and speaking, between the individual reader's attentiveness to God alone and his ecclesial and social location, simply means that scriptural reading is not properly conceived instrumentally, which is again to say it is an event over which the reader does not have final control. It is, rather, a spiritual event in which everything depends upon divine grace. The prayer that attends scriptural reading is a concrete expression of the reader's sense of unworthiness, emptiness, and neediness—as a preacher, certainly (Barth had made this point eloquently enough in the preface to the second *Römerbrief* in describing his overwhelming sense of pastoral responsibility and inadequacy), but primarily as a sinful creature confronted by a holy God. In the final instance, this prayer is quite simply and irreplaceably the calling upon God graciously to speak through this text. And when God does so speak, then—and only then—the reader may and indeed must calmly give thanks, diligently contemplate the received knowledge, and finally joyfully share what he has received with others. And thus 'the Reformed scripture principle should take form in living theological praxis'.[118]

Just so, this emphasis on prayer is not an implicit denial that scriptural interpretation is genuine human work. Indeed, Barth notes, Calvin speaks strongly, and at first glance almost naively, of the work demanded of the reader: In reading scripture, we must place our wills and minds in its service, loving it with our whole hearts and allowing it to take root there. Likewise, the Westminster Larger Catechism speaks of the intellectual presuppositions (the conviction that scripture is itself the very Word of God) and moral dispositions (the will to acknowledge, believe, and obey God's Word) required of the scriptural interpreter. But this ethical description of the task of interpretation cannot be adequately developed without the recognition that the power to do these things must come to us through the grace of God's Spirit (Calvin), or that God alone can make the text come alive to the reader, so that the self-denying attentiveness demanded of the reader is inextricably linked with the invocation of divine grace (Larger Catechism).[119]

The maintaining of this counterpoise of work and prayer, both equally grounded in prior divine action, is the practical point of Barth's appeal to the doctrine of inspiration. In prioritizing the text as such, and advocating submission to it in such strong terms, Reformed theology obviously opens itself to the charge of a certain authoritarianism or legalism. Already in the Calvin lectures Barth recognizes the dangers involved in relating scripture and ethics in the Reformed manner.[120] And of course the charge of biblicism, with which Barth was confronted almost immediately upon the publication of his first *Römerbrief*, points in the same

---

[117] Cf. Barth, *Bekenntnisschriften*, pp. 84, 101, 104–5 (ET 51, 63, 65–6).

[118] Barth, *Bekenntnisschriften*, p. 85 (ET 52).

[119] Barth, *Bekenntnisschriften*, p. 86 (ET 53).

[120] See Barth, *Die Theologie Calvins*, pp. 522–4 (ET 386–7).

direction. Now Barth finds in the Reformed tradition itself the resources necessary to answer the charge—especially in the doctrine of inspiration. Only now, rather than merely drawing out its practical implications (which in the second Romans preface boiled down to the slogan *Besinn dich!*), Barth seeks to give a faithful account of its basic theological grounding as developed in the Reformed confessions. And he does so in a threefold thesis: 'Holy scripture is the perfect revelation, or, it is the work of the Holy Spirit. But this judgment concerning scripture is also a work of the Holy Spirit.'[121]

This thesis seeks to outline the space within which the free work of scriptural interpretation takes place. And delimitations are required on all sides. On the one hand, the perfection (or sufficiency, or clarity, or even *antiquity*[122]) of scripture is the perfection of the revelation which it contains and mediates: Barth does not find in the Reformed confessions the anxiety, which features so strongly in discussions of biblical inerrancy and which decisively informed the earlier North American evangelical reception of Barth,[123] that the Bible (the truth of which is understood as a matter of correspondence to at least theoretically verifiable historical facts) must be acknowledged as equally authoritative in every detail. Historical-critical study of the text is not ruled out *tout court*. On the other hand, historical-critical study cannot overrule the basic conviction implied in the confession—viz., that in containing revelation scripture contains nothing less than the Word of God.

In confessing that scripture is God's Word, Reformed theology (in its most proper instances) cuts off any attempt to ground scripture's authority elsewhere. 'Scripture is the perfect revelation' is an axiom, a tautology, which affords no ground, or, rather, is grounded only in God. Thus the second and third parts of Barth's thesis statement: It is the work of the Holy Spirit, and is known as such only through the Spirit. God can be known only through God, and that means that where God is truly heard in scripture, the Holy Spirit in the reader has found the Spirit in the Bible.[124] In this way, Barth equates the doctrine of scripture's perfection with the doctrine of its inspiration, which in Calvin's exposition is built

---

[121] Barth, *Bekenntnisschriften*, p. 89 (ET 55).

[122] Barth, *Bekenntnisschriften*, p. 90 (ET 56): When the confessions speak of the authority of scripture in terms of its antiquity, Barth claims, they doubtless echo the Renaissance slogan '*ad fontes*'. But one must finally speak here of *the* source, of *the Urgeschichte*, so that '"Antiquissima" soll das "perfectissima" verdeutlichen als das Erste, das Ursprünglich—das Göttliche!' Cf. Barth, *Die Theologie Schleiermachers*, pp. 278–81 (ET 155–7): Where the canonicity of scripture is linked to its antiquity, and its antiquity in turn is a correlate of revelation, the contemporary reception and confirmation of the scope of the canon is a matter for the *church*. But where (as in Schleiermacher) antiquity means simply temporal beginnings, the scope of the canon is a question of textual criticism and historical reconstruction to be undertaken by experts in the academy.

[123] See Philip R. Thorne, *Evangelicalism and Karl Barth: His reception and influence in North American Evangelical theology* (Pittsburgh, 1995).

[124] Barth, *Bekenntnisschriften*, pp. 92–3 (ET 57).

on the two simple claims that God speaks in scripture and we hear God so speak by the Spirit.[125]

On Barth's reading of the Reformed tradition, it is the coherence of these two aspects of the one work of the Spirit—in the biblical authors and in the readers— that distinguishes the classical doctrine of inspiration from the later notion of verbal inspiration. In the doctrine's earliest expressions, inspiration is thought of 'as a single, timeless—or, rather, simultaneous act of God in the biblical authors *and* in us'.[126] However distant the prophets and apostles may seem to us historically, psychologically, culturally, and so on, in reality we are bound together with them in the Holy Spirit's *Selbstgespräch*. In dealing with scripture, the *Realgrund* does not differ from the *Erkenntnisgrund*; the fact that the text is canonical necessarily involves our knowledge of its authority. In short: However important it is to distinguish the activity of the Spirit in relation to the prophets and apostles from the work of the Spirit in the reader (and of course Barth does recognize such a distinction), there can be no final separation here. The tradition in Protestant orthodoxy of speaking of the inspiredness of the text in itself is problematic at precisely this point: In a misguided attempt to take seriously the historical distance between the biblical writers and contemporary readers, it spoke of the inspiration of scripture as an event that essentially concerned only the biblical authors or made it a quality of the text as such.[127]

---

[125] Barth, *Bekenntnisschriften*, pp. 95, 99 (ET 59, 62).

[126] Barth, *Bekenntnisschriften*, p. 100 (ET 63); cf. pp. 95–6 (ET 57).

[127] Barth seems simply uninterested in appropriating the classical distinction between inspiration (as the Spirit's work vis-à-vis the biblical authors) and illumination (where Reformed theology usually treated the inward testimony of the Spirit). Whether this represents a real problem in Barth's doctrine of scripture (as suggested by, for example, Klaas Runia, *Karl Barth's Doctrine of Holy Scripture* (Grand Rapids, 1981), pp. 146–168) is an issue that cannot be pursued in any detail here. For his part, Runia agrees with Barth that the hearing and understanding of the Word of God in scripture remain always a gift of the Spirit (though Runia—in implicit criticism of a perceived occasionalism in Barth?— stresses 'the continuity of the work of the Spirit', so that the Spirit's gift of understanding is permanent (p. 152)). But he suggests that Barth's emphasis on the continuing work of the Spirit in scripture causes him to illegitimately downplay 'the inspired nature of the original writings', in so doing misconstruing the deepest intentions of Protestant orthodoxy's doctrine of scripture (p. 160). As it stands, Runia's critique of Barth's doctrine of scripture almost certainly reflects a disagreement over the doctrine of revelation: 'To [Barth], the distinction [between revelation and the Bible] is not merely quantitative, but essentially qualitative. The Bible as such is not to be identified with revelation. In itself it is not part of the event of revelation. In our opinion, this use of the word "distinction" finds *no ground in the Bible itself*. It is a preconceived, dogmatical construction to which the Bible itself is a perfect stranger' (p. 33). For Runia, the apostles are, by virtue of their calling and appointment to their task, '*revelational witnesses*. They are not only witnesses to revelation, in a limiting and distinct way, but they themselves *belong to the revelation*. Their speaking and writing *is* revelation' (p. 35). For a more accurate and rounded account of Barth on

Finally, Barth concludes, whether one speaks of the objective work of the Spirit (of the *autopistia* of scripture) or of the Spirit's subjective work (of its internal witness), one must not allow the Reformed scripture principle to be brought into alignment with historicist, subjectivist, or rationalist conceptions of the knowledge of God. One must speak instead of the entirely specific sovereignty of God's revelation, of the lordship of God as he bears witness to himself in these texts. And so one is led from the doctrine of inspiration to the doctrine of election.[128] Only thus can the doctrine of scripture finally be grounded theologically, and only in recognition of this ground can it be appropriately read as the Word of God.[129]

'Recognition of this ground' does not mean simply a subjective inclination towards furthering Christian belief and practice. In his treatment of Schleiermacher's *Kurze Darstellung*, Barth notes that for Schleiermacher a 'personal interest in Christianity' and a 'philological spirit and skill' together 'are the real criteria of biblical scholarship which is legitimately theological and scientific'.[130] This claim is, of course, only a special application of Schleiermacher's general principle that all truly theological work, undertaken by definition for the sake of the proper governance of the Christian church, requires both religious interest and a scholarly spirit.[131] 'But', Barth continues:

one might ask whether a third and much more important thing beyond these subjective conditions is not totally *forgotten* here, namely, what the older Protestant theology called 'the inner testimony of the Holy Spirit', and which is completely captured *neither* by the formula 'personal interest in Christianity' *nor* by 'philological spirit and skill'. It denotes materially a partnership between the expositor and the author that he is expounding, an understanding regarding the *theme* of the text, which *neither* the *Christlichkeit nor* the *Wissenschaftlichkeit* of the expositor can provide, but which like the theme is *not* a given, so that like the concept of the canon itself it has to stand in

---

apostolic appointment and calling in relation to the doctrine of inspiration, see David Demson, *Hans Frei and Karl Barth. Different Ways of Reading Scripture* (Grand Rapids and Cambridge, 1997) and the discussion in Chapter Three below.

[128] Cf. Barth, 'Biblische Fragen, Einsichten und Ausblicke', in *WG*, pp. 70–98 (74, 76) (ET 58, 60): 'It is with the question of election that the Bible answers our question of what it has to offer us. What we call religion and culture may be things available to everybody, but the belief, simple and universal, which is offered in the Bible, is not something available to everybody: not at any time nor in any respect can any who will, reach out and take it.... Except in terms of the difficult thought of election, no word can be spoken and no word heard of what the Bible has to say to us regarding the glory of God in the face of Jesus Christ.'

[129] Barth, *Bekenntnisschriften*, pp. 101–2 (ET 63–4).

[130] Barth, *Schleiermacher*, p. 283 (ET 158).

[131] See Friedrich Schleiermacher, *Kurze Darstellung des theologischen Studiums*, 2nd ed., in *Universitätsschriften, Herakleitos, Kurze Darstellung des theologischen Studiums*, ed. Dirk Schmid (Berlin and New York, 1998), pp. 316–446 (327, 329–30)); Barth, *Schleiermacher*, p. 247 (ET 138).

correlation with *revelation*, by which the expositor knows that he is confronted, and also with the *church*, which he knows is standing behind him with its mandate as the true subject of the knowledge and exposition of *this* text. In comparison with the older church, including the reformers, a gap opens up in Schleiermacher at this point, and this gap was *not* filled by the theology of the nineteenth century, zealously though it called for Christian experience on the one side and historical criticism on the other.[132]

In one sense, the key point here—as it has been throughout the material we have been discussing—is Barth's unceasing emphasis on the inalienable sovereignty of God in his revelation and therefore on the particular theological objectivity of scripture, which must always be respected as scripture is read. But we can also detect material progress in this passage over Barth's earlier polemics against Schleiermacher's hermeneutics and also over his earlier deployment of the doctrine of inspiration in expounding the relationship of contemporary reader to ancient author—a progress perhaps most clear in the exclusive emphasis on the church as the 'true subject of the knowledge and exposition of this text'.[133] At the very least, it is crucial to our understanding of Barth's Göttingen dogmatics lectures, in which the church figures first in a list of the presuppositions of dogmatics,[134] to recognize that at this point Barth can find in the Reformed tradition—specifically, in the Reformed doctrines of revelation, inspiration, and election—a basis for speaking of the church as a privileged community of knowledge and action without thereby compromising the infrangible priority of God precisely over the church (the fatal flaw, to Barth's mind, of Schleiermacher's ecclesially oriented theology of religious consciousness as well as Lutheran symbolic theology and Roman Catholicism). Barth already hints in his Calvin lectures, specifically in his descriptions of the tension between election and ethics in Calvin's ecclesiology and of the movement between prayer and work in scriptural interpretation, that the basic problem for a Reformed theology of scripture is that the Bible as the Word of God is as such also the rule of the life of the church. The former insight (scripture is the Word of this God) stands together with the latter (scripture as canon—as the normative and norming witness of the Old and New Testaments as these are read and taught in the church), and Barth refuses to allow one side to be stressed at the expense of the other. And by the fall of 1923, when Barth delivered his address on 'The Doctrinal Task of the Reformed Churches' to the *Hauptversammlung des reformierten Bundes*, this conviction has given rise to a concrete agenda:

> For the immediate future the one serious item I see on the agenda for Reformed theology is to study towards a new conception of the *scripture principle*, which should contain much more than that term now implies. I say study, for this new conception does

---

[132] Barth, *Schleiermacher*, p. 283 (ET 158).

[133] Cf. Busch, *Die Anfänge*, p. 14.

[134] *UCR I*, p. 4 (ET 4).

not allow of any sudden creation. So far as human endeavor will have any part in making this study successful, we shall need to think through the category of *revelation* again, and learn again to read the Bible, both Old and New Testaments, from that viewpoint.[135]

In one sense, of course, this means simply the reintegration of the two insights just mentioned: *God speaks* and so rules the church in scripture; and God speaks and so *rules the church in scripture*. The one task of the church, Barth is saying, is to listen to and obey this God as he speaks through these texts. Just so, this can be seen as simply one way of describing the task that occupied Barth throughout his academic career—the task that for Barth famously meant beginning ever anew at the beginning, or, in the words of his last, unfinished address, the continual 'starting out, turning around, [and] confessing' of the church.[136] But it is also true to say that in its more immediate context it is precisely this thinking through of the scripture principle in terms of the category of revelation that Barth takes up in the prolegomena of the Göttingen dogmatics, with its trinitarian construal of the doctrine of revelation, its doctrine of the three addresses of the Word of God, and its description of scripture as Word and witness.

Perhaps without undue simplification, we might finally find that the reception of Barth's hermeneutics can also be described in terms of this characteristically Reformed tension, which in Barth becomes a dialectical relating of a relentlessly eschatological impulse with an emphasis on the concrete authority of scripture as such: On one hand, accounts of the postmodern Barth have applauded his emphasis on the nonrepresentability of God but have not always known quite what to make of his apparently authoritarian insistence that interpretation means a thoroughgoing submission to the biblical text, a submission, it is said, that is possible only if one ignores the variations within scripture itself, the patriarchal slant of the text, and so on. On the other hand, some conservative evangelical interpreters of Barth (and, in different ways, some narrative theologians), resonate with Barth's emphasis on the authority of scripture in Christian preaching and theology, but have been less comfortable with his emphasis on the freedom of the theme of scripture even over the words of scripture.[137] We might also say, taking Ingolf Dalferth's useful phrase in a slightly different direction, that if Barth's theology in general and so also his doctrine of scripture in particular can be said to involve a certain 'eschatological

---

[135] Barth, 'Reformierte Lehre', p. 199 (ET 249–50).

[136] Barth, *Letzte Zeugnisse*, ed. by Eberhard Busch (Zürich, 1969), p. 61; ET *Final Testimonies*, trans. Geoffrey W. Bromiley (Grand Rapids, 1977), p. 51.

[137] Cf. Runia, *Barth's Doctrine of Holy Scripture*. Hans Frei's well-known preference for the later volumes of the *Church Dogmatics* over Barth's prolegomena perhaps also points in this direction; see the preface to Frei, *The Eclipse of the Biblical Narrative. A Study in Eighteenth and Nineteenth Century Hermeneutics* (New Haven, 1974).

realism',[138] that some conservative evangelicals wish Barth were less eschatological, while some narrative theologians wish he were less realist. In either case, a first step in avoiding both postmodern and postliberal misreadings of Barth may be to recognize the Reformed logic in his position—that is, the Reformed insistence that 'at least *two* human words are necessary to make known the real word of God'.[139]

We can then go on to recognize that Barth's early emphasis on continual, repentant attention to the whole of scripture serves to specify his primary theological emphasis on the freedom of God, and vice versa. Thus Barth stresses the inseparability of the Old and New Testaments because recognition of the integrity of the canon inoculates the church from the sorts of domesticated or quasi-revolutionary christologies that can be spun from the gospel narratives when they are unhinged from the rest of scripture—particularly from the Old Testament witness to the sovereign God of Israel.

> The old Reformed churchmen heard the very voice of God in the Scriptures—the voice of a God jealous in the Old Testament sense, who will not give his glory to another, the one, only, unique, almighty, and all-glorious God who governs in unconditioned freedom, grants no hearings, but dispenses grace to man in perfect sovereignty. And their passionate appeal to truth and authority and salvation as they were exclusively contained in this one book was precisely not speculation but a (concrete, contingent, existentially intended) confession of this God.[140]

Further, the God whose freedom must thus be recognized is not a general principle of alterity, but the God who is known to be free precisely in his revelation as it is attested by this particular text. Thus Barth opens his discussion of the divine aseity in the Göttingen dogmatics lectures by repeating a warning issued by Melanchthon:

---

[138] Ingolf U. Dalferth, 'Karl Barth's eschatological realism', in *Karl Barth: Centenary Essays*, ed. S.W. Sykes (Cambridge, 1989), pp. 14–45.

[139] Barth, 'Reformierte Lehre', p. 203 (ET 256); though of course Barth never claimed that a dialectical method was inherently capable of adequately expressing the truth of God in human language (see Barth, 'Das Wort Gottes als Aufgabe der Theologie', in *WG*, pp. 156–78 (171–5) (ET 206–12); and further, Barth, 'Fate and Idea in Theology', in Rumscheidt, *The Way of Theology in Karl Barth*, pp. 25–61).

[140] Barth, 'Reformierte Lehre', p. 201 (ET 252); cf. *KD* I/1, pp. 422, 426 (ET 402, 405): 'The New Testament statement about the unity of the Son with the Father, i.e., the deity of Christ, cannot possibly be understood in terms of the presupposition that the original view and declaration of the New Testament witnesses was that a human being was either exalted as such to deity or appeared among us as the personification and symbol of a divine being.... Those who think, or hyperbolically allege that they think, that a man can really become God or that the real God could have a copy in a man have very little understanding of the word "God" in the Old Testament sense.'

Christ leads us to the revelation of God. When Philip asked him to show them the Father, he gravely rebuked him, called him back from speculation and said (John 14:9), 'He that hath seen me hath seen the Father'. He does not want us to ask about God in random speculations, but to fix our eyes on this revealed Son and to direct our invocation to this eternal Father, who revealed himself by sending this Son and giving the gospel.[141]

The Göttingen Dogmatics

The opening pages of the Göttingen dogmatics—as of both the *Christliche Dogmatik* and *Kirchliche Dogmatik*—are occupied largely with the twofold task of recognizing and—because this recognition is the recognition of a *temptation*— relativizing the academic context in which Barth is operating.

> 'Dogmatics' denotes a place where all the inner and outer difficulties of theology assemble and emerge, the place which almost all those have in mind who cleverly or foolishly sigh over theology and theologians, the place which in spite of all the assurances of prudent negotiators and advocates calls into question the validity of our stay at the university and even perhaps of our whole existence, the place which we theologians try as hard as we can to avoid by fleeing to history or practice.[142]

All this is, of course, an academically oriented updating of the problematic with which Barth had been occupied since at least his 1917 lecture on 'The New World in the Bible': God's revelation places us in an impossible situation—or rather the only possible situation, but one from which we seek continually to escape, not least by insulating ourselves from scripture by turning to purely historical or short-sightedly practical questions.[143] In an academic context, this means recognizing that theology must guard against the encroachment of standards of judgment or intellectual processes that are alien to its true subject matter, even or especially when those standards and processes are institutionalized in the academy and when they bear the cultural prestige of being identified as scientific.

Nevertheless, Barth does want to identify dogmatics as a science, or, in the words of his opening thesis, 'scientific reflection on the Word of God' which is spoken by God in revelation, recorded in scripture, and proclaimed and heard in the church.[144] Materially, this involves a conceptualization of science in terms of

---

[141] *UCR II*, p. 150 (ET 427).

[142] *UCR I*, pp. 4–5 (ET 4). Barth's reflections on the academic situation of theology in these dogmatics lectures are largely a refinement of the position he had outlined in October 1922 in his Elgersburg lecture on 'Das Wort Gottes als Aufgabe der Theologie' (*WG*, pp. 161–5 (ET 191–7)).

[143] Barth even speaks again in this connection of scripture's theme in terms of the burning bush of Exodus 3 (*UCR I*, p. 6 (ET 5)).

[144] *UCR I*, p. 3 (ET 3).

objectivity [*Sachlichkeit*], i.e., 'the closest possible adjustment of cognition and knowledge to the distinctiveness of its object'.[145]

> The most suitable 'method' to the securing of objective truth, the most certain guarantee of coherence in knowledge, the most unbiased critical norm, and the most consistent grounding of all knowledge will in all fields of science be the truth itself, which we do not have to produce, but which is given to us.[146]

Formally, it means that Barth is free to appropriate language and concepts from other academic disciplines, especially philosophy, to express genuinely theological insights. Such theological use of philosophical language is, Barth claims, inevitable: 'Of none of us is it true that we do not mix the gospel with philosophy.'[147] And, so long as it is done carefully, with every recognition of the dangers it poses, this is unobjectionable.

> In making this witness [of scripture] my own, I am not free of all philosophy, but at the same time I am not bound to a definite philosophy. All things are lawful for me, but nothing shall take me captive.... Practically it is inadvisable for the theologian to bind himself for too long a period or too much in principle to any conceptions. That is, it is inadvisable for him to anchor himself systematically to any technical terminology.[148]

Barth—especially the Barth of the *Church Dogmatics*—was hardly a philosophical dilettante; his unwearied refusal to invest too heavily (at least consciously) in any particular conceptual scheme is a considered strategic decision. Whether this conceptual restlessness is the only practical way to avoid the philosophical distortion of theology is another question, one over which modern theology remains divided. In general terms, the dominant approach has involved the attempt systematically to incorporate traditional theological language within a coherent philosophical vocabulary, so that the church's witness is clarified rather than compromised by its philosophical alignments. Barth waged a long-term battle in this direction, especially with Bultmann's Heideggerian existentialism. But he never fought for an abstract philosophical eclecticism. His negations are rather a reflex of, on the one hand, his belief that the Word of God is sovereign over any human witness to it (a sovereignty represented in the tangible difference between scripture and the church) and, on the other hand, a particular reading of the history of theology in which a strong correlation of philosophy and theology is seen as at

---

[145] *UCR I*, p. 10 (ET 8).

[146] *UCR I*, p. 10 (ET 8).

[147] *UCR I*, p. 316 (ET 259).

[148] Barth, *Credo. Die Hauptprobleme der Dogmatik dargestellt im Anschluß an das Apostolische Glaubensbekenntnis* (Zürich: EVZ, 1948), pp. 158–9; ET *Credo. A Presentation of the Chief Problems of Dogmatics With Reference to the Apostles' Creed*, trans. J. Strathearn McNab (New York: Charles Scribner's Sons, 1936), pp. 184–5.

once a symptom and furtherance of the domestication of God's Word. In methodological terms, these negations correspond to a theological realism in which the object—the Word of God—that authorizes and shapes properly scientific theological inquiry remains inalienably subject.

Having established dogmatics as a science whose object is the Word of God (not, as in Schleiermacher, the science of faith, religion, or the religious consciousness of the past or present; nor, as in pre-Kantian metaphysics, the science of God), Barth goes on to specify the Word of God as revelation, scripture, and preaching—three *Anreden* which in explicit dependence on the Athanasian Creed are said to be without confusion or separation the one Word of God.[149] This brief passage forms the bridge from Barth's introductory comments on the objective character of dogmatics as scientific reflection on the Word of God to his second chapter, in which the Word of God as preaching is said to be the starting point and goal of dogmatics.[150] And it introduces the distinctions on which the structure of the prolegomena is based.[151]

Barth takes up this exposition of what he will later[152] call the threefold form of the Word of God, along with the attending prolegomenal architecture, in the *Christliche Dogmatik* and the *Church Dogmatics*, developing it at much greater length and with greater precision. We will reserve detailed comment for our treatment of the relevant sections of the *Church Dogmatics*. But some initial reflections are worth registering here.

First, while Barth certainly used the opening Göttingen dogmatics lectures as an opportunity to clarify for his students (and, no doubt, his colleagues) his understanding of theology's location in the university, his interest in the lecture series as a whole lies more in providing a distinctively Reformational account of the Christian faith. And in the lectures on prolegomena, this involves developing a theology of God's authoritative presence over, to, and in the church that stands in self-conscious continuity with classical Protestantism—and so in clear distinction from Roman Catholic and modern liberal Protestant theologies.

Second, therefore, the burden of the prolegomena lies (at least in large part) in developing a trinitarian doctrine of revelation in which the scripture principle plays a central role, opening up a way of talking in a specifically Reformed way about the relative freedom and authority of the preaching church. And it is under the dialectical relating of freedom and authority that Barth finds a doctrinal location to

---

[149] *UCR I*, pp. 18–9 (ET 14–15).

[150] *UCR I*, pp. 28–51 (ET 23–41).

[151] *UCR I*, pp. 53–244 (the Word as revelation), 245–320 (as scripture), 321–379 (as preaching) (ET 43–198; 199–262; 315–475).

[152] Barth, *Christliche Dogmatik*, p. 58 speaks of 'die drei Gestalten des Wortes Gottes'; Barth finally modifies this formula to speak of one threefold form of the Word in *KD* I/1, p. 89. The word 'form' as it appears on p. 14 of the English translation of the *Göttingen Dogmatics* has no basis in the original.

discuss the interpretative posture which the Christian church must adopt vis-à-vis scripture.

Third, in these lectures we find a developing emphasis on the *mediation* of revelation in history. Thus at the beginning of this section Barth distinguishes the three iterations of God's Word in quantitative terms: 'I am distinguishing the Word of God in a first, original address in which God himself and God alone is the speaker, in a second address in which it is the word of a specific category of people (the prophets and apostles), and in a third address in which the number of its human bearers or proclaimers is theoretically unlimited.'[153] But he then goes on with special reference to the Word of God as preaching to elaborate this distinction in temporal terms:

> At this third point I have tried to indicate that God's Word is to be regarded as a living, actual, and present factor, the Word of God which now both is and should be proclaimed and heard. Now! Should be! Note in these expressions first of all the movement, the qualified temporal movement, the turning from past to present denoted by them. The Word of God is God's speaking. It is ongoing as Christian preaching. It is not ongoing as revelation in the strict sense. It never took place as such. The statement 'God revealed himself' means something different from the statement 'revelation took place'. Revelation is what it is in time, but as the frontier of time, remote from us as heaven is from earth. Nor is God's Word ongoing as holy scripture. It is in time as such. It took place as the witness given to revelation. But in itself it is a self-enclosed part of history which is as far from us as everything historical and past. Our experiences are not a continuation of those of the prophets and apostles. Theoretically one might declare the continuation of the biblical canon to be possible (e.g., if two lost epistles to the Corinthians were found again, or if an ecumenical council found it right to receive the *Didache* into the New Testament). But this would not be an ongoing of scripture, only an extension of the concept of scripture, or of what the concept means. All conceivable extensions of scripture would still belong to the past, not to the present. They would not be a step out of the past into the future. But as Christian preaching, which proceeds from revelation and scripture (as the Holy Spirit proceeds from the Father and the Son), the Word of God is ongoing. It is present. Naturally, in, with, and under Christian preaching, revelation and scripture are present too, but not otherwise. In this regard we are not restricting the term 'Christian preaching' to sermons from the pulpit, or to the work of pastors, but including in it whatever we all 'preach' to ourselves in the quiet of our own rooms. The only point is that outwardly or inwardly this must be a speaking, a mediated addressing and hearing of the Word of God from revelation and scripture. It is on account of Christian preaching, the Word of God today, that we take up the question of the Word of God and that theology in general and dogmatics in particular are a concern for us.[154]

---

[153] *UCR I*, p. 18 (ET 14).
[154] *UCR I*, pp. 19–21 (ET 15–16).

The freedom of God is secured in this passage in the first instance by speaking of revelation as in some sense a timeless event: revelation 'never took place as such'. Correspondingly, the freedom of scripture over the church is secured by describing scripture as belonging to the past. *By definition*, scripture is past, and just so it appropriately points in its concrete historical distance and difference from the present and future church to the graciously self-maintained distance of revelation from the church. That is why Barth is so keen to maintain that scripture belongs to the past even as he insists that the canon is at least theoretically open. This interrelation of scripture's authority and God's own authority is, as we have seen, a characteristic of Barth's understanding of scripture from at least 1917, and it remains a crucial feature of Barth's thought throughout the period under review. But the eschatological language he uses in this passage with reference to God's own speaking does not. Only ten days after making the statement above, Barth felt the need to modify his language in order to emphasize (against no less than Schelling, Schleiermacher, Tillich, Ritschl, Kaftan, Wendt, Haering, and Troeltsch![155]) that the historically contingent scriptural witness to revelation reflects a self-speaking of God that is sovereign precisely as it occurs '"*there* in Palestine" and "*at that time*" in the years 1–30"'.[156] 'The concealed and unique address that we call God's revelation' is, Barth now claims, history; '*qualified* history', to be sure, which is to say a history which stands over against all other history 'with principal superiority', unconditioned by the possibilities which inhere in time and space generally considered. But history nonetheless.

If Bruce McCormack is right to see just here a 'subtle but momentous shift of accent' by which we can mark the end of the eschatological model which Barth had deployed throughout the early 1920s,[157] the way in which Barth describes the formal correlation of the Word of God in revelation with scripture and proclamation in these dogmatics lectures should evolve to reflect his new emphasis. And in some cases it seems to: Barth's early articulation of the difference-in-unity of revelation, scripture, and preaching as 'the triunity of the eternal, the temporal, and the present in God's Word' gives way to the claim that the church's proclamation finds its norm in 'the historical datum of the canon' which mediates the Word which God himself speaks *in the incarnation*, so that 'the center of the concept of revelation' is, quite simply, 'the fact of Jesus

---

[155] *UCR I*, pp. 71–3 (ET 59–61).

[156] *UCR I*, p. 70 (ET 59).

[157] McCormack, *Dialectical Theology*, pp. 339–41, finds here initial evidence that the theology of the second *Römerbrief*, in which the dialectic of veiling and unveiling in revelation is accompanied and supported by a rigorous time-eternity dialectic, is giving way during the Göttingen dogmatic lectures to a new, more christologically focused theology in which the crucial 'eschatological reservation' is now elaborated in terms of the anhypostatic-enhypostatic christology that Barth had discovered through his study of Protestant orthodoxy.

Christ'.[158] Correspondingly, the *distinction* (that is, the indirectness in the indirect identity) between revelation and scripture, which cannot now simply be maintained in terms of a time-eternity dialectic, rests perhaps more heavily on the concept of *witness*, and the prophets and apostles must be distinguished very sharply from any others who might claim to bear witness to God's revelation:

> They differ in principle from all the others to whom revelation is mediated by their witness, even though the success of their mediation is that through them revelation is visible and audible and credible and authoritative for these others in exactly the same way it is for them, and even though among these others there might be those who can be called witnesses of Jesus Christ just as much as they can, and who, historically considered, might have been much more active and powerful and illuminating witnesses of Jesus Christ than these first witnesses.[159]

Further, it is precisely in the historical character of the prophetic-apostolic witness—in the relative but clear distinction between scripture and all other human words—that we find a reflection of the absolute distinction between God's revelation and all human witness to it:

> If we are not to pursue a *theologia gloriae*, then a real, authenticated, and incontestably superior *mediation of revelation* which finally answers the question of truth must stand so much above history that in keeping with the concealment of revelation and the cross of Christ, *as* the mediation of revelation and full of the divine mystery, it stands *in history itself*. What is demanded at this point is precisely a relative historical entity, that is, human beings and their human words. To eliminate this contingent entity which gives such urgency to the question of faith or offense would be equivalent to eliminating the concealment of revelation and therefore revelation itself. The recognition that revelation is not a part of human history *as such* [i.e., that it is 'qualified history'], that we have it only as we are *given* it, that our experience, even though we learn from a devout mother or a Luther or an Augustine, stands under a final *caveat*, under the crisis of the question of *truth*—this recognition, if it is to be authentic, must take the form of a recognition not merely of revelation itself, which might be the forbidden leap into immediacy, but also of a canon in the realm of mediacy, in a halting of the movement back to the sources on *this* side of revelation.[160]

The impact of Barth's increased attention to the contingency of revelation upon his description of the indirect identity of scripture with revelation is also clear in this quotation. While he had noted in the lectures on the Reformed confessions that scripture in its concrete canonical form represented the distinctness of God (and

---

[158] *UCR I*, pp. 46, 259 (ET 37, 212).

[159] *UCR I*, pp. 259–60 (ET 213); on the relation between the incarnation and the prophetic and apostolic witness, see esp. pp. 174–87 (ET 142–52).

[160] *UCR I*, p. 261 (ET 214).

indeed was the only such image of God recognized by the Reformers[161]), he now presses this point at much greater length and with much greater conviction, precisely because he now sees that revelation has taken time into itself and in so doing has authorized time to bear its own witness to revelation in the form of the prophetic and apostolic witness to Jesus Christ.

The same development is visible in Barth's reuse of some statements about the inspiration of scripture first aired in his Reformed confessions lectures. Barth still continually speaks of the presence of God to the church as the church's *contemporaneity* with revelation.[162] But history—the movement of time between incarnation and the proclamation—now occupies a higher profile in the argument. Thus Barth's parenthetical elaboration on his earlier claim that inspiration signifies a single act uniting the authors and readers of scripture: 'In view of the Holy Spirit, we can say that one must regard inspiration as a single, timeless or rather simultaneous act of God in the biblical authors and in us (even the *mediation* of revelation is real only as act!), an act in which the Spirit speaks to the Spirit, and the Spirit hears the Spirit.'[163]

Barth has not entirely given up his practice of securing the sovereignty of God in his revelation by speaking of God's act as timeless; to use McCormack's terms, the time-eternity dialectic of the second *Römerbrief* has not entirely faded from view. But notice how Barth, even as he picks up this earlier statement, balances the eschatological language of timelessness with the language of mediation, which throughout these first dogmatics lectures is bound up with the problem of history, specifically with Lessing's anxiety about the capacity of history to mediate absolute truth.

There may well be rather different and indeed more compelling ways of describing these issues from a developmental perspective. For our purposes, as we look ahead to our discussion of the *Church Dogmatics*, the important point is that we will need to be attentive to the ways in which Barth, whose understanding of the time of revelation will undergo further review and modification between 1924 and 1932, describes the relationship of the time of scripture to that of revelation on the one hand and that of preaching (and therefore of scriptural interpretation) on the other. To anticipate, Barth will in *CD* I/1 speak simply of 'God's past revelation' and of 'His future revelation', defining thereby the time within which the church recalls and hopes for God's Word.[164] And of course this theological construal of the time of scriptural interpretation has ramifications for the character of such interpretation that will need to be drawn out.

To summarize: We began this chapter by suggesting quite simply that during his gradual break with the liberal theology that had been his intellectual and

---

[161] Barth, *Bekenntnisschriften*, p. 80 (ET 49).

[162] E.g., *UCR I*, pp. 277 (ET 227).

[163] *UCR I*, p. 274 (ET 225); cf. Barth, *Bekenntnisschriften*, p. 100 (ET 63).

[164] *KD* I/1, p. 114 (ET 111).

spiritual home, and throughout his long career thereafter, Barth intended to take scripture seriously. We have tried to indicate just how this is so by reading—with help from a handful of extramural lectures; some of Barth's correspondence, both public and private; and a representative selection of secondary texts—a series of Barth's works from 1917 to 1924: specifically, an adult education lecture, a biblical commentary (in two editions), two lecture series on historical theology, and the prolegomena to a dogmatics.

We have emphasized that this reading is offered for the limited purpose of introducing and orienting our later, fuller discussion of Barth's doctrine of scripture as it is presented in the first volume of the *Church Dogmatics*. It has done so first by introducing a series of themes that run forward from these early writings through his more mature dogmatics: the description of scripture as witness to the self-revealing God; the comprehensiveness of God's judgment and grace, and the corresponding relativity of all historical distances and cultural differences; the emphasis on a continual, repentant, but therefore truly free attentiveness to scripture, which was only given a clearer theoretical grounding by Barth's increasing self-identification with the Reformed tradition.

We have also introduced some patterns of argument and textual engagement in Barth's work: the close and generous though not uncritical readings of scriptural and theological texts; the characteristic style and force of Barth's polemics, more formalized and nuanced but no less pointed or spiritually sensitive as he moved from the pulpit to the classroom.

In the next chapter, this high-level historical survey will give way to a close reading of a single text: Barth's history of modern Protestant theology, *Die protestantische Theologie im 19. Jahrhundert*. The larger themes will recur.

Chapter Two

History and the Politics of Interpretation

There are any number of ways in which to usefully read Barth's history of modern theology, *Die protestantische Theologie im 19. Jahrhundert*,[1] all of which remain to date largely unexplored. While this text has received widespread approval even among readers broadly unsympathetic with Barth's dogmatic and exegetical work (Tillich having famously called it 'a beautiful book'[2]), it has not yet been studied with anything like the rigor applied to Barth's other major works.[3]

The curious absence of sustained engagement with this text, and with it, serious discussion of Barth as a historian of Christian theology, begs a fuller explanation than can be provided here. But we can introduce themes to be explored further in this chapter by making two brief suggestions.

First, *Die protestantische Theologie* is widely overlooked precisely because it is well received. Or, more precisely, because it is received as a piece of genuine historical research. Barth's more familiar works are familiar in large part because they are, from Barth's perspective, misread: So, for example, Barth's *Römerbrief* is widely read not as biblical commentary but as free (i.e., unhistorical) theologizing, a book which is—however interesting and edifying—at best only loosely connected with the text of Paul's epistle. And so the major question facing Barth's readers becomes not how to understand his *Römerbrief* as a commentary, but how to understand why Barth would insist that it is one.

In contrast, commentators on *Die protestantische Theologie* have in large measure taken at face value Barth's claim that the book really is about the history of modern Protestant theology. The book has therefore been viewed as something of an exception to the rule; an exception that shed light on Barth's intellectual range, demonstrated his early and abiding debt to Harnack, embodied his

[1] Karl Barth, *Die protestantische Theologie im 19. Jahrhundert. Ihre Vorgeschichte und ihre Geschichte* (Zürich, 1947); ET *Protestant Theology in the Nineteenth Century. Its Background and History*, new edn (London, 2001).

[2] Paul Tillich, *Perspectives on 19th and 20th Century Theology*, ed. Carl E. Braaten (New York, 1967), p. 92.

[3] For an important recent exception, see John Webster's careful and perceptive reading, 'There is no past in the Church, so there is no past in theology: Barth on the history of modern Protestant theology', in his *Barth's Earlier Theology*, pp. 91–141. For a more wide-ranging treatment, see Ian R. Boyd, *Dogmatics among the Ruins. German Expressionism and the Enlightenment as Contexts for Karl Barth's Theological Development* (Bern, 2004).

superiority over his less talented and humane followers, etc. But as an exception it has not figured largely either in the standard critique that Barth imposes himself everywhere in his exegetical and dogmatic work or in more sympathetic treatments of Barth's intellectual development.

Certainly on one level the book is an exception, Barth's only major independent work of theological history to be published during his lifetime. Barth himself cautioned readers of the book to remember that, whatever his historical interests and views, he was not a professional historian.[4] And during preparations of lecture materials that were to become earlier sections of the book, Charlotte von Kirschbaum described the work as 'a lively and interesting—and for Karl certainly very refreshing' diversion from the dogmatics to which she, at any rate, was anxious to return.[5]

That said, it somehow remains deeply unsatisfying to bracket the book off simply as an exception or a corrective. However distinctive it is within Barth's *oeuvre*, it stands in both material and methodological continuity with his other work, and an instinctive recognition of this fact is perhaps a second, largely unexpressed reason why the book has been widely ignored. To accept Barth's historiographical commitments in the first chapter of *Die protestantische Theologie* is on a certain level to accept the corresponding claims made in Barth's discussions of biblical hermeneutics. And where the latter is not considered a live option, the only possible way to approve of Barth's historiography is to stress its discontinuity in relation to his biblical hermeneutics or (since that strategy can hardly hold up for long) simply to ignore it altogether.

In this chapter, we will explore the significance of these historical lectures for an understanding of Barth's hermeneutics from two directions. First, through a close reading of Barth's first chapter, 'Über die Aufgabe einer Geschichte der neueren Theologie', we will attempt to draw out the connections between Barth's historiographical claims and his reflections on biblical interpretation. The thesis pursued here is that Barth's theology of reading, when fleshed out in terms of the interpretation of modern theology, remains as ever a theology of the third article. But the accent here is placed on the *credo ecclesiam* rather than (or, perhaps better, in addition to) the *credo remissionem peccatorum* characteristic of his biblical hermeneutics from at least 1916 up through the early 1920s and beyond. Second, we will look at the main body of this text to analyze Barth's portrayal of what he calls the 'absolutism' of the eighteenth century and its relationship to Christian theology. Here we will highlight Barth's insistence that modernity's revaluation of its theological inheritance is primarily a reflex of moral rather than intellectual changes in western European culture, and that these moral shifts require specifically theological analysis. The importance of Barth's own analysis of the character of modern culture can hardly be overstressed: In the first place, it helps

---

[4] *PT*, p. v (ET xi).
[5] Von Kirschbaum to Thurneysen, 25 November 1932 (*B–Th III*, pp. 302–7 (303)).

us understand why Barth appears relatively unconcerned—or at least unencumbered—by the category of 'modernity' as such. Or more specifically, why he can approach scripture largely free of characteristically modern anxieties (including those encoded in hermeneutical theories of one sort or another) regarding the social impact of interpretative disputes over authoritative texts. And further, one might venture the claim that the reception of Barth's hermeneutics has been largely determined by unexplored preconceptions about the character of modernity, and that the rehabilitation of theological discourse about modernity is prerequisite to understanding what Barth is doing hermeneutically and historiographically. Later in this chapter we will examine some of the ways in which this may be the case.

The Task of a History of Modern Protestant Theology

Barth first lectured on the 'History of Protestant Theology since Schleiermacher' in the summer of 1926 in Münster. These lectures comprised an introductory section 'Über die Möglichkeit einer Geschichte der neueren Theologie'; a second section (apparently unique to this lecture series) in which Barth charted the theologically significant events and publications of the nineteenth century year-by-year; and a series of sketches of leading thinkers from Schleiermacher to Ritschl. These lectures were rewritten for the winter semester of 1929/30, at which time Barth began to explore the eighteenth-century antecedents of the Schleiermacher–Ritschl axis in lectures on Lessing, Kant, Herder, and Novalis. He also added a chapter on Hegel and thoroughly reworked the opening chapter, now titled 'Über die Aufgabe einer Geschichte der neueren Theologie'. And finally, after his move to Bonn, Barth expanded and delivered the lectures a third time, now over the course of two semesters, adding 'three new sections on the man of the eighteenth century in general—that is, in his worldliness, his Christianity, and finally his theology',[6] as well as writing a new chapter on Rousseau and revising the chapters on Lessing and Kant. These lectures from 1932–3 were first published in 1947 with only the slightest modifications.[7]

Barth's foreword to the 1947 edition of these lectures is certainly one of his more modest. He stresses the incompleteness of both sections of the book, the first on eighteenth-century background, the second on nineteenth-century theology proper. He invites the reader to reflect on what he has left out of the lectures (Barth himself mentions Goethe and Troeltsch,[8] and commentators have had much to say

---

[6] Barth to Thurneysen, 23 December 1932 (*B–Th III*, p. 320).

[7] Thanks are due here to Dr. Hans-Anton Drewes for providing details about the evolution of these lectures and for making available the manuscript of the first section of the 1926 lectures.

[8] *PT*, p. v (ET xi).

about the absence of any Anglo-American figures, not to mention Dostoevsky, Nietzsche, and, especially, Kierkegaard[9]), as well as the places where his historical judgments relied on secondary sources and where they may simply be questionable.[10] In this connection, Barth emphasizes that the book is 'a relatively old work', containing 'gaps I would not leave open today, and accents which I would now place differently'.[11] Nevertheless, Barth did endorse its publication, in part simply to meet a demand poorly met by the unauthorized copies in circulation and the individual sections of the lectures that had appeared in print. But more importantly, to Barth's mind, the book advocated (in its first, introductory chapter) and exemplified (in its two main sections) an openness and patience with the figures of the period not always exhibited by Barth's students:

> I have allowed publication because I have constantly had occasion to wish and suggest that the attitude and approach of the younger generations of Protestant theologians to the period of the church that is just past might be rather different from that which they now often seem to regard, somewhat impetuously, as the norm—misunderstanding the guidance they have received from me. I would be very pleased if they were (to put it simply) to show a little more love towards those who have gone before us, despite the degree of alienation they feel from them.... I hope that my own approach here will make clear to one and all that the better exegesis and dogmatic theology for which we are striving again today must prove itself by the way in which its advocates acquire not only a sharper but also a more impartial eye for the historical reality of their fellow theologians of yesterday and the day before. We need openness towards and interest in particular figures with their individual characteristics, an understanding of the circumstances in which they worked, much patience and also much humour in the face of their obvious limitations and weaknesses, a little grace in expressing even the most

---

[9] The more useful reviews include those by Colin Gunton (*Theology* 76 (1973): 205–6), the thesis of which is repeated in his 'Introduction' to the new English edition of *Die protestantische Theologie* (*Protestant Theology*, pp. xv–xx); D. L. Mueller (*Review and Expositor* 71 (1974): 123–4); J. Forstman (*Religion in Life* 42 (1973): 559–60); W.L. Hendricks (*Southwestern Journal of Theology* 2 (1960): 73–4); R.L. Shinn (*Union Seminary Quarterly Review* 15 (1960): 170–2); J.C. McLelland (*Studies in Religion* 3.2 (1973): 193–4); and esp. Martin Schmidt ('Karl Barths Geschichte der evangelischen Theologie im 19. Jahrhundert', *Theologische Literaturzeitung* 11 (1950): 654–64).

[10] Here Barth's quick and rather intemperate dismissal of Ritschl has been widely cited; see e.g. Jaroslav Pelikan's very good introduction to the American edition of Barth, *Protestant Thought: From Rousseau to Ritschl* (New York, 1959), pp. 7–10. (Though one might ask to what extent the brevity, if not the tone, of Barth's chapter on Ritschl has less to do with his distaste for the subject than the simple fact that Barth—here as so often—ran out of time at the end of the semester.) On Barth's reliance on secondary sources see Schmidt, 'Barths Geschichte'; cf. Barth to Thurneysen, 23 December 1932 (*B–Th III*, p. 320): 'I must collect my material bit by bit at the greatest possible speed from as many histories of the world, culture, literature, art, church, and theology as possible, and yet also at least snoop around in all sorts of primary sources.'

[11] *PT*, p. v (ET xi).

profound criticism and finally, even in the worst cases, a certain tranquil delight that they were as they were.... Above all, such an approach is in accord with the knowledge of the divine judgment on all that is called the flesh, which has rightly and necessarily come alive among us in such a different way. Whence comes historical rectitude, if not from here?[12]

Whatever the provisionality of the lectures, in other words, they remain important because of the ongoing and still under-appreciated hermeneutical significance of the doctrine of justification, or at least of a set of theological convictions regarding the universality of God's gracious judgment. The desire to demonstrate this significance unites the Barth of September 1946 (when this foreword was written) with the Barth of June 1926, when he wrote to Thurneysen of his aim to present the theologians of the nineteenth century in such a way 'that alongside the dubiousness of the whole, in every case a good word—that is to say, the forgiveness of sins promised to the whole—somehow also comes into view'.[13] And it stands immediately behind Barth's remarkable introductory comments from 1929 on the task of writing a history of modern theology.

These comments are organized in three sections: The first outlines in brief Barth's conception of the study of theological history and announces the scope of the lectures to follow; the second represents a sort of extended critical bibliography of modern books on the history of (especially recent) theology; and the third revisits both topics introduced in the first section. Rather than simply trace the flow of these comments, we will organize our treatment here around three interrelated concepts: historical understanding as an act of responsibility, of humility, and of faith.

Responsibility

'The portrayal and understanding of the history of Protestant theology from the time of Schleiermacher onwards is a *theological* task. Even as an object of historical consideration, theology demands theological perception, theological thought, and theological involvement.'[14] Thus Barth's opening thesis. Characteristically, he does not allow that the theological perception of the history of theology is simply one option among others. The theologian is not free to approach theological history nontheologically any more than she is free to approach it nonhistorically. As always in Barth, inquiry into any particular subject matter must be pursued in accord with the subject matter itself. And, as always, because the object of inquiry takes precedence over any possible mode of inquiry, methodological self-consciousness must never degenerate into self-justification:

---

[12] *PT*, p. vi (ET xii).
[13] Barth to Thurneysen, 11 June 1926 (*B-Th II*, p. 423).
[14] *PT*, p. 1 (ET 1).

'There is, of course, no method, not even a theological method, by means of which we can be sure of catching sight of theology. It can escape us in this way, too—namely, by virtue of our inadequacy to the theological task posed by it.'[15] But any successful inquiry into the history of theology does necessarily involve tackling the subject on its own terms—i.e., at once theologically and historically. Barth thus speaks in the same breath of the 'special participation' in theology required of the historian of theology and of 'the general rule of historical understanding'—namely, that knowledge of history requires participation in history.

The question of the relationship between these two aspects of the one act of responsible, participatory investigation of the history of theology mirrors that raised by Barth's comments in the *Romans* prefaces regarding the general applicability of the hermeneutics he derives from his engagement with scripture. Barth never addresses this question directly at any length, and in the present instance he simply juxtaposes the two aspects, describing each in its own terms, though concentrating somewhat more attention on the special participation required of the historian of theology.[16] And here we will limit our discussion to unpacking each in turn. So, first, we turn to Barth's description of the character of responsible historical investigation.

'We know history', Barth claims, 'only when and in that something happens to us and for us, perhaps even against us; we know it only when and in that an event concerns us, so concerns us that we are with it, that we participate in it. Any knowledge of history that proved to be merely seeing, observing, establishing, is a contradiction in itself'.[17] Why? Because history is knowledge of intentional human activity: 'Der Gegenstand der Geschichtswissenschaft, das geschichtliche Faktum, ist der lebendige Mensch.'[18]

Barth's conception of historical knowledge here trades on a sharp distinction between *Geschichtswissenschaft* and the *Naturwissenschaften*. The latter deal with facts [*Tatsachen*] which as such make no demands upon the investigator, but in relation to which she is fundamentally free. Historical understanding, on the other hand, as knowledge of living persons, is necessarily active, self-involving, responsible knowledge. The persons we encounter in history lay claim to us, their actions posing to us the question of how we will respond to them. Historical

---

[15] *PT,* p. 1 (ET 1).

[16] Much depends on how one characterizes this relationship. Chapter One above stressed the theological particularity of Barth's approach and suggested that it can be understood as a move from the particular to the general on the basis of theological convictions about the uniqueness of God's life and the comprehensiveness of his saving work. Burnett, *Barth's Theological Exegesis*, pp. 49, 113, 236–7 seems to take a somewhat more relaxed and pragmatic approach to the issue, raising the question in regard both to epistemology and to hermeneutics that if something is true of God or of the Bible, why would it not be true elsewhere?

[17] *PT,* p. 1 (ET 1).

[18] *PT,* p. 2 (ET 2).

understanding involves providing an answer to this question. 'We know history in that another's action somehow becomes a question to which our own action has to give some sort of answer. Without this responsible being-questioned, our knowledge of history would be knowledge of facts, but not of living people; it would not be history, but a form of science.'[19]

Whatever we might say in response to Barth here on the basis of more recent developments in the philosophy of both the natural and social sciences,[20] throughout the period under review this sort of distinction between the hard sciences and historical enquiry was common currency. Historians were not uniformly optimistic about actually achieving responsible historical understanding as Barth understands it; the question of whether the more or less distant past really could become alive to us was widely disputed.[21] Nevertheless a principled distinction between the interpretative responsibility of the historian and the scientist was generally observed by historians and scientists alike.

---

[19] *PT*, pp. 1–2: 'Ohne dieses verantwortliche Gefragtsein würde unsere Geschichtserkenntnis Erkenntnis von Sachen, nicht aber von lebendigen Menschen, sie würde gerade nicht Geschichts-, sondern eine Form von Naturwissenschaft sein' (ET 2).

[20] On which see the older but still important treatment of Richard J. Bernstein, *Beyond Objectivism and Relativism. Science, Hermeneutics and Praxis* (Philadelphia, 1983).

[21] Thus in his famous Storrs Lectures of 1931, Carl L. Becker spoke with a certain resignation (and enduring elegance) of the 'infinite attention and indifference' with which twentieth-century scientists, historians, and philosophers alike were condemned to read a pre-modern Christian work such as Aquinas' *Summa Theologiae*: 'We can perhaps wonder a little—although, since nothing is alien to us, we are rarely caught wondering—at the unfailing zest, the infinite patience, the extraordinary ingenuity and acumen therein displayed. We can even understand what is therein recorded well enough to translate it clumsily into modern terms. The one thing we cannot do with the *Summa* of St. Thomas is meet its arguments on their own ground. We can neither assent to them nor refute them. It does not even occur to us to make the effort, since we instinctively feel that in the climate of opinion which sustains such arguments we could only gasp for breath. Its conclusions seem to us neither true nor false, but only irrelevant' (*The Heavenly City of the Eighteenth-Century Philosophers* (New Haven and London, 1932), pp. 11–12). For Becker, while the distinction between the historical method and the scientific method is valid, both are 'results of a single impulse, two aspects of the trend of modern thought away from an overdone rationalization of the facts to a more careful and disinterested examination of the facts themselves' (p. 20). And this 'subtle shift in the point of view', 'perhaps the most important event in the intellectual history of modern times' (p. 21), so separates modern thought from the pre-modern project of reconciling experience with revealed truth that pre-modern thought (which in a certain respect extends all the way through the eighteenth century) becomes to us, for all intents and purposes, irretrievably lost. It can be an object of curiosity, but certainly not approached as the achievement of living thinkers to whom we are accountable. See further Burleigh Taylor Wilkins, *Carl Becker. A Biographical Study in American Intellectual History* (Cambridge, MA, 1961), pp. 174–209.

We are well served to ask, then, to what degree Barth's more general comments about historical involvement as a *sine qua non* of historical understanding can be understood as an expression of a general cultural mood—an ethically driven reaction against a positivism that was perceived to dehumanize the object of its enquiry. More specifically, we might ask to what extent Barth is simply appropriating a set of themes already well developed in the early-twentieth-century hermeneutic tradition—*viz.*, the distinction between life and nature, and the corresponding insistence on the autonomy of historical enquiry vis-à-vis the hard sciences.[22]

These questions bring us close to ground recently covered in detail by Richard Burnett in his fine recent study, *Karl Barth's Theological Exegesis*. On the basis of a careful reading of Barth's *Römerbrief* (drawing especially on the draft prefaces to the 1919 edition first published in the *Gesamtausgabe*), Burnett makes a strong case for seeing Barth's early hermeneutics as far more provocative and deliberate than is often recognized. In doing so, he also raises afresh the question of why hermeneutical issues dominated the reception of the *Römerbrief*, and argues that they did so '*not* because [the book] fell into a so-called hermeneutical "vacuum," but because it challenged the most influential hermeneutical tradition of the nineteenth and twentieth centuries, the hermeneutical tradition of Schleiermacher and Dilthey'.[23] In support of this thesis, Burnett rightly argues that for Barth the self-established and graciously maintained freedom of God is the fundamental hermeneutical problem, one for which psychologically and historically oriented hermeneutics[24] have thus far been unable to properly account. And he describes at length Barth's attempt to overcome this tradition, highlighting the contrast between Barth's emphasis on the hermeneutical significance of love (i.e., responsible participation with the author in the subject matter[25]) and the manifold historical-psychological evasions of this commitment, not least in the notion of 'empathy' as it is developed by Schleiermacher and Dilthey.[26]

---

[22] See here the valuable overview of the debate over the history-science distinction in post-idealist German philosophy in Herbert Schnädelbach, *Philosophy in Germany 1831–1933*, trans. Eric Matthews (Cambridge, 1984), pp. 33–108.

[23] Burnett, *Barth's Theological Exegesis*, p. 49.

[24] Represented in Burnett's study by Wernle, Herder, Schleiermacher, Dilthey, Troeltsch, Wobbermin, and the pre-1915 Karl Barth, not to mention (and here Burnett's convictions regarding the continued relevance of Barth's hermeneutics are most evident) much contemporary mainstream biblical interpretation: 'The empathetic approach to interpretation', Burnett claims, 'is as pervasive today among rank and file scholars in biblical and religious studies departments throughout [the United States] and Europe as ever, and with it the same historicizing and psychologizing assumptions' (*Barth's Theological Exegesis*, p. 261).

[25] Cf. Burnett, *Barth's Theological Exegesis*, p. 126.

[26] See Burnett, *Barth's Theological Exegesis*, pp. 142–220.

There are questions to be put to Burnett here: Whether it is useful to speak of 'the hermeneutical tradition' of Schleiermacher as such, for example, and whether this tradition is best comprehended through the term 'empathy'.[27] More importantly, we might ask whether Barth's concerns about Schleiermacher's hermeneutics are best captured by talk of the mitigation of individuality or of an anthropology of alienation, or whether these are not at most derivative notions, symptoms of more fundamental differences requiring further, more specific theological elaboration.[28] Finally, we might ask how far the textual evidence, suggestive as it often is, allows us confidently to reconstruct what Barth might have made of these questions.

Whatever we make of all this, we can certainly allow Burnett's valuable book to remind us just how important it is to take careful account of the broader intellectual traditions to which Barth was indebted. And in the present instance that means placing the preface of *Die protestantische Theologie* not only in its immediate polemical context (i.e., reading it as a reaction against his students' lack of hospitality towards their theological forbears, or as an extended response to Brunner's dismissal of Schleiermacher[29]), but also in the broader context of more

---

[27] Cf. Burnett, *Barth's Theological Exegesis*, p. 150–51: 'like other Romantic interpreters of his day, Schleiermacher saw interpretation as, among other things, a matter of getting inside the mind or soul of an author by means of aesthetic intuition', so that while 'Schleiermacher may not have used the specific term "Einfühlung" ... his hermeneutical program is clearly dependent upon this Romantic concept'. For the suggestion that 'empathy' is not central to the Romantic tradition, see Martin Fontius, 'Einfühlung/Empathie/Identifikation', in Karlheinz Barck et. al., eds, *Ästhetische Grundbegriffe, Band 2 Dekadent-Grotesk* (Stuttgart, 2001), pp. 121–42. The application of the term to Schleiermacher's philosophy of understanding is, of course, widely contested. See here Andrew Bowie, *From Romanticism to Critical Theory. The Philosophy of German Literary Theory* (London, 1997); Bowie, 'Introduction' to Friedrich Schleiermacher, *Hermeneutics and criticism and other writings*, trans. and ed. Andrew Bowie (Cambridge, 1998), pp. vii–xxxii; H.G. Gadamer, *Hermeneutik I. Warheit und Methode. Grundzüge einer philosophischen Hermeneutik, Gesammelte Werke, Band 1* (Tübingen, 1986) (ET *Truth and Method*, ed. Garrett Barden and John Cumming (New York, 1975)); Gadamer, 'Zwischen Phänomenologie und Dialektik. Versuch einer Selbstkritik', in *Hermeneutik II. Warheit und Methode. Ergänzungen, Register, Gesammelte Werke, Band 2* (Tübingen, 1986), pp. 3–23 (esp. pp. 14–16); further Claus v. Bormann, 'Hermeneutik I. Philosophisch-theologisch', in Gerhard Müller, ed., *Theologische Realenzyklopädie* (Berlin and New York, 1986), 15:108–37, and the literature cited there.

[28] See Burnett, *Barth's Theological Exegesis*, pp. 155–8, 205–6.

[29] One cannot recall too often in this connection Barth's distaste for Brunner's *Die Mystik und die Wort. Der Gegensatz zwischen moderner Religionsauffassung und christlichen Glauben dargestellt an der Theologie Schleiermachers* (Tübingen, 1924). Barth refers to it at the start of his 1926 lecture series, and it still stands as an example of the sort of historical-theological arrogance to be avoided in the 1932 lectures (*PT*, p. 7 (ET 7). It remained a source of very personal irritation for Barth as late as 1960: Upon hearing a

general claims regarding the distinctiveness and dignity of historical knowledge and the *Geisteswissenschaften*.

We can find a useful point of entry to the issue in the concept of *life*. In Barth's nineteenth-century lectures, the distinctiveness of historical enquiry over against any form of *Naturwissenschaft* is founded on a basic distinction, not simply between humanity and the nonhuman, 'natural' world, but between *die Sachen* and *die lebendigen Menschen*. In the first place, this means that historical enquiry centers on the *purposeful* expressions of human subjects; the task of history writing is not to be confused with a seeing-through of these expressions to a series of putative subconscious motivations. Nor, on the other hand, can the living person be understood simply as the point at which large-scale economic, biological, political, linguistic, or other historical and cultural forces converge and come to individual expression. In this sense, to speak of *den lebendigen Mensch* is to speak of the whole person as a free, responsible agent (the ethical component of Barth's aversion to any form of psychologism or historicism should not be missed).

Secondly, to say 'living person' is to speak of this person in the *whole* of the activity for which he is responsible. History as the study of the living person is wide-ranging in its investigation of this manifold action. Thus while Barth's *Die protestantische Theologie* necessarily focuses primarily on written texts, it includes a series of remarkably perceptive comments on, *inter alia*, architecture, gardening, music, and fashion as characteristic expressions of the eighteenth-century man's absolute will for form.[30]

But a third significance of the adjective *lebendig* would hardly have been lost on an audience conversant with broader contemporary debates over the possibility of attaining to genuine objectivity in the human sciences, largely informed as these were by Dilthey's work, in which the notion of life is thematized and placed at the heart of a thoroughgoing critique of historical knowledge.

Dilthey locates the independence and unity of the *Geisteswissenschaften* (which embrace history and the systematic social sciences as two classes of human

---

summary of his own critique of Schleiermacher, Barth responded, 'It is correct, but I don't like the impression it leaves. It makes me look like a lawyer accusing him, doesn't show that I love him as my neighbor. I should have preferred a kinder view to come across, more respectful. Never have I done such a thing as Brunner did. After his book, I said to him we should get together and study the matter. He said he couldn't [and deep, flushed emotion crept into Barth's face, halfway between tears of sorrow and rage] that he had burned his papers! He was done with him! [A sweep of the arm, a look of extreme disgust.] Imagine! For me, Schleiermacher is present, within the church, my comrade, the finest of them all!' (Terrence N. Tice, 'Interviews with Karl Barth and Reflections on His Interpretations of Schleiermacher', in *Barth and Schleiermacher: Beyond the Impasse?* ed. James O. Duke and Robert F. Streetman (Philadelphia, 1988), pp. 43–62 (50)). See further John W. Hart, *Karl Barth vs. Emil Brunner. The Formation and Dissolution of a Theological Alliance, 1916–1936* (New York, 2001), esp. pp. 44–53.

[30] See *PT*, pp. 36–9, 49–53 (ET 40–3, 54–9).

self-knowledge) in their distinct approach to a distinct subject matter: humanity, considered according to its inner nature—i.e., in its deliberate, concrete (individual), complex activity and passion, and therefore according to its inherent purpose, value, and meaning.[31]

> We can distinguish the human studies from the sciences by certain, clear, characteristics. These are to be found in the attitude of mind, ... which moulds the subject-matter of the human studies quite differently from that of scientific knowledge. Humanity seen through the senses is just a physical fact which can only be explained scientifically. It only becomes the subject-matter of the human studies when we experience human states, give expressions to them and understand these expressions. The interrelation of life, expression and understanding embraces gestures, facial expressions and words, all of which men use to communicate with each other; it also includes permanent mental creations which reveal their author's deeper meaning, and lasting objectifications of the mind in social structures where common human nature is surely, and for ever, manifest.... So man becomes the subject matter of the human studies only when we relate experience, expression and understanding to each other. They are based on this connection, which is their distinguishing characteristic. A discipline only belongs to the human studies when we can approach its subject-matter through the connection between life, expression and understanding.[32]

What is thus experienced and understood is, precisely, 'life as the interweaving of all mankind'.[33] As in Barth, the notion of life involves the variety and complexity of human achievement. But in Dilthey, this emphasis on the many-sidedness of human willing and doing is bound up with a sort of anxious optimism about the possibility of achieving objective knowledge of oneself and others not at all characteristic of Barth. The development of the *Geisteswissenschaften* depends for Dilthey on, among other things, the increasingly comprehensive understanding 'of *all* objective manifestations of mind'.[34] Because Barth's interest is more specifically theological, invested in tracing the relationships of human beings in light of their common relationship to God, the notion of 'life' does not need to function as a basic epistemological category. Rather, the point of Barth's appeal to life—to ground the call for interpretative responsibility to theologians past in recognition of a shared participation in a common task—is largely secured through ecclesiological statements to be examined below. And the significance of Barth's appeal to scripture in this context, however fleeting, should not be overlooked:

---

[31] See H.P. Rickman, ed., *W. Dilthey. Selected Writings* (Cambridge, 1976), pp. 170–5, 215–6; hereafter Dilthey, *Selected Writings*. Throughout this section I have followed Rickman's translation of Dilthey's *Der Aufbau der Geschichtlichen Welt in den Geisteswissenschaften*, ed. by Berhard Groethuysen, *Gesammelte Schriften*, vol. 7 (Stuttgart, 1958).

[32] Dilthey, *Selected Writings*, pp. 175–6.

[33] Dilthey, *Selected Writings*, pp. 177–8.

[34] Dilthey, *Selected Writings*, p. 177 (emphasis added).

'Augustin, Thomas, Luther, Schleiermacher und alle die Andern sind nicht tot, sondern lebendig.' What is the basis of this claim? Not finally the epistemological dictum that 'there is not a person or a thing which is merely an object to me, which does not represent pressure or furtherance, the goal of some striving or a restriction on my will'.[35] But rather, and quite simply, because *Ihm leben sie alle* (cf. Lk. 20.38).[36]

The lesson drawn from this one example can, despite the dangers involved in any such generalization, be legitimately applied to the broader question of Barth's relationship to the hermeneutically oriented historiographies of Droysen, Dilthey, Bultmann, and others. On a general level, there is an important conceptual overlapping: Barth accepts a principled distinction between history and science, both in the sense that history has to do with a distinctive subject matter (living humanity) and that it pursues a distinctive, self-involving course toward knowledge. And he seems to stress in *Die protestantische Theologie* the constitutive power of interpretative expectations and methods in a way that he does not—or at least not so strongly—when speaking of the biblical texts. In view of the emphasis on the objectivity and self-interpreting power of the text in 'The New World in the Bible', for example, we may be somewhat surprised to hear Barth say that 'history is made up of living men whose work is handed over defenseless to our understanding and appreciation upon their death' and that it is precisely for this reason that their words have a claim on our courtesy.[37] These and other similarities need to be factored into any comprehensive evaluation of Barth's theological historiography.

On the other hand, one cannot help but pause at the nearly pedestrian observation that Barth's historiography really appears quite modest in scope, especially when compared with Dilthey's massive if fragmentary body of work on the subject. His comments on the task of history-writing, although he will argue for their general significance, do not seem to be intended as justifications of the attempt to write a history of theology, much less of the attempt to understand historical figures in their individuality. While Barth would certainly have been aware of the epistemological problematic at the heart of Dilthey's program (viz., the recognition that others can only be objectively known through their self-expression in media which must necessarily obscure individuality precisely as they enable individual self-expression), he is not so heavily exercised by this issue that it prevents him from trusting that if he attends to the texts at hand he can in fact hear what it is the theologians of the nineteenth century have to say.

We can recall in this connection Barth's account of an exchange with Gogarten early in 1922, when the latter visited Göttingen. 'At that time', Barth recalled, Gogarten:

---

[35] Dilthey, *Selected Writings*, p. 178.

[36] *PT*, p. 3 (ET 3).

[37] *PT*, p. 8 (ET 8).

came to my lectures and listened a couple of times to what I had to say about the Heidelberg Catechism and the Epistle to the Ephesians. Even now, I can still hear him telling me, before he went off back to ... Stelzendorf: 'Do you know, Karl Barth, I don't think that things will turn out as you expect. Before we can talk about the Heidelberg Catechism and the Epistle to the Ephesians, we must first know what history is.' I asked him, 'But how will you discover what history is?' He replied, 'First I must tackle Troeltsch, Dilthey, Yorck von Wartenburg and some other great figures from the beginning of the 1920s.... Well, first of all we must find a concept of history and only on the basis of that will we be able to read texts like the Heidelberg Catechism and the Epistle to the Ephesians'... Even then, that is in the winter of 1921–22, I noticed ... that we did not think in the same way. For me it was quite the other way round: first of all I wanted to study the Heidelberg Catechism and the Epistle to the Ephesians. Only then did I want to try to understand what 'history' is. But these were two very different approaches.[38]

This simple but crucial difference in approach has any number of implications that can be discussed fruitfully on a general methodological level. But if we are not too quickly to abstract Barth's historiography from its most immediate context, we must first ask about the basis of Barth's desire to read biblical and theological texts before engaging in philosophical clarifications of the concept of history, not to mention his confidence that he can legitimately do so. And this brings us to the question of the specifically theological character of Barth's historiography. When Barth assumes that he can go about the business of actually reading the theologians of the first, sixteenth, or nineteenth century without first demonstrating the possibility of historical understanding, he is demonstrating a confidence inseparable from a perceived obligation to just these particular figures.

This is because for Barth responsibly approaching these figures means attending to and being radically implicated by the subject matter to which these figures refer. Responsible interpretation is nothing less than participation with the author in the subject matter. And this entails, among other things, standing alongside the writer and looking in the direction he indicates. This does not mean being unaware of the individuality of the author; but it does mean understanding the author as an individual in relation to just this subject matter. The crucial distinction is between viewing an author as source and viewing him as witness.[39] In the former case, the writer is of independent interest as creative personality; in the latter the crucial concept is faithfulness to the subject matter, and the reader's responsible attentiveness to the writer is initiated for the sake of and finally sustained by that subject matter itself.

We can approach the issue in a slightly different but intimately related way by examining the way in which Barth develops the notion of interpretative *objectivity*.

---

[38] Busch, *Karl Barth*, p. 137.

[39] The point is well made in Burnett, *Barth's Theological Exegesis*, p. 216.

And here Rudolf Bultmann's 1955 Gifford Lectures, *History and Eschatology*, provide a useful point of comparison.

Bultmann opens these lectures by asking whether modern historicism does not inevitably lead to historical relativism and, eventually, nihilism.[40] The urgency of this question for Bultmann stems in large part from his sensitivity to the hermeneutical principle that the results of any particular investigation are at least partially determined by the question posed by the investigator, that 'each interpretation is guided by a certain interest, by a certain *putting of the question*'.[41] At the most general level, the interpreter's enabling interest in the subject matter (i.e., his 'pre-understanding') arises from 'the simple fact that author and interpreter are living in the same historical world, in which human life is enacted as a life in surroundings, in the knowing use of objects and the intercourse of men'.[42] But more particular questions follow from the fact that investigation is always undertaken in specific circumstances by unique individual enquirers; and this raises the question of how to appropriately evaluate the plurality of interpretations that arise from these various pre-understandings, or how historical knowledge can lay claim to objectivity in any meaningful sense.

Bultmann begins his response to this question by distinguishing the objectivity to which science appeals and the objectivity appropriate in historical enquiry, a distinction which must be explicated at least in part in terms of the historian's existential involvement in history: 'The subjectivity of the historian is a necessary factor of objective historical knowledge ... History gains meaning only when the historian himself stands within history and takes part in history.'[43]

The active participation of the historian in history defines the limits of acceptable interpretative pluralism, and so grounds the notion of historical objectivity, in two ways. First, the historian as an individual human being in a specific socio-political situation brings to bear a set of unique questions, but a set of questions that nevertheless must recognizably correspond to his humanity.

> Each historical phenomenon can be seen from different points of view, because man is a complex being. He consists of body and soul, or if one prefers, of body, soul, and mind. He has appetites and passions, he feels physical and spiritual needs, he has will and imagination. He is a political and social being, and he is also an individual with his own particularity, and therefore human community can be understood not only as political and social but also as personal relationship. In consequence it is possible to write history as political history as well as economic history, as [the] history of problems and ideas as well as [the] history of individuals and personalities. The historical judgment may be guided by psychological or ethical interest and also by aesthetic interest. Each of these

---

[40] Rudolf Bultmann, *History and Eschatology. The Presence of Eternity* (New York, 1957), pp. 10–11.

[41] Bultmann, *History and Eschatology*, p. 113.

[42] Bultmann, *History and Eschatology*, pp. 113–4; cf. p. 124.

[43] Bultmann, *History and Eschatology*, p. 119.

different views is open to one side of the historical process, and from each viewpoint something objectively true will appear. The picture is falsified only if one single viewpoint is made an absolute one, if it comes to be a dogma.[44]

In short, for Bultmann objectivity is grounded anthropologically and secured ethically through the demand for perspectival generosity: Objectivity in historical enquiry means, among other things, entertaining views of all sorts so long as they are legitimately grounded in the structure of human being in the world and do not pretend to absoluteness.

This particular sort of interpretative hospitality corresponds in Bultmann to an evacuation of a traditional Christian eschatology: 'Today we cannot claim to know the end and the goal of history. Therefore the question of meaning in history has become meaningless.'[45] And in its place arises the ethical question: After eschatology, 'there still remains the question of the meaning of single historical phenomena and single historical epochs ... There remains the question of the importance of single historical events and deeds of our past for our present, a present which is charged with responsibility for our future'.[46]

This responsibility for the future is the second aspect of the historian's participation in history that grounds historical objectivity. Historical enquiry begins precisely where one feels the responsibility of acting in the present, in the light of the past, for the sake of the future.

> The genuine historical question grows out of the historical emotion of the subject, of the person, who feels his responsibility. Therefore historical research includes readiness to hear the claim which meets one in the historical phenomena. And just for this reason the demand for freedom from presuppositions, for an unprejudiced approach, which is valid for all science, is also valid for historical research.[47]

At each moment, invited and obliged to realize ourselves in the here and now, we make history and render it meaningful: 'In this responsibility, as responsibility over against the past as well as over against the future, the unity of history is grounded.'[48]

All this stands in obvious contrast to Barth's claim that objectivity—and so responsibility—in dealing with the history of Christian theology must be specified by its continual reference to the self-revelation of God in Christ as it is attested in scripture. This does not mean simply that the object to which the witness of scripture and so of scripture's authors directs us is capable of graciously grasping and holding our attention. It also means that the concept of responsibility operates

---

[44] Bultmann, *History and Eschatology*, p. 118; cf. p. 138.

[45] Bultmann, *History and Eschatology*, p. 120.

[46] Bultmann, *History and Eschatology*, p. 121.

[47] Bultmann, *History and Eschatology*, pp. 121–2.

[48] Bultmann, *History and Eschatology*, p. 144.

in a specific space to be characterized in theological terms. So, for example, in Barth the unity of history is in the first place a factor of God's faithfulness, not of our taking responsibility for our future selves. And because God's faithfulness is not a timeless attitude towards creation but the historically localized reconciling act of God in Jesus Christ who graciously confronts the church in the witness of the prophets and apostles, responsibility toward God necessarily means a responsibility to the past.

> The servant of the Word of God must be a theologian because he has to testify to that Word by his speaking in preaching, instruction, and pastoral care. It is not the Word of God that is conditioned by human knowledge and requires critical, systematic reflection, but his own service to the Word of God, this particular service to the Word of God by the witness of his own speaking. What is involved is always the hearing of the Word of God, documented in the Bible, in any given present, since that necessarily precedes any speaking. Because the present is continually changing, the theologian cannot be content with establishing and communicating the results obtained by some classical period; his reflection must be renewed constantly. For this reason, serious theological work is forced, again and again, to begin from the beginning. However, as this is done, the theology of past periods, classical and less classical, also plays a part and demands a hearing. It demands a hearing as surely as it occupies a place with us in the context of the church. The church does not stand in a vacuum. Beginning from the beginning, however necessary, cannot be a matter of beginning off one's own bat. We have to remember the *communio sanctorum*, bearing and being borne by each other, asking and being asked, having to take mutual responsibility for and among the sinners gathered together in Christ. As regards theology, also, we cannot be in the church without taking as much responsibility for the theology of the past as for the theology of the present.[49]

To the question 'Why are we concerned with theologians past?' Barth will respond: Not primarily because the field of our moral action is determined in large part by a cultural inheritance bound up with the history of Christianity in the West, however great the impact of Christian theology and Christian practice on our culture may be. Rather, we are concerned with them because they have come forward in the church of Christ claiming to speak the Word of the Lord. If one must speak of an enabling interest in the subject matter at issue in a history of theology, it certainly cannot be adequately described in pre-theological terms as participation in a world of social intercourse within the bounds of the natural world. Our responsibility as historians of theology is defined by the existence of the *church*, what Barth calls 'the only possible sphere for this undertaking'.[50] And just so it involves a confession of faith and a very specific sort of humility.

---

[49] *PT*, pp. 2–3 (ET 2–3).
[50] *PT*, p. 5 (ET 5).

Humility

Barth sees two dangers—two forms of pride—accompanying the task of historical theology. The first involves the temptation to measure the past by the present, if not assuming a general principle of progress, then at least assuming the present affords a secure basis for judging the past. We may well recognize this as an inescapable instinct of modernity,[51] but Barth in this context is interested in drawing attention to the particular form this temptation takes for students of theology (and perhaps for students of any academic discipline in which the *truth* of history is at issue).

> The moment of one's own theological knowledge is always to some extent an intoxicating one, not only when a student in his middle or later semesters has the experience, at the hand of a guide or through his own initiative, of having discovered what is going on behind the sphinx-like expression of theology, but truly and really only when many an argument has been held and half, or even the whole, of a life devoted to scholarship lies in the past. The intoxication of such a moment represents a temptation.... Will it remain clear to us at this moment that while the present can always be right over against the past, we can give no satisfactory answer to the question whether it is right in actual fact? If that is forgotten, if in the intoxication of the moment the consciousness of being able to be right turns into the consciousness of actually being right, then our hearing of the voices of the past will be objectively wrong, however much it may be subjectively right.[52]

Why is such a hearing objectively wrong? Because it involves one illegitimately adopting the posture of a judge to whom others are accountable. This is to be avoided above all because God has reserved judgment for himself, and the failure to recognize this methodologically would be to fail to give God his due glory and so would trespass a basic hermeneutical principle of any Reformed theology. But it also short-circuits the possibility of historical understanding: 'The one who is all too sure, illegitimately sure, that "we have brought it to so glorious a conclusion" cannot and may not notice carefully "what a wise man thought before us".'[53] The other is not respected as other, and history becomes a monologue, or a game of chess in which one player plays both white and black pieces.[54]

---

[51] Cf. *PT*, pp. 39–40 (ET p. 44), where Barth describes the eighteenth-century origins of the critical study of history, 'a highly problematical affair' that became possible when 'man began axiomatically to credit himself with being superior to the past, and assume a standpoint in relation to it whence he found it possible to set himself up as a judge over past events according to fixed principles, as well as to describe its deeds and to substantiate history's own report'.

[52] *PT*, p. 5 (ET 5).

[53] *PT*, p. 5 (ET 5).

[54] *PT*, pp. 5–6 (ET 5–6).

Barth sees this problem in a wide variety of histories of modern theology, 'a whole series of accounts where it is all too evident that the authors are not guiding us in a shared investigation of what the men of the past may be saying to us', but are speaking as those who have already had done with listening and are now content to report to others the results of their own discoveries.[55] These results may be either dismissive or adulatory; the temptation to canonize sixteenth-century Reformed theology mirrors the temptation too quickly to reject nineteenth-century culture-theology. In either case the issue is that the results are one-sided because the investigation, which may have started out well enough as a genuine engagement with the material, has stagnated. If it has the appearance of continued historical work, this is only because it is retracing the steps of an earlier excursion whose outcome is already known and which leads to a destination in which the historian already feels at home.

What is the alternative? A 'tranquil, attentive, and open hearing of the involved participant' that recognizes an obligation to hear voices of the past in their own terms; 'a claim that their own concerns should be heard and that they should not be used simply as a means to our ends';[56] a continual returning to these voices with the expectation that we may hear something genuinely new from them, and therefore with the discipline to set aside the cherished results of our past work if required.

In this aspect, at least, Barth's account of the task of historical investigation parallels Schleiermacher's ethics of understanding, outlining an ideal that reflects and serves to inspire an engagement with the sources that is never finally complete.[57] (Thus while he was preparing a chapter on Lessing for the 1933 lectures, Barth wrote to Thurneysen asking, 'Wouldn't you also love to spend a second lifetime as a historian?'[58]) And concretely, Barth's emphasis on humility gives rise to some very sober and practical advice:

> The condition for a legitimate concern with the theology of the past is ... that we should escape again from the unavoidable intoxication of the moment of our own theological recognition as quickly as possible and with the utmost speed meet up again with our fathers, with those whose voices we think that we have heard often enough before.[59]

---

[55] See *PT*, pp. 6–8 (ET 6–8).

[56] *PT*, pp. 5, 8 (ET 5, 8).

[57] Cf. Bowie, *From Romanticism to Critical Theory*, p. 125: 'understanding is for Schleiermacher primarily ethical: it does not derive final foundations from already existing rules, but rather imposes a continuing obligation upon free actors to attempt to see the world from the viewpoint of the other'.

[58] Barth to Thurneysen, 10 February 1933 (*B-Th III*, p. 357). A temporarily bed-ridden Thurneysen responded six days later with the somewhat floral wish that Barth could have ten lifetimes to devote to his historical work (see pp. 364–5).

[59] *PT*, p. 10 (ET 10).

Humility proves itself—not in an overly deferential posture toward either one's sources or one's contemporaries, but—in hard work: continual, repentant attention to even the most familiar texts. The inevitable pride in one's accomplishments, the institutional pressure to build upon and validate one's own past research—all this must be fought: above all by prayer (though this is not explicit in the present passage), but also in countless, unmarked hours of study.[60]

The second, related form of theological pride against which Barth warns involves the presumption that the boundaries of the Christian church are as available to us as they are to God. In practice, this means dismissing individuals, schools of thought, or ages in the history of the church as, if not heretical, at least not worthy of serious consideration in the present work of hearing and proclaiming the Word of God.

> An explicit judgment, the feeling that for better or worse we can be 'finished' with this or that, always means the closing of a door that ought to remain open, the silencing of a voice that ought to continue to speak, and that is not only to our detriment, but also to the detriment of the church. By transgressing the prohibition once formulated by Overbeck, to the effect that men are not called to hold the last judgment on one another, people violate the mystery of the body of Christ and at the least cut themselves off from a source of knowledge.[61]

As a function of the church which exists as a community of faithful and hopeful witness between the time of Christ's ascension and his return, theology must for Barth operate with an eschatological reserve that does not prevent one from making affirmations and denials but characterizes them as the decisions of a church that awaits the judgment of its coming Lord. The humility that takes the

---

[60] That the voices of the past were really living voices was for Barth finally an ecclesiological (and therefore pneumatological) claim; but simply on the level of personal sensibilities Barth was inclined to think of Schleiermacher and other figures from the tradition as present companions in his theological work. And for both these reasons one should avoid thinking that Barth conceived of this devotion to historical scholarship in individualistic terms, however much individual work it necessarily involves. This corresponds to Barth's steady refusal to accept that reading could only serve as the occasion by which we remember a truth already within us, a view he (notoriously) sensed in pietism and Roman Catholicism, and which receives perhaps its most evocative modern expression in Proust's *Sur la lecture* (ET *On Reading*, trans. and ed. Jean Autret and William Burford (New York, 1971)).

[61] *PT*, p. 9 (ET 9). Barth goes on to reject (almost certainly in response to Brunner, *Die Mystik und das Wort*, p. 390) the standard distinction between a person and his work as *sophistische*. 'One can and must distinguish between creator and creature where the creator is God. To distinguish between a person and his work, between the sinner and his sinful act, is an impossible abstraction, which does not become more possible by virtue of its popularity. In the measure that one commends or rejects a work one also commends or rejects a person. This must stop.'

form of careful historical scholarship must recognize these limits of the sphere in which this work occurs.

> History writing cannot be a proclamation of judgment. In that case, it would seem that prophetic inspiration warranted us to presuppose not only that our age could be right, but that it was right. We shall do well not to claim this possibility too hastily or too often. It is appropriate for us to leave on one side what the Son of Man will do in his future, namely to divide the good from the evil.[62]

In particular, 'it is necessary to remind ourselves that it has in no way been revealed to us that the nineteenth century was in whole or in part a time in which God withdrew his hand from the church'.[63] Historical scholarship undertaken in the church operates with the assumption that a unity of subject-matter and concern unites the church at all times and places, despite the very real differences of expression and cultural location that of course also characterize the church in the world:

> Over and above the diversity the unity can continually be seen, the unity of embarrassment and of worry, but also a unity of richness and hope, which in the end binds us to the theologians of the past. It would represent an unchurchly and therefore an untheological attitude [*eine unkirchliche und darum auch untheologische Haltung*] if we were not to approach a particular period on this presupposition, or were to put it in doubt.[64]

Barth invokes a version of Pascal's wager to describe the consequences of this interpretative posture (though not, it should be said, to justify it): If I act as though even the most immediately troubling figures in the tradition were genuinely concerned with the revelation that constitutes the church ever anew and I am mistaken, I will lose nothing by it. Whatever errors they entertain will become apparent soon enough if I take them seriously in this way. But if I allow my suspicions to prevent me from taking them at their word, I may miss something that I need to hear in and for the sake of the church.[65]

What makes Barth so sure the church today will not simply repeat past heresies if it entertains voices in the tradition that have been widely regarded as suspect? The first and final word here would be the prayer that the Spirit would preserve the church of Jesus Christ. But we should also note the significance of the scripture principle in this context: When Barth claims the places where the tradition has erred will certainly come to light on the basis of this 'as if',[66] he presupposes an

---

[62] *PT*, p. 9 (ET 9).

[63] *PT*, p. 13 (ET 13).

[64] *PT*, p. 13 (ET 13).

[65] *PT*, p. 14 (ET 14).

[66] *PT*, p. 14 (ET 14).

irreversibly ordered relationship between the church and scripture as the self-authenticating witness to God's Word. The distinction between canon and community is constitutive of the identity of this community across time (it is the community that hears its call to be in just this text), and recognition of precisely this distinction frees one to a generous reading of the tradition. Conversely, a recognition that no theological school or program can domesticate the revelation to which scripture authoritatively refers prevents a Protestant theology from deploying the scripture principle itself as a theological weapon. One may truly protest against the apparent conflation of church and scripture (Barth often did so, especially in dialogue with pre-Vatican II Roman Catholic theology), but in doing so one is protesting in the name of and for the sake of the *church*, and one may not presume to know whether or not in God's eyes the one against whom one is protesting is a member of it.

Rather, one must act on the assumption that he or she is in the church precisely because one may not limit the scope of God's saving act. 'I have to count all these people as members of the Christian church and, remembering that I and my theological work are in the Christian church only on the ground of forgiveness, I have neither to dispute nor even to doubt that, like me, they were ultimately concerned with the Christian faith.'[67]

Faith

We have already begun to cross over into that aspect of historical enquiry that is best comprehended by the statement that theological history-writing is an act of faith. Faith that one's own sins have been forgiven; faith that the God who so forgives has called others to fellowship in the body of Christ and sustains this fellowship by his Spirit; faith, therefore, that this church does truly exist in the world despite the many conflicts and confusions that mark all things human; faith that we can relate to one another across time and place as fellow members of just this community and recipients of just this grace; and faith, finally, that the God who calls this community into being and gives its members to each other is the one, true God who rules over all history and so allows us to speak meaningfully of history as such. Whatever Barth says about interpretative responsibility and humility finds its *Grund* in this faith. *Credo unam sanctam catholicam et apostolicam ecclesiam* is, Barth claims, the basis for the mutual conversation that is historical theology, the reason why we are not allowed to ascribe alien motives to witnesses of another time and place, but must believe that every period in church history really is and wants to be understood as 'a period of the *church*, that is, as a time of revelation, knowledge, and confession of the one Christian truth'.[68]

---

[67] *PT*, p. 14 (ET 14).
[68] See *PT*, pp. 13–14 (ET 13–14).

This movement towards unification in Barth's historiography is balanced by an emphasis on the internal variety of just this history. The burden of these introductory comments taken as a whole is, of course, to remind Barth's students of the abiding value of listening to the voices of the past precisely in their otherness. A theological historiography that emphasized the unity of the church in time so strongly that it was unable to trace its historical variations would not be dealing with *this* church—the church that exists by and in order to bear witness in history to the revelation of God in Jesus Christ. Or, in the interrogative terms more characteristic of this particular lecture, the church that exists as response to the question raised by the revelation that is the foundation of the church.[69]

> Now, however, on the basis of our unity with our predecessors, we must also take quite seriously the difference between them and ourselves. Even when we give full weight to the *credo ecclesiam* and take it specifically, we cannot mistake the fact that they obviously speak a wholly different language [*eine ganz andere Sprache*] from us— naturally not only grammatically, syntactically, and stylistically different (though significant distinctions make themselves felt here also), but materially in view of the wholly different stress, evaluation, use, classification, and interpretation of the common, received vocabulary of the Christian church [*des gemeinsamen, schon von ihnen übernommenen Sprachschatzes der christlichen Kirche*]. We may and must grant that in the end their intentions were not different from our own. Nevertheless, we cannot ignore the fact that they set out to do the same thing in a wholly different way. They were involved in the same embarrassment and worry, the same richness and hope towards the divine revelation that are also ours—in a wholly different way. They have translated and interpreted the same text specially and differently than we do. In this encounter they were troubled in quite a different way from us. The church means that the eternal revelation entered not only into time but also in to the sequence and the changes of time.... It cannot be disputed that on the basis of its unity, the various periods of the church are special and other, so that real historical knowledge of another period must consist in an awareness of its peculiarity and otherness, of its subsidiary themes, as well as of the main theme which it shares with us. [Therefore,] in theology ... we must always—under the presupposition of the unity of the church—investigate the special and other context and concern of the past and understand this from its own relative center and not from ours.[70]

The continued and continually evolving existence of the church and its theology across time, in other words, are to be explained in terms of the character of the divine act. Because revelation entered into time without thereby ceasing to be the one eternal revelation of God, the church exists in time while yet remaining the one church of Christ. Of course this theological depiction of the identity of the church and its theological tradition does not as such exclude all other descriptions—of the church as a convictional community whose theological

---

[69] See *PT*, p. 13 (ET 13).

[70] *PT*, pp. 14–15 (ET 14–15).

tradition is constituted by a series of practical and theoretical negotiations of a set of shared questions, for example. But Barth's own approach to the issue cannot be understood without attending to the fact that he consistently and clearly grounds the dynamic continuity of theology as a function of the church in the essentially historical character of revelation.

Obviously all that we have said about Barth's historiography in this section applies, *mutatis mutandis*, to the theological interpretation of scripture, which is no less an act of responsibility, humility, and faith than the theological interpretation of the history of theology. Equally obviously, a full understanding of both Barth's historiography and his scriptural hermeneutics requires further work in (at least) two directions: The first involves investigation of the doctrinal bases of Barth's hermeneutics, i.e., his dogmatic elaborations of Trinity, incarnation, church, etc. This will be a major focus of the following two chapters, where we turn to examine Barth's doctrine of the Word of God in the first volume of the *Church Dogmatics*. The second, which will occupy us in the final sections of this chapter, involves attending to Barth's actual historical work, partly to see how his historiographical commitments work themselves out in practice, but also—and for our purposes perhaps more significantly—to see how his characterization of modernity impacts his understanding of the necessity and limits of the church's dogmatic self-examination of its reading practices.

Modernity as a Category of Theological Thinking

At the beginning of this chapter we ventured the rather ambitious statement that 'the rehabilitation of theological discourse about modernity is prerequisite to understanding what Barth is doing hermeneutically and historiographically'. This section will attempt first to qualify and then—however inadequately—to support this claim.

First, the qualification: My interest here lies in the intersection of general hermeneutics, modernity as a political and intellectual construct, and the reception of Barth's account of biblical interpretation. So rather than attempt to survey the vast and vexing literature on the origins and character of 'modernity' (or its equally contested correlative 'postmodernity'), we will simply refer to the uncontroversial claim that general hermeneutics has a history of its own, and that this history is bound up with a dynamic complex of modern instincts and institutions.[71] The task

---

[71] Among the many useful overviews and histories, see Dilthey, 'The Development of Hermeneutics', in Dilthey, *Selected Writings*, pp. 247–63; H.-G. Gadamer, *Hermeneutik I. Warheit und Methode*; Gadamer, 'Klassische und philosophische Hermeneutik', in *Hermeneutik II*, pp. 92–117; Kurt Mueller-Vollmer, ed., *The Hermeneutics Reader. Texts of the German Tradition from the Enlightenment to the Present* (New York, 1985); Anthony O'Hear, ed., *Verstehen and Humane Understanding* (Cambridge, 1996); Richard E. Palmer,

then becomes asking how to account for this mutual implication of modernity, general hermeneutics, and what can often appear as a pervasive impatience with Barth's account of biblical interpretation.

We can begin by observing that general hermeneutics in its various forms can be usefully understood as one of the many ways in which modernity has sought to defuse potentially (and, tragically, often actually) violent disagreements over the interpretation of scripture. Thus Odo Marquard, in a characteristically elegant and widely overlooked essay, speaks of modernity as the 'Age of Neutralizations' and of modern general hermeneutics as involving a transformation of the dogmatic relationship to the text into an interpretative one, 'an understanding of the text that is open—*ad libitum*, if necessary—to discussion' precisely because 'someone who is open to discussion may possibly stop killing'.[72]

The Thirty Years War is an important landmark here, both as a specific historical event that precipitated a series of important philosophical, political, and theological adjustments by a generation of seminal modern thinkers, and as a proof-text of the modern doctrine that publicly sustained religious convictions are prone to compromise by military or other disciplinary involvements. Of course we can hardly speak of modernity simply as the attempt to resolve the sixteenth- and seventeenth-century 'problem of many authorities'[73] through other than military means; but the wars of religion did at least help an anxious and fragmented age to suspect that 'religion, rather than solving the spiritual crisis, was at the heart of the turmoil'.[74] And the characteristic urgency of modern thought derives in large measure from the conviction, born out of the experience of these conflicts, that traditional confessional language must be recontextualized in the name of the social stability that preserves space for personal and cultural development (including private or publicly innocuous religious activity, as well as scientific and technological progress).[75] The cultural burden of modern general hermeneutics, in

---

Hermeneutics. Interpretation Theory in Schleiermacher, Dilthey, Heidegger, and Gadamer (Evanston, 1969).

[72] Odo Marquard, 'The Question, To What Question Is Hermeneutics The Answer?', trans. Robert M. Wallace, in *Contemporary German Philosophy, Volume 4*, ed. Darrel E. Christiensen ([n.p.], 1984), pp. 9–31 (22). Marquard's use of the phrase 'Age of Neutralizations' is indebted to Carl Schmitt's classic *Der Begriff des Politischen* (Berlin, 1932), §8 (esp. p. 79) (ET *The Concept of the Political*, trans. George Schwab (New Brunswick, 1976), p. 69).

[73] See Jeffrey Stout, *The Flight from Authority: Reason, morality and the quest for autonomy* (Notre Dame, 1981), p. 43.

[74] Louis Dupré, *Passage to Modernity. An Essay in the Hermeneutics of Nature and Culture* (New Haven and London, 1993), p. 114.

[75] And thus, extending a point made by Paul Ricoeur, hermeneutics and ideology critique do indeed belong together, precisely because while one privileges cultural inheritance and the other a vision of future social liberation, both are equally motivated by an ethical concern arising from a historical self-understanding articulated in nonconfessional

other words, is a sad series of instances in which, in Erasmus's words, the 'interpreter of the divine mind musters the apostles fully equipped with spears, slings, siege-machines [and] canons, to preach Christ crucified'.[76]

If we allow ourselves, at least for the moment, the luxury of this aerial view, we can fairly easily read the specific methodological pronouncements of hermeneutical thinkers such as Schleiermacher, as well as more purely rationalist or pragmatist models of modern discourse, in terms of an overarching ethical concern that is bound up with a commonly available narrative about the political volatility of the strong religious identity. Schleiermacher's hermeneutic appeal to the literary and Dilthey's appeal to 'life' both involve—just as surely as Descartes's epistemological foundationalism,[77] Montaigne's urbane and conservative skepticism,[78] and Spinoza's 'conception of a science which comprehends both God and nature'[79]—'the search for the context that relativizes the controversy over the absolute understanding of the text in favor of what is uncontroversial, or controversial without consequences, in the understanding of the text'.[80] And we can further discern a broad distinction in the contemporary hermeneutical literature between those who stress the continuing importance of the methodological as intrinsic to the ethical task of hermeneutics and those—less optimistic about the viability of metacriticism—who advocate a more transparent

---

terms. See Ricoeur, 'Hermeneutics and the Critique of Ideology', in *Hermeneutics and Modern Philosophy*, ed. Brice R. Wachterhauser (Albany, 1986), pp. 300–39.

[76] Desiderius Erasmus, *The Praise of Folly*, trans. Clarence H. Miller (New Haven and London, 1979), p. 126.

[77] On which see especially Stephen Toulmin, *Cosmopolis. The Hidden Agenda of Modernity* (Chicago, 1990).

[78] For a taste of which, see Michel de Montaigne, 'Apology for Raimond Sebond', in *The Essays of Montaigne*, trans. E.J. Trenchmann (New York, 1954), pp. 368–525 (486–9): 'How variously we judge of things! How often we change our opinions!... Our faulty condition should at least make us behave with more moderation and discretion in our changes. We should remember that whatever we receive into our understanding, we often receive untruths, and that we receive them with the aid of those same tools that often prove false and deceptive.... Now, being conscious of this my liability to change, I have accidentally cultivated in myself a certain steadfastness of belief, and have hardly altered my original and natural opinions. For however much new fashions may appeal to me, I do not readily change, for fear of losing by the exchange. And since I am not capable of choosing for myself, I accept the choice of others, and remain in the state wherein God has placed me. Otherwise I could not keep from perpetual rolling. Thus, by the grace of God, I have kept wholly, without being stirred or troubled by conscience, within the ancient tenets of our religion, amidst the many sects and divisions that our times have brought forth.'

[79] Alasdair MacIntyre, *Three Rival Versions of Moral Enquiry. Encyclopedia, Genealogy and Tradition* (Notre Dame, 1990), p. 23.

[80] Marquard, 'To What Question is Hermeneutics the Answer?', pp. 22–3.

appeal to local political and ethical considerations.[81] Marquard unapologetically identifies himself with the first of these approaches: If general hermeneutics has recently come under increasingly severe attack, that is, he claims, 'because the Thirty Years War seems very far away and the French Revolution at least far enough away that the Terror begins to be a problem that one can skip over'.[82] And while he admits that a recovery of the political and ethical significance of a general (or literary) hermeneutics is not sufficient to prevent interpretative conflicts from turning violent, he certainly thinks it necessary.

> I consider the predominance of literary hermeneutics to be something we cannot relinquish.... It is the answer that lives and lets live by reading and letting read.... This literary hermeneutics, as a pluralizing hermeneutics, operates with liberalism's technique of the *separation of powers*, in accordance with which the individual—while no doubt he cannot, using Adorno's formula, 'be different *without* fear'—can at any rate be different with *reduced* fear, ultimately—*divide et fuge!*—by separating the powers of texts and interpretations as well, that is, by dividing even the authorities that stories are, and separating even the powers that texts are.[83]

But we may well ask whether there is finally any ultimate difference between Marquard's hermeneutical call for 'the salutary superficialization of questions of truth and salvation'[84] and Richard Rorty's rather more complacent suggestion that we are free 'benignly to neglect' philosophical (and theological) topics that are not evidently necessary for the workings of a just democratic society.

> Such a society will be accustomed to the thought that social policy needs no more authority than successful accommodation among individuals, individuals who find themselves heir to the same historical traditions and faced with the same problems. It

---

[81] For a much more sophisticated discussion of this distinction in contemporary hermeneutics, see Anthony C. Thiselton, *New Horizons in Hermeneutics* (London, 1992), a text at once sensitive to the theological issues involved and wholly uninterested in Barth's contribution to them.

[82] Marquard, 'To What Question is Hermeneutics the Answer?', p. 25.

[83] Marquard, 'To What Question is Hermeneutics the Answer?', pp. 24, 26–7. Similar concerns and assumptions appear to underlie a great deal of the criticism directed towards Barth's hermeneutics: Werner Jeanrond, for example, finds in Barth a failure to 'deal with the possibility and the consequences of a pluralism or even conflict of possible interpretations', and suggests that theology today requires 'a more critical analysis of our hermeneutical condition' than Barth provides, one that recognizes the distorting effects of unexamined ideologies and attempts to prevent or ameliorate such distortions through ongoing methodological critiques of our vulnerable reading practices (see Jeanrond, 'Karl Barth's Hermeneutics', in *Reckoning with Barth: Essays in Commemoration of the Centenary of Karl Barth's Birth*, ed. Nigel Biggar (London and Oxford, 1988), pp. 80–97 (95–6)).

[84] Marquard, 'To What Question is Hermeneutics the Answer?', p. 24 n. 40.

will be a society that encourages the 'end of ideology', that takes reflective equilibrium as the only method needed in discussing social policy. When such a society deliberates, when it collects the principles and intuitions to be brought into equilibrium, it will tend to discard those drawn from philosophical accounts of the self or of rationality. For such a society will view such accounts not as the foundations of political institutions, but as, at worst, philosophical mumbo jumbo, or, at best, relevant to private searches for perfection, but not to social policy.[85]

Obviously on more than one level Rorty's pragmatism is worlds away from Marquard's earnest appeal for a revitalized general hermeneutics. But both finally share a cultural memory of confessional conflict which both are anxious to avoid, and both finally believe that the philosopher must help the responsible modern citizen (who as such is also the responsible modern reader) temper his appropriation of the canonical text by demonstrating ways of talking about his situation in nontheological terms.

On this reading, perhaps the most interesting contrast in contemporary hermeneutics is between these self-consciously secular circumstantial descriptions and attempts to speak in specifically theological terms of modernity. So rather than circumscribing Christian language in ostensibly broader, more neutral, and more inhabitable contexts (such as Marquard's generally available recognition of a common human frailty), Gianni Vattimo speaks of unlimited divine self-giving as the most comprehensive context of modernity, in so doing implying that a present concern for the peaceable future of the world is best informed by an appropriation of just those scriptures that modernity seeks in the name of peace to avoid or neutralize.

Speaking theologically of modernity involves for Vattimo giving voice to the progressive weakening of Being as the fulfillment of the Christian notion of the divine *kenosis*. The increasing secularism of post-Reformation European culture is understood here as 'a "drift" inscribed positively in the destiny of *kenosis*' and just so as 'the authentic destiny of Christianity'.[86] For the incarnation of God in Jesus Christ—which continues in the descent of the Spirit on the interpreting community and has culminated in the secularization of the modern West—authorizes every other symbolic representation of God: 'Christ does not undermine the myths and stories of false and lying gods: he makes their signification of the divine possible for the first time.'[87] All this corresponds with what Vattimo calls 'the guiding thread of nihilism', viz., 'the reduction of violence, the weakening of strong and aggressive identities, the acceptance of the other, to the point of charity'.[88] The

---

[85] Richard Rorty, 'The priority of democracy to philosophy', in *Objectivity, Relativism, and Truth. Philosophical Papers Volume 1* (Cambridge, 1991), pp. 175–97 (184).

[86] Gianni Vattimo, *Beyond Interpretation. The Meaning of Hermeneutics for Philosophy*, trans. David Webb (Stanford, 1997), pp. 50–1.

[87] Vattimo, *Beyond Interpretation*, p. 55.

[88] Vattimo, *Beyond Interpretation*, p. 73.

context of this characterization of the ethical burden of nihilism is a discussion of the relationship between religion and art, in which Vattimo suggests:

> If art can rediscover its own essentiality by becoming aware of its own constitution as secularized religion, religion could find in this connection a reason to think of itself in terms that are less dogmatic and disciplinarian, and more 'aesthetic', more in line with that third age, the 'age of the spirit'.... We are at that point once again, and there is no reason to be ashamed of it.[89]

In other words, rather than speaking of modernity simply in political-religious terms as the 'Age of Neutralizations', we need to recognize that it is precisely as the Age of the Spirit that modernity unites us in the common confession that God is vulnerable to time and death, and that we are all responsible for interpreting—nothing more—the world we share.

But here again (setting aside questions about the appropriateness of Vattimo's Heideggerian treatment of the doctrine of the incarnation) we note the underlying and unexamined assumption that Christian theology, however robustly deployed, is answerable to a generically describable story of religious conflict in the tradition, and that to be responsibly appropriated today it must align itself with a modern or perhaps postmodern response to it—in this case hermeneutic philosophy understood in terms of its originary 'nihilistic vocation':

> Recognizing the nihilistic implications of hermeneutics seems to liberate us from the generality of a philosophy of culture that continually oscillates between relativism and transcendentalist metaphysics (depending on whether one identifies the horizon of interpretation within the lifeworld understood as a particular culture or as a universal normative reference point). But it also opens the way to a conception of the world as a conflict of interpretations that seems dangerously close to the Nietzschean celebration of the will to power. What the nihilist ontology of hermeneutics provokes, we might say, is not so much theoretical opposition as legitimate ethical concern. Yet, given that the world is plainly nothing more than a conflict of interpretations, is it still possible for interpretations to emerge that are so compelling as to precipitate violence and struggle in the current sense of the word?... The interpretations that lead to violent struggle are those that do not recognize themselves as such—and which, as in the tradition, regard other interpretations simply as fraudulent and wrong.[90]

All this can help illuminate at least one major trend in the reception of Barth's hermeneutics, where one can trace an increasingly common appreciation of its thoroughly theological character alongside widespread criticism of Barth's broader doctrinal configurations precisely because they do not properly address modern anxieties about religious dogmatism. In one sense these critics prove much more fruitful dialogue partners with Barth than those who refuse to believe that any

---

[89] Vattimo, *Beyond Interpretation*, pp. 73–4.

[90] Vattimo, *Beyond Interpretation*, p. 28.

hermeneutics is legitimate unless it appeals to resources external to the Christian tradition. And this helps explain why, although it remains important to carefully situate Barth's hermeneutics vis-à-vis the characteristic features of historical-critical exegesis dominant in the first half of the twentieth century, it is precisely among those more interested in postmodern interpretative theory and practice that Barth has gained a more sympathetic if not always a more discriminating audience. But the rough survey offered thus far should serve to reinforce the point that it is not enough simply to ask whether tinkering with Barth's dogmatic framework (e.g., by moving closer to a social model of the trinity, developing a stronger emphasis on the divine self-giving in the incarnation, or providing an account of the relationship of the church to the resurrected Christ in somewhat less Reformed terms) would allow him to more easily meet contemporary concerns about a perceived biblicism and general authoritarianism. Rather, we need also to ask how Barth's own account of the political problematics presented by the modern experience of interpretative pluralism and violent religious conflict relate to the doctrinal framework he actually did develop. In other words, before accepting that Barth's language of scriptural reading as an act of obedience immediately marks his hermeneutics as involving an uncritical and needlessly authoritarian biblicism, we need to take account of his own construal of the modern history of interpretative conflict, the nature of fruitful and open theological dialogue, and the role of ideology critique.

Conflict, Freedom, Prayer

First, then, the modern crisis of authority: According to Barth, the problem of interpretative pluralism and the conflicts it engendered in the sixteenth and seventeenth centuries were not the result of the Protestant scripture principle but rather followed from the 'enthusiastic belief in a direct access to revelation granted to the church'—a belief most obvious in the mystics and Radical Reformers, but common also in Lutheran and Reformed churches, which failed to take the scripture principle seriously enough. 'And in view of this', Barth claims:

We must say of the much deplored difficulty of explaining the Bible and of the fact of the many variations and contradictions in the explanations found, that what has always so widely divided the minds of men in the exposition and application of holy scripture has not been too great but too small a faithfulness in the perception that the church must hear in scripture and only in scripture the Word of God. What Catholicism has for the most part done is classically typical of all heresies. In the exposition and application of scripture it thinks that outside of Christ and the Holy Spirit as self-attested in scripture it can also claim a Christ who may be known directly and a Holy Spirit who can be received and works directly—he may sometimes go by other more secular names, he may even be identical with one's own reason or one's feeling for life [*Lebensgefühl*] or nature or historical consciousness. And where this happens, then scripture, which is clear in itself and in subject matter, becomes obscure, the demanded freedom in exposition and application becomes self-will, and a divergence of the various expositions and applications becomes inevitable. There is no more dangerous subjectivism than that which is based on the arrogance of a false objectivity. Not the fact that holy scripture as the Word of God is obscure and ambiguous, but the fact that it is the Word of God for the church on earth, and therefore a teacher of pupils who are all lost sinners, is what makes the much deplored divergence in its understanding possible, and, unless the miracle of revelation and faith intervenes, quite inevitable. But this divergence can be avoided only by this miracle and certainly not by denying it in advance. It will not be avoided if, instead of accepting in faith the grace which meets them in scripture, the pupils give way to their own sin, renouncing the relationships as pupils in which all their hope should be set, and each trying to be the teacher of scripture or at least an equal partner in discussion. But even if in so doing they appeal to Christ and the Holy Spirit, even if ever so many of them should enjoy the finest *consensio* among themselves—on this path they can only increase the fragmentation and make it incurable.[91]

We will unpack some of the doctrinal positions presupposed in this statement in the next two chapters. For now the important point is to note the distinctive convergence of theological and historical judgment: It is not simply that Barth reverses the usual historical narrative—the real problem is not taking *sola scriptura* seriously enough!—but that he thinks it possible to responsibly describe the political realities in view (and Barth never denies their gravity) in spiritual and so theological terms as a sinful and therefore divisive human arrogance that pretends, in one form or another, to an immediate knowledge of God. For Barth, the social fragmentation so characteristic of early modernity is not a basic datum of theology that dictates the shape of any responsible contemporary talk of God, but something to which theology can really speak on its own terms.

The possible objections here are only too obvious: An underestimation of the sheer social benefit of leaving religious fanaticism behind (or, put slightly differently, an inattentiveness to human suffering in God's name); a failure to recognize the value of interdisciplinary and intercultural dialogue in containing the social ramifications of exclusivist truth-claims; perhaps even, and ironically, a hint of self-justification that (given Barth's theological position) is rhetorically illegitimate just as it is (given the political reality of the church in the world) ethically irresponsible. But it is not our immediate task to address these and related concerns, which were well familiar to Barth and which have been well and widely treated in the literature. Here we will simply register the point that Barth is willing

---

[91] *KD* I/2, pp. 615–16 (ET 553). The reference to heresy typified in Roman Catholicism notwithstanding, this is not a simple repetition of sixteenth- and seventeenth-century Protestant polemics: 'Not too little but too much traditionalism, i.e., enthusiastic belief in a direct access to revelation granted to the church, was always true of the older Protestants as well.'

to accept the risks attendant upon an 'uninterruptedly theological'[92] account of the modern history of interpretative pluralism and conflict. And it is precisely this move that goes some way towards freeing him to read scripture in ways (at once literally and prayerfully, for example) that appear largely unavailable to those sharing the political-ethical instincts and commitments inscribed in modern general hermeneutical theory.

The original context of the phrase 'uninterruptedly theological', which may well serve as a general descriptor of Barth's historiography, is the methodological reflection with which Barth opens his (in)famous discussion of 'The Revelation of God as the *Aufhebung* of Religion' in the first volume of the *Church Dogmatics*.[93] And in this connection we can make some observations about a second topic of central concern in Barth's account of the task and scope of a theological hermeneutics—viz., his description of the character of free and open dialogue in modernity and in Christian theology.

At first glance, the boundaries of this free discussion (to use an only apparently self-contradictory phrase) are more apparent than their legitimate basis. What could be more striking (and unsettling) than the imperious claim that 'revelation is denied where it is treated as problematic'—where it is, as the standard English translation has it, 'regarded as open to discussion'?[94] But in context, this claim is simply another way of speaking of the axiomatic priority of God's initiative in church proclamation and theology, a logical extension of the thesis, central to Barth's entire discussion of religion, that religion is a predicate of revelation, not vice versa. And of course this is simply an application of the basic theological claim that the creator cannot be a predicate of the creature.[95] Whatever else we go on to say about freedom of thought and speech, we must at once recognize that this freedom exists in the context of the irreversibly ordered relationship between God and the world. Our freedom to speak of God is at once a gift and a task, and seen from either perspective it is something we must receive. When Barth says revelation is not open to discussion, he means in the first place that we cannot ask God to step out of the room while we debate the reality of his presence.

We can hardly afford to forget here that Barth's treatment of religion—and within it, of open discussion—occurs in the course of the treatment of the doctrine of the trinity that occupies the second major section of the prolegomena to his dogmatics. And Barth's statements about the limits of free thought in theology are

---

[92] *CD* I/2, p. 296 (*KD* I/2, p. 323).

[93] See *KD* I/2, §17.1, 'Das Problem der Religion in der Theologie', pp. 304–24 (ET 280–97); §17.2, 'Religion als Unglaube', pp. 324–56 (ET 297–325); §17.3, 'Die wahre Religion', pp. 356–97 (ET 325–61).

[94] *CD* I/2, p 296; cf. *KD* I/2, p. 322: 'die Offenbarung wird geleugnet, wo sie als problematisch behandelt wird'.

[95] Or put slightly differently, 'Revelation is not a predicate of history, but history is a predicate of revelation' (*KD* I/2, p. 64 (ET 58)).

closely related to the anhypostatic/enhypostatic christology developed within this trinitarian exposition.[96] More closely still, his discussion of religion takes its place within a doctrine of the Holy Spirit as the subjective reality and possibility of God's self-revelation to humanity in which he asserts at length that human beings cannot be viewed either *in abstracto* or simply in terms of their createdness. According to Barth, our existence is given and clarified anew in revelation; we have no grounds on which to speak of our independent existence. 'Man's existence is involved only as the humanity of Christ is involved in the doctrine of the incarnation, or the *virgo Maria* in the doctrine of the mystery of the incarnation. The existence of man or particular men comes into consideration here only as it is posited by God, indeed as it is newly posited in the act of his revelation.'[97] Again, if we can legitimately recognize an analogy between Christ's anhypostatic existence as true man and our own existence, that is because our existence is truly grounded in his, as in the Holy Spirit we are incorporated into Christ and so into the life of the triune God. 'From God's side, and from God's side in a new way, which transcends their obscure creaturely being, on the basis of the revelation which comes from God, there exist men who in their existence are the subjective reality of revelation.'[98] If we take this 'are' in full seriousness, any attempt to secure our own identity (even through a bald appeal to our createdness) is revealed as sinful rebellion, an attempt to identify ourselves as God's partners in his work of redemption. And it is on the basis of these doctrinal convictions that Barth can go on to say that in speaking of religion in its relation to God's revelation:

> Our basic task is so to order the concepts revelation and religion that the connexion between the two can again be seen as identical with that event between God and man in which God is God, i.e., the Lord and Master of man, who himself judges and alone justifies and sanctifies, and man is the man of God, i.e., man as he is adopted and received by God in his severity and goodness. It is because we remember and apply the christological doctrine of the *assumptio carnis* that we speak of revelation as the *Aufhebung* of religion.[99]

From this angle we can see that Barth's rejection (or rather recontextualization) of the modern concept of open dialogue is rooted in a rejection of an anthropology that may well be characteristic of modernity but is so only because it is characteristic of all people in all ages who rebel against the God who will not share his glory with another. Open dialogue in its modern sense does not mean simply a serious and civil exchange of ideas; it implies the existence of self-positing (and so

---

[96] See *KD* I/2, §15.2, 'Wahrer Gott und wahrer Mensch', pp. 145–87 (ET 132–71), including the historical excursus on the anhypostasis/enhypostasis doctrine on pp. 178–80 (ET 163–5).

[97] *KD* I/2, pp. 256–7 (ET 235).

[98] *KD* I/2, p. 257 (ET 235).

[99] *KD* I/2, p. 324 (ET 297).

self-justifying) conversation partners, and therefore of a discussion which can never properly respect the truth that our existence is not our own, however much we may go on to invoke that truth within the conversation at hand. The basic distinction here is not between open discussion and a flavorless or oppressive conformity of thought and opinion, but between open discussion and confession, praise, and witness. Barth protests against undisciplined open discussion in large measure because the bland discourse of tolerance, while it may well perform useful service in the public sphere, can never be allowed to replace the sound of what in 'The New World in the Bible' he had called 'the chorus of prophets and apostles' and the dynamic, multivocal reiteration of their witness in the church's theology. In this way, theology can speak lovingly and patiently of humanity in its many historical, cultural, and religious contexts. But it may not speak untheologically— i.e., 'openly'.

> A theological evaluation of religion and religions must be characterized primarily by the great cautiousness and charity of its assessments and value-judgments. It will observe and understand and take man in all seriousness as the subject of religion. But it will not be man apart from God, in a human *per se*. It will be man for whom (whether he knows it or not) Jesus Christ was born, died, and rose again. It will be man who (whether he has already heard it or not) is intended in the Word of God. It will be man who (whether he is aware of it or not) has in Christ his Lord.[100]

This theological construal of the existence of the person for whom both truly open dialogue and true confession are both inherently impossible but for whom the former is revealed as finally impossible and the latter as graciously real corresponds to Barth's comments on the limitations of ideology critique. If, as we argued above, the project of modernity broadly conceived involves an attempt to secure its continuance in the face of threat from religious violence, again broadly conceived, then central to the modern identity is the belief that we are capable in one way or another of protecting ourselves from ourselves. Again, one may think of this protection in many ways, and in contemporary discussions it remains an

---

[100] *KD* I/2, p. 324 (ET 297). Cf. p. 326 (ET 299): 'A truly theological treatment of religion and religions, as it is demanded and possible precisely in the church as the locus of the Christian religion, will need to be distinguished from all other forms of treatment by the exercise of a very marked patience with its object. Now this patience must not be confused with the moderation of those who actually have their own religion or religiosity, and are secretly zealous for it, but who can exercise self-control, because they have told themselves or have been told that theirs is not the only faith, that fanaticism is a bad thing, that love must always have the first and last word.... Tolerance in the sense of moderation, or superior knowledge, or skepticism is actually the worst form of intolerance. But the object of religion and the religions must be treated with a tolerance which is informed by the patience of Christ, which shows itself to be a patience which derives from the knowledge that by grace God has reconciled to himself godless man and religion.'

open question how far methodological self-consciousness plays a part. But if it is true that our existence as particular members of the church which must bear witness to the whole world of the reconciliation accomplished in Christ is unthinkable apart from the divine revelation that comes to us as sinners, lost to God, ourselves, and others, then it follows that this belief is misplaced. We recognize ourselves to be incapable of generating or maintaining true community because such community actually has come to us in Christ through the Holy Spirit. And so the ethical and political burden of ideology critique is lifted from us. Rather, on the basis of what God has done for us, we are to occupy ourselves with that unique passive action that is perhaps most easily comprehended by saying that we must pray for the outpouring of the Holy Spirit. This prayer will necessarily be attended by the most rigorous thinking, the most civil dialogue, and the most careful political engagement: 'To pray for someone or something means the most intensive participation possible. I cannot pray for something if I am not at the same time ready to participate in it and to—where the possibility arises for me—commit myself to it.'[101] But it will never be supplanted or even complemented by these other activities, which while genuinely given to us are not simply continuous with God's work in gathering his people to himself and just so to each other.

We arrive at the same point, and begin to bring our discussion back more directly to Barth's nineteenth-century Protestant theology lectures, if we say that Barth insists on giving theological definition to the term 'humility'. We have seen how this concept plays an important part in Barth's historiography, where humility means recognizing the relativity of one's own historical location and the exclusive privilege of God to sort wheat from chaff. In his prolegomenal discussion of some problems in the history of christological dogma, Barth makes the further point that Christian humility means humility in response to God's revelation, and therefore both that it is not coincident with public modesty and that it is not finally within our control. As modern readers of the patristic and Reformational christological controversies, it may well be that 'we can only look back with a forgiving leniency if also with some head shaking ... in sincere amazement to see how stubbornly theologians of those days defended their views, how keen they were to clear matters up to the last detail'.[102] But if so, this is not simply because we inhabit a different 'climate of opinion' than they, nor may we simply resign ourselves to (or perhaps even celebrate) our sheer distance and difference from them. Rather Barth argues that the modern inability to meaningfully enter these debates reflects a modern christological deficiency that can only be described as both error and sin. That is, we suffer from a spiritualistic and arbitrary moralism that cannot accept the realism of the biblical testimony to the incarnation, 'a horror of the being of

---

[101] Frank Jehle, *Ever against the Stream. The Politics of Karl Barth 1906–1968*, trans. Richard and Martha Burnett (Grand Rapids and Cambridge, 2002), p. 108 (original emphasis removed).

[102] *KD* I/2, p. 143 (ET 130).

God in his revelation' and a rejection of the ontological significance of the classical claim that Jesus Christ is true God and true man. Where the standard modern histories speak of the intellectualism and dogmatic fanaticism of the tradition, Barth speaks of the modern appeal to theological humility as an ethical veneer for a rejection of the New Testament witness to the mystery of Christ.

> From this point of view it is very understandable that they [viz., Harnack, Herder, Ritschl, and Schleiermacher as exponents of modern Protestant christology] could and had to arrive at the humility which renounces beforehand all serious and responsible inquiry for the truth and every attempt to appropriately answer it. For such humility there is rather an immense wealth of possibilities, all equally good and acceptable in themselves and in their respective places, and over which there can be no serious quarrel. We are bound to say that this humility may be ever so sincere and admirable. In many an instance, from the standpoint of human morality, it may actually stand out from that of so many of the orthodox zealots as the better attitude. But we must roundly contend that it is not Christian humility, i.e., not the humility that is faced with the mystery of God's revelation. On the contrary, however high our praises of it in other respects, it rests upon a fundamental circumvention and conjuring away of this mystery, and upon a consciousness of human control over God, which necessarily has to be described as pride rather than humility.[103]

If this pride which masquerades as humility really can be described on a certain level as a civic virtue and preferable to a misguided fanaticism, this is not because we are free to suspend theological judgment in the face of the evident moral superiority of modern secularism. Rather (and though Barth does not explicitly make this move here, it resonates with the larger argument developed in his christology), we must recognize here a divine patience both with the excesses of patristic or Reformation-era fervor and with neo-Protestant banalities. And the appropriate response to this recognition centers on prayer—confession of our errors and praise to the God who gives us time to turn from them (cf. Rom. 2.4).[104]

---

[103] *KD* I/2, pp. 143–4 (ET 131).

[104] On a closely related topic, note *KD* I/2, pp. 117–18 (ET 106–7): 'The judgment of God, which Christ's community sees visited upon the world about it, as upon a wicked world ordained to dissolution, is no less severe than that which finds expression in the exclusiveness of Israel compared with the Gentiles and their gods. The bloody wars of Yahweh against Baal have now, of course, ceased; not because the radical nature of the rejection of the "form of this world" (Rom. 12.2) has been mitigated, but because now it has become so utterly fundamental. This aeon has been overcome in Christ with all its principalities and powers. Christ has in his body taken it to the cross and borne it to the grave. Therefore now the form of the struggle in the Old Testament which it still presupposes can and must fall to the rear. As such it is pointless. It has become a sign which can be dispensed with as such and even disappear, now that the thing itself has been brought to the fore in Christ's triumph over all his enemies (Col. 2.14–15). The secularization of nature, history, and civilization is now, in view of the cross of Christ, no longer a problem.

Thus Barth on post-Reformation interpretative pluralism, open dialogue in modernity, and the status of ideology critique. In treating these topics, each of which is central to the common conception of the task of a contemporary theological hermeneutics and which therefore together have decisively shaped the reception of Barth's own account of the tasks and aims of scriptural interpretation, we have found a common thread in Barth's attempt to think through the consequences of his theological convictions in writing the history of modernity. Not a history of modernity as such, of course; we have abstracted what appear as pertinent responses to our three questions from various historical excursuses in the prolegomena to the dogmatics, each of which was composed in response to a particular issue thrown up in the course of Barth's doctrinal work. But the examples adduced here should at least illustrate the distinctiveness of Barth's attempt to develop an 'uninterruptedly theological' portrayal of certain salient features of modernity. And we can now go on to fill in this picture, at least in broad strokes, by looking at Barth's own description of some ways in which the eighteenth and nineteenth centuries attempted to neutralize the power and distinctiveness of the gospel.

The 'Age of Absolutism'

We begin with a few general observations by way of introduction and review. First, 'modernity' is not a basic category for Barth. On his terms, the church that attends to God's revelation can speak meaningfully of specific historical ages and trends. And it will inevitably employ general historical categories when pursuing its own task. But history as such and whatever periods we discern (or interpretative models we construct) within it really are comprehended by God's revelation and must be articulated in relation to it. Thus Barth's history of modern Protestant theology is first an account of the Word of God, of divine speaking and human hearing. And just because it is a story of the career of the *living* Word, it is a story of its gracious encounter with humanity in specific, unrepeatable historical contexts which themselves are legitimately of genuine theological interest.

Second, as the story of the speaking of the *reconciling* Word, the Word of God's mercy to sinners, the story is one of divine grace and human sin. It is a history of the human failure to recognize God's revelation or, to use more active language, of human attempts to evade this revelation. This evasion takes many forms, and again a theological history will trace its various instances in careful

---

The program of the Old Testament has been carried through to a finish. For that reason, and not because of the increase in *Humanität, Toleranz* or *Kulturfreudigkeit*, the church's attitude to the world is so utterly different, so much calmer and so much more superior than Israel's once was. If the old aeon has been done away, as is the case according to the New Testament *kerygma*, we no longer need to fight against it. Or rather, the armor in which it is combated has now become the purely spiritual kind described in Ephesians 6.'

historical detail. But at the same time, such a history will be attentive in *hope*, always looking for those events in which faith recognizes the true reception and knowledge of God's revelation by just these sinners.

Third, this theological-historical orientation, outlined in the foreword to *Die protestantische Theologie*, stands in the lectures on the 'Vorgeschichte der neueren protestantischen Theologie' alongside a distinctive judgment about the primacy of the moral over the intellectual in the modern revaluation of Christian doctrine. It 'is very important to me', Barth reported to Thurneysen in late 1932, 'that the famous *Dogmenkritik* of the eighteenth century, for example, demonstrably is not to be attributed, as we learned in our time, to a breakthrough of truthfulness in view of the changed perception of the world, etc., but very simply to a sentimental self-consciousness, to a definitely moral, not an especially intellectual, adjustment to the time'.[105] Or, as he generalized this insight for his students: 'The Christian man of the eighteenth century ... was primarily a citizen and a moralist and then, as a consequence, a philosopher, doubter, critic, inventor of a new, scientifically purified, type of Christian teaching'.[106] This somewhat unusual emphasis helps explain why Barth's account seems rather less occupied with the role of science in the emerging modern world than many other theologically inclined discussions of modernity,[107] and more closely why Barth, if he does not intentionally downplay the significance of *Wissenschaft* and *Technik*, at least sees *Politik* as relatively more important as a key to the eighteenth century.[108]

Correspondingly, Barth does not understand the eighteenth century primarily as the Age of Enlightenment, despite the fact that it was largely so understood by those who first succeeded it and reacted against it. For Barth, while this slogan has its usefulness, it can serve to obscure those apparently less 'enlightened' yet no less characteristic events and cultural products of the time (the founding of the

---

[105] Barth to Thurneysen, 23 December 1932 (*B–Th III*, p. 320).

[106] *PT*, p. 80 (ET 86–7).

[107] As, for example, Colin Gunton, *Enlightenment and Alienation. An Essay towards a Trinitarian Theology* (Grand Rapids, 1985). On this whole question see Stephen Williams, *Revelation and Reconciliation. A window on modernity* (Cambridge, 1995), which, despite sharing modernity's 'sick revulsion at dogmatism masquerading as virtue and proving its style in feud and blood' (p. 52), still thinks it possible and indeed more historically responsible to tell the story of the origins of modernity as 'a conflict between a moral sense that powered reason and a doctrine of reconciliation, which revelation protected' (p. 53). Williams suggests Barth's own exposition in *Die protestantische Theologie* would have been more consistent to his own deep convictions if, instead of concentrating on theological epistemology, Barth had told the story in terms of the contrast between, e.g., human self-definition (as that which powers reason) and the gospel of Christ (revelation as an act of grace) (p. 78). Whether *Die protestantische Theologie* should in fact be read as inconsistently preoccupied with theological epistemology seems to me an open question, but one which does not fundamentally impact Williams' constructive thesis.

[108] See *PT*, pp. 24–5 (ET 28).

Freemasons in 1717, Mozart's *Magic Flute* of 1791, etc.) which could easily lead one to describe the period as an age of mysticism.

Instead, Barth speaks of the Age of Absolutism, which he thinks to be a more comprehensive category, and one that draws attention to the basic self-understanding of the significant figures of the period as expressed in their most revealing efforts and achievements.

> 'Absolutism' in general can obviously mean a system of life based upon the belief in the omnipotence of human ability. Man, who discovers his own power and ability, the latent potentiality in his humanity (that is, in his human being as such), and looks upon it as the final, the real and absolute, I mean as something 'detached' [*Gelöstes*], self-justifying, with its own authority and power, which he can therefore set in motion in all directions and without any restraint—this man is absolute man. And this absolute man … is eighteenth-century man, who appears to us more or less distinctly, more or less open or veiled in conventional drapings, in all the human faces of that century which are so different amongst themselves.[109]

Here again we see Barth's emphasis on the responsible, active agent—the living person—as the subject of history. And as the living man of the eighteenth-century expresses himself in various spheres, relating the history of the period involves tracing his manifold activity in varying detail. Thus Barth works out the notion of absolutism in a wide-ranging series of psychological, scientific, political, and cultural connections before turning his attention specifically to the characteristic theological problems of the age.

As a psychological characteristic of the age ('the thing which is regularly recurrent in the makeup of the great number of individuals of that time who are known to us'[110]), absolutism involves a peculiar 'joy in man's intellectual, technical, and moral capacities'—i.e., a 'general unquestioning confidence' in European culture.[111] This confidence at once underlies and is confirmed by the development of the modern sciences. The Copernican cosmological revolution leads to a new sense of one's place in the universe, but not to a new humility; that the earth revolved around the sun rather than vice versa was perhaps a new and controversial idea, but man, who had the ability and responsibility to discover, evaluate, and decide in this matter, was in any case firmly at the center of the universe. And the modern man who has newly learned where he is now learns how to control his environment, to make himself at home. Eighteenth-century man begins to travel and to colonize, extending the physical boundaries of his knowledge and his control. And along the way, he develops new scientific and technical expressions of this control.[112]

---

[109] *PT*, pp. 19–20 (ET 22–3).

[110] *PT*, p. 53 (ET 59).

[111] *PT*, p. 192 (ET 203).

[112] See *PT*, pp. 20–24 (ET 23–7).

More importantly, eighteenth-century man is 'the man who no longer has a *Kaiser*'. Insofar as the empire represented an authority that could check the political ambitions of individual member states, it was 'the concrete veto on political absolutism in any form'.[113] With the loss of the imperial ideal, this political constraint disappears. It gives way first to an 'absolutism from above': Here (the classical example is Louis XIV) the will of the absolute monarch is identified with the good of the state; and in this equation the prince is equally free to express his power through territorial wars, architectural indulgences such as Versailles, or misdirected if not intentionally patronizing social reforms. This in turn invites a revolutionary 'absolutism from below', in which the state is identified with the people or the nation. The revolution may occur in the name of the individual (so the liberal) or the collective (so the nationalist) or some combination of the two, but in any case it shares the absolutist principles against which in another form it reacts. 'Politically, absolutism means the determination of law by that class in the state [whether royalty, nobility, middle class, or peasantry] which in contrast to the others possesses the effective power.'[114]

And finally, in relation to the cultural preoccupations of the time, absolutism means 'a striving to reduce everything to an absolute form' or, more simply, an 'absolute will for form'.[115]

Inanimate nature especially, in all its realms, but human bodily existence too—the sound that could be spontaneously called forth, with all the possibilities for coloration and different rhythmic patterns which it presented, human language in all its adaptability as a means of expression, social intercourse, individual development, and the individual in relation to society—this whole wealth of the given is in the eyes of eighteenth-century man a mass of raw material, of which he believes himself to be the master.[116]

---

[113] *PT*, p. 25 (ET 28); cf. p. 30 (ET 33–4): The imperial ideal is 'the policy, which not only exercises dominion, but bestows freedom, which not only dispenses favors, but establishes justice, and establishes it by means of justice, a policy whereby the best possible is done for the people with the people, and therefore as a matter of principle just as much through the people as through the king; a policy therefore in whose eyes as a matter of principle no person is merely an object; again, a policy subject not only to an abstract responsibility, but to a concrete one—a policy therefore which might well deserve the title "by the grace of God"'.

[114] *PT*, p. 25 (ET 28). We can only note in passing that these and the many other political comments in these lectures take on an added significance when we remember that they were delivered as the Weimar Republic was falling apart under the weight of a widespread economic crisis and an astonishing series of political misjudgments that helped clear the way for the National Socialist rise to power. Among the many good summaries of this period, see Ian Kershaw, *Hitler 1886–1936: Hubris* (London, 1999), esp. pp. 379–427; Walter Laquer, *Weimar: A Cultural History, 1918–33* (New York, 1980).

[115] See *PT*, pp. 37–8 (ET 41, 43).

[116] *PT*, p. 37 (ET 41). In what must have been one of the more engaging lectures of the series, Barth goes on to illustrate this thesis in relation to the various cultural expressions—

Thus far absolutism as a general historical *Stichwort*. But the notion of absolutism also has in Barth very specific spiritual and theological resonance. And in speaking of absolutism as an attempt to assimilate the revelation of God into the cultural project of the age, Barth is, in his own way, developing a distinctive theological account of the neutralizing strategies of the eighteenth and nineteenth centuries. We can approach this distinctiveness vis-à-vis the approaches introduced earlier in this chapter from two complementary angles. First, by noting that the issue in Barth is not competing religious adherences and their social ramifications (the strong identity as such) but the human attempt to control and so evade God's revelation. And second, by attending to the fact that Barth identifies this domestication of revelation in characteristic and instructive doctrinal terms.

Absolutism as Humanization

In introducing his account of 'the problem of theology in the eighteenth century', Barth paraphrases the term 'absolutism' as 'humanization'. The terms of the problematic are not one cultural project, philosophical inclination, or political program in relation to another, but a human self-understanding on one side and everything else on the other. And among this 'everything else', Christianity occupies a special place. Not necessarily in the self-consciousness of the time: In relation to all other problems, the eighteenth century widely believed it had achieved (or was at least well-positioned to achieve) a quite reassuring mastery, and 'the magnificent attempt of the eighteenth century, undertaken with a magnificent self-confidence, to treat everything given and handed down in nature and in history as the property of man, to be assimilated to him and thus to be humanized—this attempt is extended also and not least to the subject-matter of theology, to Christianity'.[117] But 'in his attempt to come to grips with Christianity in his own way, we see him hesitate and stumble at various points'.[118] And the question arises whether this hesitation—this interruption into the otherwise apparently undisturbed self-confidence of the age—might not have a wider significance, so that when cracks appear elsewhere in what is then revealed as a façade, one might reasonably suspect that the source of the general disturbance lies precisely here, in the subject-matter of Christianity.

And in this connection, Barth suggests that the eighteenth century instinctively recognized despite itself that its confidence was ill-founded unless it could successfully deal with Christianity as it had everything else: 'The serpent makes an attempt even at this morsel. Perhaps this is the most profound significance of the

---

horticulture, architecture, fashion and social comportment, historiography, pedagogy, the formation of free societies, language and literature, and musical artistry as technical proficiency—comprehended in this summary.

[117] *PT*, p. 62 (ET 68).

[118] *PT*, p. 61 (ET 67).

whole historical process, perhaps everything else is merely preliminary or incidental to it: that it first and last and above all has to make an attempt at this morsel.'[119] For in confronting terms such as creation, sin, grace, gospel, and above all the name Jesus Christ to which the Bible bears appropriately contingent and concrete witness, eighteenth-century man confronts a reality which apparently calls into question the power of self-realization in which he had placed his trust.

> If humanization had to present any problem, then this was evidently the one. Did not the man of the eighteenth century, the man who believed in the omnipotence of human capability, for whom there could be no object in the strong sense of the term, find himself confronted here *in nuce* with the problem of the nature of the object? Was not the attack which he had carried out so victoriously on all fronts against the object a failure if it was a failure here? But humanization on this decisive front had to mean: the experience and knowledge of that superior authority as a reality that was not ultimately and absolutely but only provisionally and relatively *different* from man himself, viz., from his capability in the widest sense. Humanization had to mean, if not the sublimation [*Aufhebung*], at least the incorporation [*Einbeziehung*] of God into the sphere of sovereign human self-consciousness, the transformation of the reality that came and was to be perceived from outside into a reality that was experienced and understood inwardly. Experienced and understood inwardly, but that meant appropriate for man, incorporated into human capabilities, comprehended as such a reality as can be begotten of man's capability and must so be begotten to count as reality. Experienced and understood, but that meant comprehended as material whose form man was in a position to treat in the same way that he was able to impose himself upon nature and history.[120]

How then does the eighteenth century seek to neutralize Christianity and thus confirm that its self-confidence was justified? How does the eighteenth century, in other words, attempt to humanize the problem of theology? By recontextualizing it, Barth suggests, in individualistic/pietistic, scientific/philosophical, ethical, and political terms.

Politically, 'all along the line the church was led and claimed by the state in such a way that the state was primarily concerned for itself and for the church only to the degree that this concern matched its own interests'.[121] The state may think it best to encourage and finally enforce religious pluralism (the absolute state is the absolute church, elevating 'the idea of the relativity of all confessions to the status of a universally valid truth') or religious uniformity (the state prosecution of dissenters often enough being 'attributed to the intolerance of the church which is

---

[119] *PT*, pp. 62–3 (ET 69).

[120] See *PT*, pp. 63–4 (ET 69–70). It obviously follows from all this that Barth interprets both pietism and the Enlightenment as 'two forms of the one essence, of Christianity as shaped by the spirit of the eighteenth century, two forms which are equally close to the Reformation and distant from it' (p. 65 (ET 71)).

[121] *PT*, p. 68 (ET 74).

apparently being protected in this way') or some mediating political-religious compromise. But in any case, 'the church and Christianity are *in the state* and receive their outward form and movement entirely *from the state* and not from their own being and laws'.[122]

The eighteenth-century *moralizing* of Christianity is bound up for Barth with the increasing religious activity of the bourgeoisie, who brought to their understanding of and (remarkably active) participation in the church a 'typical middle-class ideology' as well as a very particular sense of their own historical location and so of their stake in preserving the political conditions of the time.

> The gentrification [*Verbürgerlichung*] or moralizing of the problem of theology in the eighteenth century consists essentially in this: that it was regarded all along the line or at any rate also as the problem of altering and shaping life in a visible and tangible way, that could be experienced and established concretely and directly, inwardly and outwardly, accomplished by man in particular thoughts, actions, and behaviors. The identification of Christianity with this alteration and shaping of human life is, from this perspective, the great attempt of the time at humanizing. When the Christian citizen or the bourgeois Christian of the time hears the great words of the Christian creed founded upon the Bible as the fundamental record of divine revelation, he feels as well and honestly and seriously as Christians of all times that he is confronted here with the announcement of things which are supremely new and shattering, which at the same time claim him with supreme authority and power. But he can also see a past, in the sixteenth and seventeenth centuries, disturbed by a series of supremely devastating, offensive, and repulsive wars of a spiritual and political nature which at their climax, in the Thirty Years War, made Germany into a wilderness and cost Europe not only rivers of blood but also whole rivers of ink and printers' ink poured out in a highly questionable fashion. He also knows of the damnable moral brutalization of the upper classes on the one hand and of the great mass of lower classes on the other, which followed the wars of religion. He knows that these wars were all waged in a more or less honest or hypocritical way over this very Christian creed, over the new, shattering, demanding things which the men of this desolate, sorry past thought that they could find in the Christian creed. And now he also knows and sees that the Christian creed, as the men of this dark past thought they understood it, had insufficient power to combat the brutalization. As a man with a historical horizon, he knows further that a similar understanding of the Christian creed in other, more distant times, has caused similar wars and has equally failed the moral demands made upon it. But the Christian citizen of the eighteenth century certainly does not wish such wars and such moral brutalization to be repeated or continued in any way, and therefore rejects the view of the Christian creed that caused such wars and did not prevent such brutalization. And he believes that he can see the mistake which crept in during all those dark times: the way in which people understood the Christian creed then was wrong, perverse, and evil. Understanding in those dark times was theoretical and only theoretical; Christianity was made into a collection of conflicting doctrines and precepts, dialectic subtleties which merely occupied the mind and heated the head, but left the heart empty and the

---

[122] See *PT*, p. 66–70 (ET 72–6).

conscience in perplexity. The supreme verities of faith had been robbed of their real content and had been changed into barren theological maxims whose contradictions inevitably aroused the direst passions. Proclaiming and accepting them could help no one, because he either failed to understand them, as being too scholarly and learned, or if he did understand them, could not understand them for his salvation. In short, the Christian citizen of the time invented—and it was a truly significant and momentous discovery—the theory of the barrenness, indeed the danger of the theological theory.[123]

Here we see Barth's account of the historical motivation underlying the modern moralizing of Christianity—viz., the consciousness that the creed has proved politically destabilizing precisely when it has been appropriated as a description of given truths or facts and not primarily as a catalyst for personal and social improvement. And it naturally follows on this reading that with the criterion of true Christianity (the evident flourishing of the modern citizen and the social conditions that foster it) thus firmly in place, it becomes a secondary if strategically important question how to employ it: The creed could be simply rejected, of course, though such a revolutionary cultural change would entail obvious social risks. Or (and this was the course that was adopted, at least initially) one could adapt Christianity to bourgeois life by distancing oneself from past disputes over theoretical irrelevancies and promoting instead the practical use of the creed: 'through all the pores of orthodoxy there begins to seep the conviction that the change and transformation of life that is so desired is the real meaning of Christianity, the true mystery of revelation, which has only now been understood correctly'.[124]

In other words, bourgeois self-interest gives rise to the eighteenth-century hermeneutics of transformation: The transformation of Christian society from a confessionally divided and overly theoretical culture to a unified community of personal virtue and civic hospitality becomes the basis and goal of a correct interpretation of scripture, the creeds, and church history. This interpretation may appear to move from text to world (as in pietism) or from world to text (so rationalism), but in either case 'the desire is to put all the emphasis, not on the saving facts as such, but on the improvement of life that is associated with them and understood in a more or less concrete way'.[125] And while Barth can genuinely appreciate the pastoral warmth and social benefit that attended both the individually oriented pietist and socially conscious rationalist moves, he nevertheless sees here a devaluation of the objective that is finally nothing less than an undermining of the Christian creed.[126]

At this point, Barth more closely specifies the manner in which the modern *intellectualizing* of Christianity follows from this attempt at a moralizing reduction of the creed—indeed from the failure of this attempt: 'The price for this Christian

---

[123] *PT*, pp. 71–3 (ET 77–8).

[124] *PT*, p. 74 (ET 80).

[125] *PT*, p. 76 (ET 83).

[126] See *PT*, pp. 77–8 (ET 83–4).

moralism is that it has itself to be given a theoretical foundation and justification. Probably because it does not completely succeed in reaching the reality for which it longs so much, it must in turn manage to confirm that it is at least the truth.'[127]

The development here is from a relative weighting of the subjective elements of traditional belief to an increasingly bold criticism of the creed itself. In both cases the modern citizen is finally guided by the will to foster a civic commerce undisturbed by confessional conflict and authoritarianism, but it becomes increasingly clear that this goal is best served by freeing oneself altogether from the authority of the Bible, dogma, and Christianity—precisely by subjecting these traditional authorities to a thoroughgoing reinterpretation. The tradition is now read through the categories of 'nature' and 'reason', understood not in contrast to 'miracle' and 'revelation', but rather 'with what man could not realize, what was not the object of his willing and his action, material that could not be shaped by his will for form'.

> For the man of the eighteenth century, 'nature' was the embodiment of what was at the disposal of himself, his spirit, his understanding, his will and his feeling, what was left for him to shape, what could be reached by his will for form. And 'reason', reason was the embodiment of his capacity, his superiority over mater, his ability to comprehend it and appropriate it for himself. Thus naturally Christianity simply means a Christianity that presents itself to man in a manner appropriate to his capacity, and reasonable Christianity means a Christianity that is understood and affirmed by man in accordance with his capacity.[128]

And, finally, the political and ethical/intellectual domestication of Christianity is accompanied by a new *individualization*, 'the making inward of what is external, objective to man' so that it might 'be the object of his domination'.[129] Here Barth thinks especially of pietism, which in striving for an immediate, individual relation to God is unable to adequately respect the historical integrity of the incarnation (and scripture as its witness); the church as a community in which one is genuinely confronted by the other; the external authority of church, dogma, and scripture; the concreteness of the divine command; and the objectivity of the sacraments.[130]

Doctrinal Revisions of Modernity

This rehearsal of Barth's exposition of the eighteenth-century neutralization of revelation sets up a very brief sketch of his account of what might be called the

---

[127] *PT*, p. 81; cf. 144–5 (ET 87; cf. 151–2).

[128] *PT*, p. 85 (ET 91).

[129] *PT*, p. 93 (ET 99).

[130] *PT*, p. 93–103 (ET 99–109); the reference to prayer in place of command in Barth's summary of this on p. 111 of the English translation probably follows from an understandable misreading of the original (mistaking *Gebot* on p. 105 for *Gebet*).

doctrinal shape of modernity. This phrase can be understood in two senses: First, as a recognition that eighteenth-century absolutism results in the more or less successful revaluation of a series of central Christian doctrines, a process Barth describes in some detail not only for its inherent theological interest but as a way of gaining some purchase on the deepest moral, intellectual, and spiritual impulses of the period. We have seen how Barth speaks of the cultural and theological impact of the quest for immediacy, with all that it implies for the concepts of revelation and church, authority and obedience. But Barth also identifies doctrinal loci on which the absolutist program of the eighteenth century runs aground, points at which it is unable to complete its 'great process of assimilation'. Thus he speaks of eighteenth-century deism as an indication of the fact that the age could not completely erase the concepts of transcendence and encounter from its theology, and so rejected Spinoza's panentheism rather than welcoming it as the 'expression of its own most absolutist tendency achieved at the most decisive point'.[131] Similarly, the 'blood and wounds' theology of pietism points to a subterranean influence of the Reformed doctrine of justification which persisted despite the eighteenth century's 'pious and sensible Pelagianism'.[132] And again, the age could not avoid a certain preoccupation with eschatology, even if this often took form in unrefined millenarianisms or rationalist appeals to immortality. In each of these cases, the fate of the dogmatic locus is at once illuminated by and illustrative of the larger intellectual and spiritual trends of the time.

Second, we can also speak of the doctrinal shape of modernity to once again draw attention to Barth's remarkably carefree appeal to traditional theological formulations in telling the story of modernity, and specifically of its varied attempts to reshape the inherited material of the Christian tradition to its own ends.

We can illustrate this second point by reviewing two examples that seem particularly relevant for a doctrinal description of biblical reading, beginning with Barth's reference to eighteenth-century Pelagianism and its refinement in Rousseau and Goethe. We have seen Barth claim that in the eighteenth century, even where Christianity was publicly affirmed (and it largely was), 'men affirmed it with a secret sovereignty which already seemed to make it questionable whether what was being affirmed was still Christianity'.[133] And where Christianity was rejected or reformulated (in morally and civically useful, intellectually respectable, and personally satisfying terms), this was not finally because the modern thinker felt compelled by modern biblical criticism, scientific progress, historical objectivity, and so on to develop a more intellectually honest and rigorous set of beliefs.

All this is not a foundation and a cause, but an instrument, indeed one might go so far as to say a garb, for the criticism. Fine and impressive reasons are given so that men in the

---

[131] See *PT*, p. 110 (ET 117).

[132] *PT*, p. 113 (ET 120).

[133] *PT*, p. 84 (ET 91).

modern world *can* no longer believe the teaching of Christianity in its traditional form, without a deliberate intention to deceive, but in fact because people no longer *want* to believe it. Man makes the opposition to older Christianity which had come about through his new moralism into a contrast between the modern and the obsolete presuppositions for cosmology and epistemology—in order to justify himself.[134]

Here the connection between the moralism and intellectualism of the time is sharpened by a spiritual judgment: The moralism that drives intellectual objections to traditional Christian doctrine is itself a reflex of a tendency towards self-justification born of a desire (and here the parallels with Barth's *Römerbrief* and other early work are clear) to exempt oneself from God's judgment on all human aspiration and endeavor. The moral and intellectual characteristics of the time, in other words, are rightly seen in spiritual and theological perspective.

On a psychological level, this anxious, energetic self-confidence of the eighteenth century finds needed support in the nineteenth-century discovery of the intrinsic significance and freedom of the inner life of the individual.[135] But again, on Barth's analysis, the modern subject first attempts to resist the realism of God's judgment and *then* discovers a sphere of interiority—a place, fundamentally untouched by external relations, to which one can retire in order to confirm one's integrity and identity and then, if one is so inclined, authentically exert oneself in the world.[136] This discovery, which 'was completed, in the last assessment, simply in Rousseau's biography, in his more or less pathological method of existing as such', marks the culmination and end of the eighteenth century and the beginning of the age of Goethe. But this development, though important in its own right, should not obscure the neo-Pelagian impulse shared by both periods. In Rousseau's discovery of the inner life the age begins to learn that the subject enjoys 'the simultaneous capacity to take the object completely seriously and not take it seriously at all'.[137] And this claim for the sovereignty of the subject—obviously so significant for a description of the status of the scriptural reader and so closely aligned with Barth's complaints about the cold-bloodedness of historical-critical enquiry—is simply 'a splendid, radiant, and at the same time profound Pelagianism'.[138]

The modern subject who is free to confront the world and God in the confidence that neither can finally disturb the person he is and knows himself to be is free to confront others in communities of his own choosing. Thus (and here we move to our second example) the *church* is understood by modern man as one

---

[134] *PT*, p. 87 (ET 94).

[135] See especially the conclusion of Barth's treatment of Rousseau: *PT*, pp. 196–207 (ET 207–19).

[136] *PT*, p. 190 (ET 200). For Barth, the distinction between Lessing and Rousseau is to be found primarily in the strength of this inclination (see pp. 209–10 (ET 222)).

[137] *PT*, p. 204 (ET 216).

[138] *PT*, p. 205 (ET 217).

voluntary society among others, its authority corresponding to its nature as the place or event in which self-sufficient subjects gather with a common interest and intent. Of course on this conception the church cannot meaningfully insist on any real correspondence between God's authority and its own, not least in matters of salvation. 'Applied to such a church, the *extra ecclesiam nulla salus* would in fact be an enormity. In face of such a church we should all have not only the right but the duty to faith, to appeal to the free grace of God to be made blessed outside of it. In face of such a church we should have to insist at least upon civil toleration, not only in the name of humanity but in the name of God.'[139] But this is not finally what the church is, even though the church as we know it may well be patient of this description too. 'We can say quite simply that a church of that description is not the church but the work of sin, of apostasy in the church.'[140] Rather, as the life of the children of God is a life of utter dependence upon the incarnate Word of God, it is 'primarily and radically' communal life: 'A church community or congregation, as distinguished from all mere association, is grounded in the essential being of those who are united within it. But they are what they are from and by the Word, indeed, their being is none other than that of the Word. Therefore they are one, and originally one, as surely as the Word in which they exist is one.'[141] We will return to this claim and some of its implications in the following chapter. For now, we simply note the fact that for Barth soteriological considerations that illuminate the character of the reader of scripture relate to ecclesiological reflections that impinge on the question of authority in scriptural reading, and that the question of the authority of this church in the modern world really can be addressed meaningfully in theological terms.

Summary

What does all this mean for our understanding of Barth's theology of interpretation? First, in broad terms, it helps illuminate something of what Barth means when he claims that the hermeneutics he derives from his engagement with scripture is generally applicable—even if he will go on to say that this claim to general applicability is itself a specifically theological statement, referring to the divine truth about human understanding presented to us in scripture. So in reading the preface to these historical lectures, we need first to appreciate fully the simple fact that Barth insists we deal carefully, patiently, and hopefully with the texts of the eighteenth and nineteenth centuries, even and especially if we wish to move beyond them towards what we perceive to be a more theologically responsible posture towards scripture and a more discriminating assessment of our cultural

---

[139] *KD* I/2, p. 233 (ET 213).
[140] *KD* I/2, p. 233 (ET 213).
[141] *KD* I/2, p. 237 (ET 217).

context. But we must also attend carefully to the grounds of this insistence: a vivid awareness of God's judgment and our solidarity in sin and grace; an active sense that God has called us to exist as members of his church, which precisely as his church precedes us as we take up for ourselves the task of reading scripture, so that we graciously find ourselves together with those who have spoken from and of it before us; a conviction that God's wisdom in reserving for himself the task of judging the church and the world evokes in us a genuinely objective modesty (and exposes the manifold hermeneutical forms of our pride and despair). All of this is unintelligible as a self-standing hermeneutical proposal, and deliberately so. The points of reference are God and church and therefore history and interpretation, not the other way round.

This means, secondly, that for Barth 'modernity' (or any other historical construct) is not basic to a description of the context of scriptural interpretation. In this chapter, we have developed this point by speaking of modernity, or at least the modern development of a general hermeneutics, as a negotiation of questions about the social impact of publicly enacted religious convictions generated in part by the seventeenth-century wars of religion. And so we emphasized that Barth simply refuses to concede that the early modern history of violent interpretative conflict is either (as a historical reality) resistant to theologically and politically responsible description or (as a historiographical construct) a value-neutral narrative to which Christian theology must answer.

Instead, he simply gets on with the business of reading scripture, presuming that the church is basically correct in its confession that scripture is the Word of God and as such worthy of trust, despite the questionable causes for which it has been enlisted and despite the church's own evident failures at just this point. The freedom to read scripture with this relative lack of regard for the political anxieties that underlie the specific methodological entailments of modern hermeneutical theory (though this is not to say a disregard for any specific method or set of methods) is pointedly not a function of an alternative hermeneutical doctrine (e.g., the notion of a post-critical naiveté). It is, prior to any general hermeneutical commitments, a venture of faith, grounded in the church's confession that God is actively present in scripture, freeing the church for service in the world. But if the characteristic confidence and freedom of Barth's approach to scripture is not simply a reflex of a particular reading of the history of its interpretation and of the Christian community's cultural location, his reading of scripture and of the tradition does issue in a portrayal of modernity of considerable hermeneutical significance.

One way of focusing this observation is to say that Barth presents us with alternative anthropologies of reading. On Barth's account, the eighteenth century is described as the age of absolutism, where absolutism is understood as humanization, the attempt by the self-positing subject to treat everything given in nature and history as material which he may bend by his own means to his own ends. Thus the modern reader approaches scripture with an unquestioning assurance of his own competence in the face of these texts. If scripture must be read like any other text, this is because scripture simply is like any other text, which is to say subject to the conditions of the possibility of understanding that we as readers bring to it. Among these conditions: The text must be subject to our summons, able to be brought before a native standard of judgment that exists prior to our encounter with it. And, following from this, it must be amenable to use as the focal point of any number of reading communities, so that any particular reader, having passed judgment on the significance and worth of this text, may freely associate himself with a group of like-minded, similarly self-possessed individuals. Here the scriptural text, which thus far is understood primarily as a historical inheritance, can be construed as the product of our capacity to build and sustain community; so language of scripture's canonicity refers to the church's appropriation of these texts, just as language of scripture's textuality may reflect the state's (and so the university's) appropriation of the church's canon—in each case the fundamental competence and self-reflexive transparency of the reading community being assumed.

As we will see more fully in the following chapters, in place of the sovereignty of the modern reading subject, whose presumptions regarding this hermeneutical self-sufficiency he regards as neo-Pelagianism, Barth speaks of God's prevailing authority in scripture, and so of reading as an act of humility and gratitude in which the church is genuinely confronted by scripture's specific and comprehensive claim—a claim that evokes the self-forgetful attentiveness of faith. In place of the competence of the reader, he speaks of the hiddenness of God in his revelation and of Christ's promise to be with his church in the witness of the apostles of his choosing, so that the church's reading of scripture is a prayerful venture of faith. And in place of the inclusiveness of the reader who can fully comprehend himself within and without his associations, he speaks of the life of the church under the Word, and so of a reading together that is not an ethical-hermeneutical ideal pursued by self-sufficient individual readers but a gracious reality from the start—a common hearing and being-identified in faith.

Chapter 3

Revelation and the Grounds of Interpretation

In our first chapter, we attempted to highlight some of Barth's earlier accounts of scriptural reading from the 1917 lecture 'Die neue Welt in der Bibel' through his first dogmatics lectures in Göttingen. We noted his early attempts to describe the relationship of scripture and scripture's reader in terms drawn from scripture itself. And we drew attention to the hermeneutical significance of the universality of divine judgment and the forgiveness of sins in the *Romans* commentary. Finally, we observed Barth's increasing investment in the Protestant scripture principle, as he began to deploy with greater confidence and nuance the dogmatic resources of the early Protestant theologians in describing the encounter with God in scripture.

We then devoted a chapter to Barth's lectures on the history of modern Protestant theology. Here we recognized mutually illuminating parallels between Barth's theological historiography and his biblical hermeneutics: The historical work illustrates (in part) what Barth means when he says that the hermeneutics derived from scripture is generally applicable, while the coherence of the historiography with the biblical hermeneutics helps us recognize the theological specificity of Barth's historiography in spite of its clear and important conceptual relationship to broader debates regarding the character of historical rationality in early twentieth-century hermeneutics. And we argued at some length that the reception of Barth's hermeneutics has been heavily influenced by an assessment of the political problematics of modern interpretative pluralism that Barth did share, and that some attention to Barth's own portrayal of the deepest instincts of modernity is an important part of a contemporary appropriation of his work.

All of this is a way of saying that we have in a sense only now reached the start. For the broad thematic survey in the first chapter and the closer textual analysis in the second were both self-consciously partial treatments designed to provide an orientation to the doctrinal account of scriptural reading in the first volume of the *Church Dogmatics* that forms the focus of this chapter and the next.

In examining this material, we will necessarily revisit some of the ground surveyed or at least indicated in the preceding chapters. But we will largely avoid any explicit discussion of the relationship of the relevant portions of *Church Dogmatics* I to the corresponding material in the dogmatics lectures from

Göttingen and the *Christliche Dogmatik.*[1] We will also, with a few exceptions, limit our exposition strictly to Barth's doctrine of the Word of God, side-stepping questions about the extent and character of the continuity between this and later volumes of the *Church Dogmatics.* This qualification applies especially to Volume Four, whose masterful treatment of the prophetic office of Christ is so illuminating for many of the themes first raised in the prolegomena, and whose treatment of the sacraments stands in such sharp contrast with the position developed in Barth's earlier work. The following reading quietly presupposes that despite these and other developments, the *Church Dogmatics* can be read as a coherent whole, but as I have consciously avoided bringing material from the later volumes to bear in my discussion of the prolegomena, it does not seem necessary to test or defend that assumption at any length here.

Providing a reading of the prolegomena that is recognizably responsive to the material is one matter. Presenting Barth's argument in a serviceable way is another. The *Church Dogmatics,* while a rare joy to read, is notoriously elusive of engaging commentary.[2] And if one can hardly take comfort in others' professed struggles at this point, one can at least take some courage in noting that those who seem most nearly successful are those who have moved along the material in their own manner, proceeding on the assumption that if someone really wants to read Barth, one should read: Barth. In any case, I have felt free to arrange the following exposition along thematic lines, focusing in this chapter on the question of the theological necessity of scriptural interpretation and in the next on the character and limits of interpretation as an act of obedience by the reading church.

But in order to help set these questions in context and avoid completely obscuring the flow of the argument of Barth's doctrine of the Word of God, we will focus first in this chapter on the wider dogmatic context of Barth's explicitly hermeneutical material, beginning with a very brief account of the architecture of the first volume of the *Church Dogmatics* as a whole.

The Dogmatic Function of Prolegomena

Barth opens the *Church Dogmatics* with two introductory sections on 'The Task of Dogmatics' and 'The Task of Prolegomena to Dogmatics'. Here he defines dogmatics as the Christian church's examination of its own distinctive talk about God,[3] talk ventured in the belief that God, in making himself known in Jesus Christ, has placed upon the church the inescapable duty of bearing appropriate

---

[1] On which see Kirschstein, *Die souveräne Gott,* pp. 246–70.

[2] Cf. Hans Frei, 'Afterward: Eberhard Busch's Biography of Karl Barth', in *Karl Barth in Re-View: Posthumous Works Reviewed and Assessed,* ed. H. Martin Rumscheidt (Pittsburgh, 1981), pp. 95–116 (esp. p. 109).

[3] *KD* I/1, p. 10 (ET 11).

witness to this self-giving. Dogmatics thus follows the church's proclamation as that proclamation follows God's self-revelation, and this means both that it is not an attempt to justify the church's speech—a way of getting preaching and sacramental practice off the ground—and that dogmatics does not concern itself, at least not programmatically, with the church's social work and worship. It simply investigates the *Christusgemäßheit* of church proclamation, asking whether or not the church's proclamation is appropriate to its object, that is, to Jesus Christ, 'God in his gracious revealing and reconciling address to humanity'.[4]

Following these introductory sections, Barth moves directly into the doctrine of the Word of God proper, in four chapters. This material comprises two main parts: The first is a preliminary definition of the criterion of dogmatics (Chapter 1, §§3–7), the second a fuller definition of this criterion and with it a definition of its correct employment in the dogmatic task (chapters 2–4, §§8–24).[5] In the first chapter, Barth defines the criterion of church proclamation as the Word of God, and focuses this definition in §4, where he describes this one Word in its threefold form as revealed, written, and preached. Here scripture as the written Word is identified as the immediate norm of church proclamation, and the task of dogmatics as the critical evaluation of the agreement of proclamation with scripture. Here Barth also sketches the contours of the context in which the dogmatic task is carried out by providing preliminary characterizations of the location, forms, nature, and knowability of the Word of God. And in the subsequent three chapters, constituting the second major section of the prolegomena, Barth develops an extended characterization of the dogmatic task itself—i.e., he asks how dogmatics relates the Word of God in its form as church proclamation to the Word in its written form as the church's scripture. He does so, crucially, by providing a second, much more extensive, description of the Word. And so the central section of the first chapter (§4—'The Word of God in its Threefold Form') is taken up, the order of its exposition reversed, and its content greatly expanded in chapters 2–4.

This formal balance, along with the sheer scale of the argument, the catholicity of citation, and Barth's deliberate, self-possessed prose, gives the book a certain classical feel. But for all that it is clearly also a polemical piece, progressing in large part by means of a series of broadly-drawn distinctions between Barth's own evangelical position on the one hand, and what he takes to be the two major living alternatives (Roman Catholicism and modern Protestantism) on the other.[6]

---

    [4] *KD* I/1, p. 3 (ET 4).

    [5] See the summary statement and prospect on *KD* I/1, pp. 305–10 (ET 287–92).

    [6] Thus Thurneysen can, on reading drafts of the prolegomena, speak of 'a quite exceptional fluency of exposition' and marvel at the 'simplicity and power' of Barth's writing while also claiming that the lectures on the doctrine of the Trinity will be read 'for the next hundred years' precisely because they rescue the church from the 'superficialities of

Dogmatics, Barth claims, investigates the agreement of the church's act with its being: Its basis is God's self-communication to sinful humanity, the divine Word which commissions and sanctifies the church's speech (in preaching) and symbolic action (in baptism and the eucharist); its goal is *wirklich Verkündigung*—the proclamation that not only intends to be but really is a genuine and effective repetition of the divine promise received in faith; and, when the question of this agreement of human act and divine being is put appropriately, it is characteristically *wissenschaftlich*—i.e., it is a public, persistent, methodologically self-aware function of the believing church. But *prolegomena* to dogmatics—and this is the point at issue here—is a reflex of the *division* of the church. If dogmatics presupposes Christian speech as human speech, prolegomena presupposes speech which claims to be Christian but is not recognizable as such—that is, it presupposes heresy. And for Barth, heresy means concretely Roman Catholicism in the form it attained in the sixteenth-century conflict with the Reformation and pietistic and rationalistic modernism as it developed in the post-Reformation evangelical church.[7] So whatever the truth of Robert Jenson's claim that 'the *Kirchliche Dogmatik* is an enormous attempt to interpret all reality by the fact of Christ',[8] we should not forget that on Barth's own account the first volume of the *Kirchliche Dogmatik*, at least, is simply an attempt to restate with the necessary force and clarity 'that which the older Protestant theology, in its resistance against Catholicism and soon thereafter also against an emerging modernism, dealt with under the title *De scriptura sacra.*[9]

---

modernism' and 'the enticements of Thomism'. See the letters of 21 August 1931 and 18 August 1932 (*B–Th III*, p. 170–71, 252).

[7] *KD* I/1, p. 33 (ET 34). See already *UCR I*, p. 257 (ET 211): 'I would hazard the statement ... that Roman Catholicism with its church principle and modern Protestantism are counterbalancing heresies, and if I had to choose between them I am not sure whether I would have to prefer the classical heresy to the nonclassical one.' Cf. *KD* I/1, §7: 'The Word of God, Dogma, and Dogmatics'; *KD* I/2, pp. 607, 685–6, 746–9 (ET 546, 613–14, 666–9). Valuable background to the underlying conception of the theological enterprise can be found in Barth, *Anselm: Fides Quarens Intellectum. Anselm's Proof of the Existence of God in the Context of his Theological Scheme*, trans. Ian W. Robertson (Richmond, 1960), pp. 59–72. On the polemical and ecumenical character of the *Church Dogmatics*, see G.C. Berkouwer, *The Triumph of Grace in the Theology of Karl Barth*, trans. Harry R. Boer (Grand Rapids, 1956), pp. 166–95; Hans Urs von Balthasar, *The Theology of Karl Barth. Exposition and Interpretation*, trans. Edward T. Oakes, S.J. (San Francisco, 1992), pp. 3–55. More generally, see Richard A. Muller, *Post-Reformation Reformed Dogmatics. Volume 1: Prolegomena* (Grand Rapids, 1987) for useful background on the genre of dogmatic prolegomena in the Reformed tradition, including the historical relationship of prolegomena to ecclesial polemics, institutionalization, and the role of theology in the university.

[8] Robert W. Jenson, *Systematic Theology. Volume 1: The Triune God* (New York and Oxford, 1997), p. 21.

[9] *KD* I/1, p. 43 (ET 43).

The first volume of the *Church Dogmatics* is perhaps best read, then, when it is read with a firm sense of its rhetorical directedness. And this means, secondly, that it is best read with a sense of its self-appointed material limitations. Its *Kardinalsatz* is the Protestant scripture principle. But Barth also believed that in the theological climate of the day this principle could only be properly articulated when its larger doctrinal context was made explicit,[10] and so he develops the doctrine of scripture as part of an extended treatment of the doctrine of revelation. But this means that the several tracts of doctrine that are put to work here (the doctrine of the trinity, the christology, etc.) are developed solely in terms of their formal significance—i.e., as they allow Barth to speak of God's free, personal act as the ground of the church's being-in-proclamation and its dogmatic self-reflection.[11] So if, as Barth so famously insisted (and insisted in reaction both to modern conceptions of a pre-theological ontology and to what he understood as the Roman Catholic doctrine of the analogy of being), prolegomena is already part of dogmatics, it still part and whole is prolegomena, and should be read as such.

The Scripture Principle and the Doctrine of Revelation

Barth's claim that the scripture principle requires careful articulation within a larger doctrinal context remains uncontroversial, if perhaps only because often overlooked; objections have centered, rather, on the material implications of Barth's decision to develop the doctrine of scripture as part of a trinitarian doctrine of revelation at the outset of his dogmatics. Thus the predominance of language about 'revelation' and 'knowledge of God' in the prolegomena is seen as evidence that Barth is caught up in a characteristically modern preoccupation with epistemological issues, and that this preoccupation leads Barth to distort the trinitarian material he introduces to address it.[12] The charge—at least in its less qualified forms—almost certainly does not stick. But as it stands it can help us

---

[10] On the continuing significance of this point, see John Webster, 'The dogmatic location of the canon', *Neue Zeitschrift für Systematische Theologie und Religionsphilosophie* 43 (2001): 17–43.

[11] Cf. *KD* I/1, p. 43 (ET 43–4).

[12] See, e.g., Alan J. Torrance, *Persons in Communion. An Essay on Trinitarian Description and Human Participation* (Edinburgh, 1996). Torrance's own interest lies in asking whether a worship-oriented dogmatics, one that begins with a recognition that we participate through the Spirit in Christ's communion with the Father and just so share the mind of Christ, would provide a more adequate basis for speaking of trinitarian mutuality and human participation in the divine life than Barth's own revelation- and proclamation-focused prolegomena. In evaluating these issues, much depends on how one understands the relationship of the prolegomena to the later volumes of the *Church Dogmatics*, which Torrance recognizes develop a more thorough account of the inner-trinitarian relations (see *Persons in Communion*, p. 365; cf. 314 n. 16).

focus on some implications of Barth's doctrinal arrangements that require further attention.

We begin by noting that if our emphasis on the centrality of the scripture principle to Barth's dogmatic intentions is correct, this reinforces the argument that Barth does not in fact develop his doctrine of revelation primarily as an answer to the question of how we know God, so that we can read it without loss simply as another chapter in the larger story of post-Kantian epistemology. The overarching question posed in the prolegomena is, rather, how properly to describe the manner in which God relates to the preaching church as its merciful Lord, at once truly encountering it and maintaining his self-grounded distinction from it in this encounter. (The meaningfulness of the task of dogmatics—the critical evaluation of church proclamation in the light of scripture as its immediate norm—depends upon a recognition that the initiative in and judgment of the church's proclamation proceeds from God alone and just so that it can be a matter for human work and reflection.) The 'concrete and decisive question' in a doctrine of revelation, to use Barth's own terms, is not 'How do we know God?' but 'Who is God?'—i.e., who is this God who according to scripture reveals himself as Lord?[13] And, Barth continues, if we properly put the question of who God is—that is, if we frame our dogmatic enquiry in strictly scriptural terms—we must necessarily go on to ask how it is that this God reveals himself and what that means for those to whom this revelation is addressed. Whatever we might say about the concept of revelation in general terms, perhaps in the context of a comparative theology of religions, in dealing with the church's scripture, we must first ask who reveals himself here, who God is here, and subsequently two further questions: 'what this God does' and 'what he effects, accomplishes, creates, and gives in his revelation'.[14] And according to scripture, God is the one who brings it about that he really does exist with and for specific human beings, and they for him, in true relationship but not in more or less secret identity.

For Barth, because the revelation with which Christian proclamation has to do is God's *self*-revelation, the doctrine of revelation necessarily takes trinitarian form, and the doctrine of the trinity necessarily is a distillation of the history of salvation—a history authoritatively attested by scripture.[15] It is true that Barth was not always entirely successful in communicating the scriptural orientation of his

---

[13] *KD* I/1, p. 318 (ET 301).

[14] *KD* I/1, p. 313 (ET 297).

[15] See Christoph Schwöbel's illuminating brief treatment of the trinitarian turn in recent theology, 'Trinitätslehre als Rahmentheorie des christlichen Glaubens', in *Marburger Jahrbuch Theologie X. Trinität*, ed. Wilfred Härle and Dieter Lührmann (Marburg, 1998), pp. 129–54. Of course the use of the term 'necessarily' in this context does not imply any restriction of God's freedom in his self-giving or any mitigation of creation's contingent integrity in Barth's theology. The basic theological distinctions at issue are well rehearsed in Paul D. Molnar, *Divine Freedom and the Doctrine of the Immanent Trinity. In Dialogue with Karl Barth and Contemporary Theology* (London, 2002).

trinitarian theology of revelation. Thus he felt obliged to counter misrepresentations of his published claim in the *Christliche Dogmatik* that the doctrine of the trinity can legitimately be approached through a grammatical analysis of the sentence 'God speaks'.[16] But even a fairly cursory reading of the trinitarian material in *Church Dogmatics* I shows that the biblical text is always the intentional source and *telos* of the formal dogmatic statements. Thus it is precisely 'the God who reveals himself in the Bible' who 'must also be known in his revealing and his being revealed if he is to be known'[17]; and it is precisely 'according to the biblical understanding of revelation' that the one, true God 'is the revealing God and the event of revelation and its effect on man'.[18] In short: Barth intends these formal trinitarian statements to serve as entrances to the biblical material, statements which—while they undoubtedly bring with them some very definite conceptual entailments—are not to be accorded independent dignity or force, but rather are to be measured by their adequacy as indications of the scriptural texts.[19] All of which is to say quite simply that in reading this material we need to recognize the extent to which the scripture principle is presupposed throughout.

Again: Barth claims that God's revelation to us and the distinction between God's initiative, act, and achievement revealed in this revelation, is not something merely apparent. While he remains the one, true God in this revelation, scripture nowhere allows us to conceive of the holiness of God as something that can be predicated of only one aspect of his being-in-act or of some other divine reality hidden from us. The one, true God is himself revealer, revelation, and

---

[16] See *Christliche Dogmatik*, p. 166; *KD* I/1, p. 312 (ET 296).

[17] *KD* I/1, p. 314 (ET 298).

[18] *KD* I/1, p. 315 (ET 299).

[19] The progress over the corresponding discussion in the *Christliche Dogmatik* is largely if not wholly in the clarity and consistency with which Barth makes this point (as Thurneysen notes in his letter to Barth of 18 August 1932, which speaks of 'a broader and deeper connection with scripture' in Barth's handling of the doctrine of the trinity (*B–Th III*, p. 252)). Compare, for example, the opening moves in §9.1 of the *Christliche Dogmatik*, in which Barth very briefly (and without explicit appeal to scripture) relates the doctrines of revelation and trinity via the *Deus dixit* formula before proceeding to a fairly thorough review of the dogmatic location of the trinity in the tradition (see *Christliche Dogmatik*, pp. 165–72), with the strong, practical reassertion of the scripture principle in the opening sentences of *KD* I/1, §8 (p. 311 (ET 295)): 'When in order to clarify how church proclamation is to be measured by holy scripture we first of all ask after the prior concept of *revelation*, we are already bound in this question itself to holy scripture as the witness of revelation. Perhaps more important than all that dogmatics can say about the Bible's distinctive place in and over against the church is the example that it itself has to give in laying its foundations.' And note that this programmatic statement opens up to a series of highly condensed but materially significant rehearsals of the naming and narrative identification of God in the Old and New Testaments (*KD* I/1, pp. 314–16 (ET 298–300)).

revealedness, so that to this God 'there is also ascribed in unimpaired differentiation within himself this threefold mode of being'.[20] Thus 'it is only—but very truly—by observing the unity and the differentiation of God in his biblically attested revelation that we are set before the problem of the doctrine of the trinity'.[21] The appropriateness of the conceptuality Barth employs here is one issue; the intention to direct attention exclusively towards revelation precisely as it is biblically attested is another. And it is this theological intention, which is simply another way of speaking of the intellectual and spiritual discipline that corresponds to an affirmation of the scripture principle, that is our main concern. But we can also note in passing two broad consequences of the fact that Barth locates the scripture principle in a trinitarian doctrine of revelation and that he presupposes this principle while developing this doctrine: On the one hand, in his account the doctrine of the trinity is not prone to the vast systematic inflation it suffers in some more recent theologies, where it is called upon to diagnose and solve all manner of conceptual problems—and in the process is transformed into something very like a general recommendation of a relational ontology. On the other hand, Barth's treatment of the doctrine of scripture is less prone to the strange abstractions of some modern foundationalist theologies, in which descriptions of scripture's character and function proceed largely without meaningful reference to the God of Christian confession.

In sum: By bringing together the doctrines of the trinity and revelation, Barth preliminarily establishes a basic conception of the authenticity of revelation (it is grounded in and true to the very life of God), its content (God himself in his saving presence), and its effect (our acknowledgement in the Spirit of God's comprehensive sovereignty). All this does implicate the processes of knowing appropriate to theology, so that Barth is being perfectly consistent when he says, 'All that I know of God and can know and should know and indeed ought to know, I know by an exercise of his lordship, of which I am the object'.[22] But this is itself a confession of faith ventured in the church that is ruled by scripture, not the establishment of an abstract epistemological basis for proclamation or dogmatic reflection.

Further, by locating the doctrine of scripture within a trinitarian doctrine of revelation (if our emphasis on the self-limitations of Barth's prolegomena are correct, we should not reverse this and speak of a revelation-model doctrine of the trinity without qualification), Barth is guarding against the possibility that the scripture principle will be set up as a norm without content. That is to say, he is trying to ensure that his description of the fact of scripture's normativity follows strictly from a description of the content of the scriptural witness. Put otherwise, the doctrine of scripture belongs in the doctrine of revelation because the latter is

---

[20] *KD* I/1, p. 315 (ET 299).

[21] *KD* I/1, p. 315 (ET 299).

[22] *KD* I/2, p. 428 (ET 389).

inseparable from the doctrine of reconciliation. And the doctrines of revelation and reconciliation belong together because both are simply two indications of the one reality which scripture names Jesus Christ.[23]

Revelation and Incarnation

These broad architectural observations serve to secure a few basic points that can help guide the more detailed exposition to follow. In the first place, the doctrine of scripture belongs within a doctrine of revelation, where revelation is understood not as the communication of some abstract rules for human conduct and reflection, nor as some precognitive motivational pressure, but as God's sovereign kindness to a sinful creation. This means, secondly, that the decisive statements about what scripture is—and, therefore, how it should be read—will be statements about who God is, what form his self-revealing takes, and what this revelation achieves. Thirdly, the trinitarian shape of the doctrine of revelation refers us at every point to God's comprehensive freedom in his actions *ad extra*. As the incarnate Word of the Father, Jesus Christ is present to his people as Lord, always on his own terms. No fate befalls him: As the obedient Son of the Father he is entirely his own. Again, the Spirit of God is present in the church not as the elevation of the human spirit but as the Lord of life, sent by the Father and the Son and just so acting when and where it wills. Precisely this God remains completely himself in his revelation, and is nowhere dependent upon creaturely assistance to actualize a divine potentiality or to complement a divine initiation. Perfect in himself and in all his works, God reveals himself to be unhindered by creaturely inadequacy and opposition, so that as he creates and sustains a people for himself, they truly can live to the praise of his glory.

Insofar as we identify—however indirectly—the scriptural texts with the self-revelation of this God, we are confronted with the question of how we are to understand our own creaturely agency as readers and interpreters of these texts. If scripture is revelation, and revelation is reconciliation, the opening of blind eyes and the reorientation of estranged thoughts and desires, how are we to understand ourselves as interpreters of scripture, and how are we to describe the space within which we deliberate about the nature and function and meaning of these texts? What are the grounds for speaking of the church's interpretative work not simply as possible—as a divine concession to the human tendency to 'stop awhile and

---

[23] Cf. George Hunsinger, 'Karl Barth's doctrine of the Holy Spirit', in *The Cambridge Companion to Karl Barth*, pp. 177–94 (178): 'Just as revelation without reconciliation could only have been empty, so reconciliation without revelation could only have been mute. Revelation in fact imparted the reality of reconciliation, even as reconciliation formed the vital truth that revelation made known. Neither could be had without the other since both were identical with Jesus Christ.'

play among secondary things'[24]—but as genuinely necessary, a concrete responsibility laid upon the church in the world?

On Barth's terms, any meaningful response to this line of questioning will simply involve renewed attention to the basic statement that God is himself in his revelation, the Lord who desires and enables and makes indisputably real a relationship with his people to his glory and their salvation. Concretely, just because Christian theology speaks of Jesus Christ as God's reconciling Word, it must speak also of scripture as the prophetic-apostolic witness to the incarnate Word and of the church as the community given time and space to hear God's Word in scripture and to proclaim it. In the remainder of this chapter we will examine some of the reasons why this is so.

Revelation as Reconciliation

> The work of the Son or Word is the presence and declaration of God which, in view of the fact that it takes place miraculously in and in spite of human darkness, we can only describe as revelation. The term reconciliation is another word for the same thing.... [T]he concept of reconciliation coincides with that of revelation though not with that of redemption.[25]

To repeat: One of the main burdens of Barth's treatment of the doctrine of revelation is to stress against Roman Catholic ecclesialism and modern Protestant culture-theology the inalienable freedom of this God in his self-giving. But this freedom is not an independent principle; it can be properly acknowledged only as we trace the actual history of God's dealings with us.[26] And of course for Barth this history centers on Jesus Christ, on God's presence with and for us in this specific human being.

> Revelation in fact does not differ from the person of Jesus Christ nor from the reconciliation accomplished in him. To say revelation is to say 'The Word became flesh'. ... But to say 'God with us' is to say something which has no basis or possibility outside itself, which can in no sense be explained in terms of man and man's situation, but only as knowledge of God from God, as free and unmerited grace.[27]

Revelation is properly Jesus Christ, the incarnate Word. But incarnation means God's coming to us in hiddenness. As such it is the revelation of God's judgment

---

[24] Barth, 'Die neue Welt', p. 22 (ET 34).

[25] *KD* I/1, pp. 429–30 (ET 409).

[26] Thus the trinitarian rule that 'statements about the divine modes of being antecedently in themselves [which secure recognition of the graciousness and reality of God's revealing, reconciling work] cannot be different in content from those that are to be made about their reality in revelation' (*KD* I/1, p. 503 (ET 479)).

[27] *KD* I/1, pp. 122–3 (ET 119–20).

(because he hides himself we know that we who cannot see him and live are in the wrong before him) and of his mercy (in hiding himself he really has come to us as we are, as he had to come to us to be our God). We might say: God makes himself known to us as our future. His revelation is not our undoing, but the establishment of a relationship in which he is and remains our Lord and we become and remain his people.

His revelation is thus an act of grace. 'The majesty of God in his condescension to the creature—that is the most general truth always told us by the reality of Jesus Christ.'[28] So if we say God had to hide himself in order to make himself known to us and effect this relationship with us—that he had to be the God-man and as such our mediator—this is a strictly theological statement in which the indication of this necessity is a confession of our need and God's mercy, not an elaborations of conditions to which God is subject. Talk of the 'necessity' of God's actions serves to discipline theological reflection, not to make God dependent on his creation.[29] In recognition of this freedom, we must say that 'God could have revealed himself immediately, in his invisible glory', or in the form of a creaturely reality previously and otherwise wholly foreign to us. But in fact, God mercifully reveals himself to us as a human being, and therefore we are compelled to confess:

> this very veiling, kenosis and passion of the Logos has to take place in order that it may lead to his unveiling and exaltation and to the completion of revelation. God's revelation without this veiling or in the form of an unknown being from another world would not be revelation but our death. It would be the end of all things, because it would mean the abolition of the conditions of our existence.[30]

---

[28] *KD* I/2, p. 35 (ET 31).

[29] Cf. *KD* I/2, pp. 36, 38–9 (ET 32–3, 35) and more generally *Fides Quarens Intellectum, passim.*

[30] *KD* I/2, p. 40 (ET 36); cf. *KD* I/1, pp. 175–6 (ET 168–9), where Barth develops an extended contrast between Luther's *theologia crucis* and the doctrine of the *analogia entis* as a variety of *theologia gloriae*: 'Revelation means the incarnation of the Word of God. But incarnation means: Entrance into this worldliness. We are in this world; we are ourselves worldly through and through. If God does not speak to us in a worldly manner, he does not speak to us at all…. It is not the case that at some point God was hidden from us through some unfortunate disturbance but then revealed himself by removing this veil. On this assumption human attempts to, as it were, come to God's aid by encroaching on the mystery would be—if not actually necessary—all too understandable and excusable. But it is in fact the case that *God himself veils himself and thereby unveils himself.* And this is why we must not dream of intruding on the mystery. It is good for us that God acts exactly as he does, and it could only be fatal to us if he acted otherwise, if he was revealed to us in a manner we would think appropriate: directly and without a veil, without a worldliness or only in the harmless, transparent worldliness of the *analogia entis.* It would not be greater love and mercy, it would be our end and the end of all things if the Word were spoken to us thus. That it is spoken to us in this way, as is actually the case—revealed in its hiddenness—that is the decisive way of saying that it really has come to us instead of requiring us come to it,

It belongs to God's love for us, then, that he comes to us in this concealment. But this means he comes to us in a form we can overlook or misunderstand.

> By becoming flesh the Word enters the hiddenness, the 'servant form', which in respect of the knowability of God undoubtedly signifies an 'externalization' [*Entäußerung*] (*kenosis*) compared with the 'divine form' in which God knows himself, in which the Father knows the Son and the Son the Father. It is in this veiling—which after all is a veiling in a form familiar to man—that the majesty can meet men and thus make knowledge of itself possible through men. But it may also fail of recognition in this its 'servant form'. Its actual exposure to this failure to be recognized is the 'externalization' which the Word allows to befall himself in becoming flesh. Knowledge of it becomes real to men only in virtue of a special unveiling through Jesus' resurrection from the dead, or through all the sayings and acts of his life so far as they were signs of his resurrection. Thus God's becoming man means undoubtedly in the first instance that his divinity becomes latent.[31]

This latency of God's divinity in his revelation identifies us as the objects of his judgment and mercy, as those who must and can live with revelation without necessarily recognizing it as such. We quite simply are those who live with revelation; our overlooking or misunderstanding of God's Word in its servant form does not in any sense undermine the sheer reality of his revelation as the Word by which alone we can live. But we can and do live with it as those who do not recognize it as such (just as, Barth claims, we live alongside other human beings whether or not we recognize them in their otherness).[32] God's mercy in his revelation, in other words, means for us that revelation is in the strictest sense objective for us. It neither spells the end of our existence nor gives itself to be simply dissolved into it. It continually establishes itself in its distinction from us, and it does so for our sake.

But this means that God's hiddenness in revelation is the ground of meaningful and responsible human activity. Revelation can be misunderstood, but this does not mean that it presents us with an insoluble riddle, to our endless frustration; rather, it moves on its own accord towards its own resolution (the movement from cross to resurrection is, as the progress of the Son of Man, God's own movement). And by this movement, God evokes genuine, purposeful, and hopeful human effort, including real theological enquiry—scripturally focused intellectual work that stands under the promise of God's self-manifestation even as it runs up against the impenetrable depth of God's hiddenness.

Already we can begin to see the hermeneutical implications: Scriptural interpretation is both possible and necessary, in the most serious sense of these

---

an attempt in which we could only fail. Precisely in its worldliness it is, therefore, in every respect a word of grace.'

[31] *KD* I/2, p. 42 (ET 37–8).
[32] Cf. *KD* I/2, pp. 44–9 (ET 39–44).

words—not because the church must sustain itself in the face of competing appropriations of these texts; nor because all written texts are inherently interpretable; nor because we know quite apart from any christological considerations that interpersonal communication is prone to distortion in every case; but—because God hides himself in his revelation to us sinners.

Further, because this hiddenness is the event of the Word becoming flesh, it is the hiddenness of Jesus Christ in all his historical particularity as a unique human subject who is as such universally significant. We can therefore specify the hiddenness and mercy of God by speaking of the specific *time* of revelation. According to Barth, revelation has its own time, in two senses. First, the time of revelation is distinguished from the time of the original creation and the time of our rebellion. And second, the time of revelation is distinguished from the time of the prophetic-apostolic witness to revelation (the time of scripture) and the time of the church—of those who believe through the words of the prophets and apostles. This latter point will lead us to Barth's conception of scripture as the written Word of God and of the mediation of revelation through the words of the prophets and apostles. But first we need to unpack this twofold distinctiveness of the time of revelation as a way of asking after the theological necessity of scriptural interpretation. Why is it that the Christian church can and must interpret scripture? The answer involves a description of the church's location—of the time God has given it. As God's time for us, revelation establishes the conditions of our continuing existence as a community charged with bearing witness in history, with all its internal variations and cultural-linguistic differences, to the work of God in Christ. And the church that exists in this time lives with and from scripture.

The Time of Revelation

The opening moves in Barth's argument are, sketched in outline, relatively straightforward:[33] Revelation is event. As such, it has its own time. The theological proposition 'God reveals himself' thus means 'God has time for us'.[34] As this time is the time of the Lord of our life, we cannot seek to ground this time in another or live in an alternative time; we have no other time than the time God has for us. But we can truly live in this time because God has no other time for us than the time of his revelation.

As sinful creatures, however, we refuse God's time in favor of our own, and it belongs to God's mercy in his revelation that he does not simply abolish our time in revealing himself to us. Rather, in assuming flesh the Word of God assumes our

---

[33] Though of course this is not to deny that 'the conception of divine and human temporality ... is much more complicated, much more interesting, and much more profound in Barth's theology than has usually been recognized' (Hunsinger, *How to Read Karl Barth*, p. 227).

[34] *KD* I/2, p. 50 (ET 45).

fallen time. As God's time, revelation penetrates and comprehends our lost time, thereby distinguishing itself as a third time alongside the time God originally created and our fallen time.[35] The time God originally created is now closed to us. And so also, in a somewhat different sense, is our fallen time. We live in the time God has for us in his revelation. But because of God's hiddenness in his revelation, we continue to live in the old time which has been bounded by the new. 'Neither the old nor the new time ... exists abstractly and solely as such; they exist because the new time which already exists triumphs over the old which therefore exists also.'[36]

The triumph of revelation time over our time, even though it is the triumph of grace and so the triumph of God's mercy in his revelation, means our time is taken from us—it means our death. Again, this is not to say it is simply the end of our time: revelation and reconciliation are not redemption. It is rather the announcement of the end of all things, and so we who receive this announcement live as those who have had their future taken from them, i.e., as those who have been judged as sinners. 'Infinite time (and in this infinite time all infinite, absolute values and magnitudes!) exists only for a time-consciousness which is unaware of or forgetful of revelation.'[37] But as faith sees that we live in this old time because of God's patience, and that in taking our time from us God gives us his own, it refuses to rest in any immanent ambitions or attainments, including its own knowledge.

> It lies in the nature of God's revelation and reconciliation in time, it lies in the nature of the *regnum gratiae*, that having *God* and our *having* God are two very different things, and that our redemption is not a relation which we can survey in its totality, i.e., which we can understand in both its aspects, God's and our own. Paradoxically enough we can understand it only in its divine aspect, i.e., in faith we can understand it only as it is posited by God.[38]

The faith that seeks understanding, in other words, aware of the provisionality of all understanding in this time, continually refers away from itself in renewed, repentant attention to God's revelation. Concretely, the church cannot rest content simply reciting, in resignation or presumption, the witness that comes to it from the past. Nor can it presume a principled growth in knowledge of God across time, an increasing approximation to divine truth, so that the fullness of knowledge granted to us at the end of all things can be anticipated here and now through some form of theological extrapolation. Rather, faith accepts both the limits set for it and the responsibility laid upon it in this time, and it continually returns to the scriptural witness for its orientation. In this sense, the necessity of interpretation as a

---

[35] See *KD* I/2, pp. 52–8 (ET 47–53).

[36] *KD* I/2, p. 62 (ET 56).

[37] *KD* I/2, p. 76 (ET 69).

[38] *KD* I/1, p. 485 (ET 462).

continual, restless engagement with scripture and with the tradition is a function of the church's awareness of its time.

Thus far the time of revelation as the time of reconciliation. As such, it is the time of the incarnation. And so the time of revelation is also to be distinguished from the time of the prophets and apostles and the time of the church which believes through their words. The point of these distinctions in time is generally to deflate systematic appeals to 'history': Barth thinks such appeals often involve entirely questionable assumptions about our ability to survey and position ourselves in relation to divine revelation. More closely, he thinks the interpretative posture implicit in a good deal of historical-critical exegesis is bound up with a defective view of historical integrity and variation. And he recommends in response an account that trades on a sharp distinction between time of the incarnation and all other time. This distinction brings with it a second: The era of prophetic-apostolic witness is not simply continuous with the era of the church that receives and repeats this gospel witness. Crucially, this latter distinction is not established and maintained by the church's reading strategy: Simply identifying scripture as a historical norm of church proclamation is not to the point. The distinctions that matter are established by God and are articulated theologically with reference to the particular shape of God's action. God's taking time in the incarnation is one thing; his giving time for prophetic and apostolic witness another; his giving time for this witness to be heard and received yet another.

> These are different times distinguished not only by the difference in periods and contents, not only by the remoteness of centuries and the disparity in the men of different centuries and millennia, but distinguished by the different attitude [*Stellung*] of God to men.... This different position [*Stellung*] in God's order differentiates these three times as human times are not differentiated elsewhere, as they are differentiated only here, as only the times of God's Word are differentiated. One can, of course, dissolve the difference in time by ignoring the differentiation of the times in God's order, by viewing and presenting them, not as times of God's Word but only immanently, i.e., by taking into account only the difference of the periods and their human contents as such. Estimating the difference along these lines need then be no obstacle to a direct insight into the continuity and unity of the times, to an insight into our contemporaneity with Christ and all his saints. Indeed, it rather facilitates and establishes this insight by teaching us to see and understand the man of the past, be he Jeremiah or Jesus or Paul or Luther, as a fellow-man, to criticize him as such, but also to respect and love him, in short, to treat him as companion of one and the same time.[39]

Again, the recognition of the distinctiveness of these times is part of the church's proper acknowledgement of the objectivity of the Word of God; it prevents us from blunting the otherness of God's revelation through the concept of

---

[39] *KD* I/1, pp. 150–1 (ET 145–6).

history.[40] But it also orders the theologically mandated recognition of the historical-cultural location of the prophets and apostles. The real, effective relationship in time (the contemporaneity) of the church's proclamation with scripture and with the incarnate Word is not brought about by the effort of the preacher or by some other communal practices, ecclesial or academic. It has 'nothing directly to do with the general problem of historical understanding [*Verstehen*]'.[41] It is always a victorious act of the self-revealing Word through the Holy Spirit, apart from which no historical analysis or inhabitation will finally prove effective.[42] But as this divine act exposes the real limits of the interpretative pretensions sometimes ingredient in our appeals to history, it also establishes the legitimacy of sturdy historical work:

> Of course there is always some historical understanding when the Word of God is manifest to us in its contemporaneity.... [T]here is and has to be a specific relation of historical understanding with all the relevant components, from philological analysis to the art of what is called 'empathizing' [*bis zur Kunst der sogenannten Einfühlung*]. Proclamation is possible only in this relation of understanding, just as there could be prophecy and apostolate only in a specific relation of understanding.[43]

The specific historical *Verstehenverhältnis* of the apostles to Jesus Christ (Barth refers here to the *kata sarka* of 2 Cor. 5.16) involves a real historical distance between them and us. 'To put it quite concretely, the statement "God reveals himself" must signify that the fulfilled time is the time of the years 1–30.'[44] But as this historical distance is grounded in the economy of salvation (in the free becoming-flesh of the Word), and as revelation is never to be considered a predicate of history, so the historical location of the incarnation (ca. 1–30 CE) is not in itself fulfilled time. The contemporaneity of the apostles with Christ is not simply 'according to the flesh'. The distance between the apostles and the church here and now, and thus between scripture and the church's ongoing preaching, is not simply a temporal distance. Indeed, one can say that Barth will reject as theologically naive any attempt to speak in this connection of historical distance 'as such'.

---

[40] For Barth's assessment of tendencies in this direction in modern Protestant theology, a tendency Barth sees linked to a deficient trinitarian theology, see the trinitarian statement on *KD* I/1, pp. 155–6 (ET 150) alongside the treatment of Lessing immediately preceding it (pp. 151–2 (ET 146–7); further the discussion of the *filioque* in *KD* I/1, pp. 496–511 (ET 473–87) and *KD* I/2, pp. 272–5 (ET 250–2).

[41] *KD* I/1, p. 153 (ET 147).

[42] *KD* I/1, p. 150 (ET 145).

[43] *KD* I/1, pp. 153–4 (ET 147–9).

[44] *KD* I/2, p. 64 (ET 58).

Again, the revelation of God in Christ is historically located and locatable.[45] And this means that in correspondence with this revelation the church's witness must be historically located, sensitive to the particular time and place of its service. But the church cannot allow its perception of this aspect of its location to blind it to the fact that all its times are comprehended in the time of God's grace, just as it cannot play off the truth that Jesus suffered under Pontius Pilate against the mystery that he suffered 'so that we might die to sin and live for righteousness' (1 Pet. 2.24). So the church's interpretation of scripture in the service of proclamation here and now cannot be understood as an exercise in cultural retrieval—an attempt to rehabilitate the language of Zion or to render scripture's worldview meaningful to a more or less receptive world. Theologically, the basis of scriptural interpretation is, quite simply, the commission laid upon the church by God to exist as a community of witness in the world—a commission that corresponds to God's gentleness or hiddenness in revelation. That God's decision to be present to the world in these terms proves offensive (the so-called 'problem of particularity') simply means that it is part of the church's task to proclaim to the world and to itself that this offensiveness is to our salvation, as God allowed us to take offense at his grace and in raising his Son has quite literally put our rebellion behind us.

Revelation, Canon, Witness

As it establishes and limits the times of creation and fallen creation, the time of revelation continues until the consummation of all things. But as the time between the times of prophetic expectation and apostolic recollection, the time of the incarnation has a definite terminus within history. The ascension of the crucified risen one means that Jesus is no longer present to us as he was to the apostles. He is present to us through the apostles' witness—specifically through their written witness, the New Testament scriptures, and the Old Testament scriptures they presuppose. That he is present to the church *only* in this way means that the scriptures are in the most serious sense the canon. And to remind the church that scripture is canon in this sense is the basic point of the scripture principle, which contains within it the practical interpretative dictum *Besinn dich!* that Barth so strongly emphasized as the point of the doctrine of inspiration in the *Römerbrief* and the Calvin lectures. In continuing to unpack Barth's dogmatic treatment of the scripture principle and the theological basis for the church's interpretative activity, then, we need to consider both his account of the concrete form of the scriptural canon and the notion of apostolic succession that informs it. In both cases, we will see Barth attempting to ground a doctrine of scripture in the incarnation—the

---

[45] With more or less precision: the point is the self-identifying concreteness of revelation, not chronological tidiness, and in the light of the commanding mystery of revelation, Barth is largely unconcerned with pinning down exact dates.

existence of the apostles and their written witness representing in some sense a continuation of God's merciful hiddenness in his revelation—without simply conflating scripture and Christ.[46] Or, put slightly differently, Barth wants to speak of an indirect identity between the written Word and the incarnate Word without compromising the sovereignty of God in his revelation (e.g., by grounding the identity between Christ and scripture in a third thing—a general concept of symbolic transparency to the divine, perhaps, or a putative 'incarnational principle').

In keeping with our stress on the polemical character of Barth's prolegomena, we can also say Barth is attempting to think the scripture principle all the way through, in an explicit renewal of the Protestant engagement with the Roman Catholic doctrine of the insufficiency of scripture.[47] Naturally, it is all too easy to speak of the debate over the relative theological authority of scripture and tradition in terms that ignore the historical contingencies—including the manifold political realities—that attend this debate in every instance. This is especially true when we consider more recent communitarian and postmodernist conceptions of textual instability or vulnerability alongside earlier Roman Catholic and pietist positions. When Stanley Hauerwas claims that '*sola scriptura* is a heresy rather than a help in

---

[46] Or, what on some accounts may amount to the same thing, conflating Christ and the church. This is another point at which we do well to consider how Barth might react to more recent narrative theologies, in which a quasi-Barthian emphasis on a literal reading of the final form of the canonical text (the reading community's master narrative) is often accompanied by a quite un-Barthian identification of the risen Christ with the church that embodies or performs the gospel story. Thus, for example, Stephen Crites ('A Respectful Reply to the Assertorical Theologian', in *Why Narrative? Readings in Narrative Theology*, ed. Stanley Hauerwas and L. Gregory Jones (Grand Rapids, 1989), pp. 293–302), who 'do[es] not think the incarnation is confined to the thirty-odd years of "phasic" time from the birth to the death of Jesus'. Rather, he thinks that the resurrection implies 'that the Logos is made flesh, his flesh, wherever his story "is told, sung, sacramentally celebrated," or modelled in play-dough'. So while he does refer to Christ's session and to that extent distinguishes the risen Christ from the church, he places all the stress on the fact that according to 1 Cor. 12 the church 'is his risen body', and talk of Christ's ascension and of apostolic commissioning simply recedes from view.

[47] Or, more precisely, the Roman Catholic notion of the *formal* insufficiency of scripture, i.e., the claim that the church exercises a formal and constitutive authority that cannot simply be equated with the scriptural basis and norm of faith. That scripture is *materially* insufficient, that there are gaps in its faith-content that must be filled by developments in the tradition, is a further question, and 'a clear, fully thought-out, universally accepted answer to this precise question is not to be found in the tradition of Catholic theology' (Karl Rahner, 'Scripture and Tradition', in *Theological Investigations. Volume VI: Concerning Vatican Council II*, trans. Karl-H. and Boniface Kruger (London, 1969), pp. 98–112 (105)). See further Yves M.-J. Congar, *Tradition and Traditions. An historical and a theological essay*, trans. Michael Naseby and Thomas Rainborough (New York, 1967), pp. 409–22.

the Church',[48] he is clearly not fighting quite the same battle, or not fighting it in quite the same way as, say, Jean Gerson or François Veron, though each rejects this slogan because each is in his own particular context deeply committed to the integrity of the Christian tradition, deeply bothered by freewheeling exegesis, and deeply worried about the impact of the latter on the former. Conversely, Barth's concerns are not simply identical to Luther's or Calvin's, though each is committed (no less deeply than his Roman Catholic and Anabaptist counterparts) to the integrity of the Christian tradition and to the unity of the church in the world, a unity each believes threatened when the church cuts itself off from a real confrontation with scripture as the written Word of the church's Lord and rests content in communal self-reflection, however venerable and vibrant. Specifically, a full treatment of Barth's discussion of the sufficiency of scripture would require at the very least a thorough discussion of his engagements with both German-speaking Roman Catholic theology of the 1920s and 1930s and the German Christian movement.

That said, here we can only give a sidelong glance to these contextual specifics in registering the fact that Barth's position is at least in part consciously formulated in dialogue with what we are rather bluntly calling the Roman Catholic doctrine of the insufficiency of scripture, a doctrine that entails three basic objections to the scripture principle, or rather three components of the one objection that it is logically incoherent.[49] Roughly, the objection runs thus: First, identifying these texts and not others as 'scripture' immediately takes us beyond what the Christian church recognizes as scripture; lists of canonical books appear in the tradition but never in scripture itself. Second, scripture does not itself contain a statement of the scripture principle. And third, scripture nowhere dictates the terms on which it is to be interpreted and applied. So in formulating the scripture principle, the Protestant church is simply denying what it must presuppose, or presupposing what it denies: that scripture and tradition are mutually conditioning concepts, neither of which can be given absolute priority in a coherent account of scripture's authority. In the remainder of this chapter, we will structure our exposition with the first two aspects of this threefold objection in mind. The question of interpretation, which

---

[48] Stanley Hauerwas, *Unleashing the Scripture. Freeing the Bible from Captivity to America* (Nashville, 1993), p. 27.

[49] Overlooking for the moment the crucial point that this logical incoherence is seen as a symptom of a fundamental spiritual irresponsibility that threatens the unity of the church and therefore the stability of Christendom (here Hauerwas' Anabaptist traditionalism parts ways with the so-called Constantinian politics of classical Roman Catholicism). Thus according to the third session of the Council of Trent it is precisely those 'impudent clever persons' who 'rely on their own judgment in matters of faith and morals' who 'distort sacred scripture according to their own opinion' (in anonymously published texts) and who must therefore be subject to sanction by both church and state. See Henry Denzinger, *Enchiridion Symbolorum* (Freiburg, 1954), §786 (ET *The Sources of Catholic Dogma*, trans. Roy J. Deferrari (St. Louis and London, 1957).

we will only begin to approach here, will occupy us further in our fourth and final chapter.

The Concept and Scope of the Canon

The obvious point of departure for a discussion of canonicity in the *Church Dogmatics* is §19.2, 'Scripture as the Word of God'. Barth opens this section with the characteristic and important qualification that the church's decisions in recognizing scripture as the written Word, and specifically in its decisions regarding the concept and scope of the canon, are unavoidably fallible human decisions. Therefore the canon cannot be considered absolutely closed. In this Barth is conceding both the general fallibility of human knowledge to date ('for all we know … there may be things awaiting us in the sands of Egypt'[50]) and the pressing spiritual fallibility of the church's hearing of God's Word in scripture.

But positively, Barth's claim that the church cannot pronounce the canon absolutely closed is a reflex of his concern to consistently recognize the spiritual priority of scripture over the church.

> In no sense of the concept could or can the church give the canon to itself. The church cannot 'form' it, as historians have occasionally said without being aware of the theological implications. The church can only confirm or establish it as something which has already been formed and given…. In and with the church we obey the judgment which was already pronounced, before the church could pronounce its judgment and which the church's judgment could only confirm.[51]

Barth is, of course, perfectly aware that the process of fixing the canon was a thoroughly messy affair, proceeding by fits and starts at different speeds and to different effect in the several early Christian communities. And he recognizes that even where one can begin to achieve some historical clarity (e.g., at the council of

---

[50] *KD* I/2, p. 529 (ET 478).

[51] *KD* I/2, pp. 524–5 (ET 473–4). Note also that, while we have approached this through Barth's engagement with a so-called Roman Catholic doctrine of the insufficiency of scripture, Barth's stress on the freedom of the text over against the church (as a correlate of the divine freedom over and for the church) is directed also towards neo-Protestantism as a full-grown version of an undisciplined Protestant orthodoxy. See, e.g., *KD* I/2, p. 532 (ET 480): Protestant orthodoxy 'claimed too much, and plunged too far, when it equated the canon which it recognised with the canon revealed by God. It had no right to make the church take up any other position in relation to the canon (in flagrant contradiction with its own accusation of the Roman church) than that of a witness and sentry, i.e., that of a guarantor of its divine authority. To the extent that it did this, the orthodox doctrine of scripture … simply prepared the way for neo-Protestantism. It gave to the church, that is, to men in the church, power and assurance, which, according to its own presuppositions, could only be the power and assurance of God as opposed to all men, and therefore men in the church.'

Carthage or with the completion of the Vulgate and its subsequent liturgical influence), the ethical and political factors apparently at work are not always transparent or particularly edifying. In short, 'the church was always affected *in concreto* by historical, theological, and even ecclesiastico-political considerations',[52] considerations no less operative in the Reformation contraction of the medieval Roman Catholic canon than elsewhere. But these considerations are not of independent significance for Barth; they point to the fallibility of the church's hearing of the Word of God in scripture, but they do so truly only when we recognize the freedom of God to speak in the texts of his choosing, a freedom uncompromised by the fact that he does so speak in these texts. So whatever we go on to say about the deliberative processes by which the church decided to publicly recognize these texts and not others as principally authoritative, we can speak of scripture as canon in the proper sense—as rule in the church—only as we speak of God actively ruling the church through scripture: 'The Bible is God's Word to the extent that God causes it to be his Word, to the extent that he speaks through it.... [W]e cannot abstract from the free action of God in and by which he causes it to be true to us and for us here and now that the biblical word of man is his own Word.'[53]

From this perspective, at least, we might almost think of 'scripture' or 'canon' as verbs, or at least as terms denoting (in the sense of remembering and expecting) acts of God that evoke corresponding human response. The church's recognition of the canon cannot, on these terms, be confused with the establishment of the canon any more than obedience can be confused with command.[54] The church cannot close its eyes to the ambiguities and frictions of human decision-making, but in light of them must fight two related temptations: to despair that the church is simply a religious agency whose publicly enforced decisions are exhaustively described in terms of their cultural entanglements; or to presume that these decisions can be put beyond dispute by identifying them with the divine rule. In

---

[52] *KD* I/2, p. 524 (ET 474).

[53] *KD* I/1, p. 112 (ET 109–10).

[54] That this point could be so badly missed by those who read Barth's event-language, not least as it functions in his doctrine of scripture, as evidence of a modernist subjectivizing of the Word of God is cause for continued astonishment, even if (at least in North America) it can be partially explained by the intellectually and spiritually corrosive politics of some earlier twentieth-century modes of evangelicalism (on which see, e.g., Gary Dorrien, *The Remaking of Evangelical Theology* (Louisville, 1998), esp. pp. 49–152; cf. the representative and influential critique in Gordon H. Clark, *Karl Barth's Theological Method* (Philadelphia, 1963), e.g., pp. 160–73; and see already Holmes Rolston, *A Conservative Looks to Barth and Brunner* (Nashville, 1933), p. 101: 'On Barthian premises, there is no way to prevent men from falling into a position which the Barthians themselves would abhor. The system would inevitably tend to a vast subjectivity in which each man decided for himself just what portion of Scripture had authority for him.').

both cases, Barth argues, the proper course is to respect and acknowledge them for what they really are—fallible human acts that aspire to the obedience of faith.

On the other hand—and here we find him directly addressing an individualism more typical of modern Protestantism—Barth does stress that the concepts of canon and church (or scripture and tradition) are inextricably linked. With regard to the scope of the canon, this means first that while the church cannot pronounce the canon finally closed, it equally cannot abrogate its responsibility to publicly evaluate proposals from individuals or groups within the church to effect a change in the constitution of the canon. That said, the church need make such decisions only when these proposals are put forward by individuals who are speaking seriously to and in the name of the church. Individual church members in each age are responsible for actively appropriating the tradition; in this sense the person who acknowledges the canon as identified in the tradition is no less responsible for her decision than the one who seriously and publicly proposes change. But the church must act in the latter case as it need not in the former.

Clearly a change in the constitution of the canon, if it arises as a practical question, can take place meaningfully and legitimately only as an action of the church, i.e., in the form of an orderly and responsible decision by an ecclesiastical body capable of tackling it. Individuals can think and say what they like on theological and historical grounds. But what they think and say can have only the character of a private and non-binding anticipation of the church's action.... As long as no decision is publicly reached in the church, we have steadfastly to accept the force and validity of decisions already taken both in respect of the faith and also of the canon. In the decisions already taken, the church still tells us that this or that, this particular corpus, is holy scripture. The individual in the church certainly cannot and ought not to accept it as holy scripture just because the church does. He can and should himself be obedient only to holy scripture as it reveals itself to him and in that way forces itself upon him, as it compels him to accept it. But he still has to remember that scripture is the Word of God for and to the church, and that therefore it is only in the church that he can meaningfully and legitimately take up an attitude to scripture. Whatever his private judgment may be, even his private judgment of faith, however much it may diverge, he must always listen to the church. The so far unaltered judgment of the church radically precedes as such the judgment of the individual, even if it is the judgment of quite a number of individuals who have to be reckoned with seriously in the church. It is not, of course, the absolute judgment of God, but the judgment of the *majores*, the πρεσβύτεροι (Irenaeus![55]), the

---

[55] Almost certainly referring to *Against Heresies*, 4.26.2: 'Wherefore it is incumbent to obey the presbyters who are in the church—those who, as I have shown, possess the succession from the apostles; those who, together with the succession of the episcopate, have received the certain gift of truth, according to the good pleasure of the Father' (*The Ante-Nicene Fathers*, ed. Alexander Roberts and James Donaldson (Grand Rapids, 1956), vol. 1, p. 497). For a prominent use of this passage in a different direction, see Leo XIII's 1893 encyclical *Providentissimus Deus*, §14: 'St. Irenaeus long since laid down, that where the charismata of God were, there the truth of God was to be learnt, and that Holy Scripture

judgment of those who were called and believed before us. As such, so long as the church does not revise it, i.e., restrict or widen it, we have to respect it. As such, it has the character of a direction which no one can simply ignore.[56]

The conception of theological responsibility towards the tradition expressed in this passage clearly presupposes the existence of functioning mechanisms of church governance, even if these are indicated only in passing. But if we can legitimately conclude from this that at least on some level Barth thinks of the Bible as the church's book, such an observation resists quick translation into general communitarian terms. The theological force of his argument resides rather in the claim that the individual in the church can freely obey scripture in the church, and in so doing freely confess that these texts are properly canonical in the church, only as she remembers that scripture is the Word of God for the church and only as such a Word addressed personally to her. And in the prolegomenal discussion of canonicity, this claim is fleshed out in the material on incarnation, resurrection, and apostolic succession that falls under the heading of scripture's self-witness. And in turning to this material, we will take up the objection that the scripture principle is not itself a scriptural concept.

Scripture's Self-witness

Barth distinguishes two forms of scripture's self-attestation. The first, which Barth passes over very quickly, involves a what we might call a christologically focused restatement of the classical Protestant doctrine of the inward testimony of the Spirit. The argument here is that scripture indirectly attests its own uniqueness and normativity by uniquely bearing witness to 'the true humanity of the person of Jesus Christ'. 'What else is the Bible but the proof of the existence of the historical environment of this reality and, to that extent, of the historicity of the reality itself? But of all world literature it is only the Bible which offers this proof: or other literature offers it only because it has first been offered by the Bible.'[57] At first

---

was safely interpreted by those who had the Apostolic succession. His teaching, and that of other Holy Fathers, is taken up by the Council of the Vatican, which, in renewing the decree of Trent declares its "mind" to be this—that "in things of faith and morals, belonging to the building up of Christian doctrine, that is to be considered the true sense of Holy Scripture which has been held and is held by our Holy Mother the Church, whose place it is to judge of the true sense and interpretation of the Scriptures, and therefore that it is permitted to no one to interpret Holy Scripture against such sense or also against the unanimous agreement of the Fathers'" (*The Papal Encyclicals 1878–1903*, ed. Claudia Carlen (Raleigh, 1990), p. 331). And note that Barth himself, in a more sober mood, acknowledges that Irenaeus was 'one of the first of many who coordinated and subordinated scripture to tradition' (*KD* I/2, p. 611 (ET 549)).

[56] *KD* I/2, pp. 530 (ET 478–9).
[57] *KD* I/2, p. 538 (ET 485).

glance, this can seem an odd and rather unpromising piece of historical apologetics. But in making this claim Barth speaks specifically of Jesus as the incarnate Son of God, thus grounding the uniqueness of scripture in the uniqueness and contingency [*Einmaligkeit und Kontingenz*] of the revelation attested in it. The emphasis falls once again on the fact that the historical Jesus to whom scripture witnesses cannot simply be located in terms of more general historical constructs or structures—either as an individual whose time is without qualification the years 1–30 CE or as a truth that is historical only insofar as it is properly timeless. *This* reality is recognized only on its own terms, which is to say Jesus is known only in the faith that looks to and is possible from the resurrection, so that it is in fact a confession of faith that these texts are not simply more or less unique historical source-books but are uniquely authoritative witnesses to Christ's resurrection as the revelation of God. 'In the final analysis, therefore, we have to say that holy scripture testifies to and for itself by the fact that the Holy Spirit testifies to the resurrection of Christ and therefore that he is the incarnate Son of God.'[58]

This argument from scripture's 'general and implicit self-witness' is complemented by a much more extensive reference to its 'specific and explicit' self-witness, which 'consists in the fact that, from the standpoint of the form in which its content is offered and alone offered to us, it is the witness of the existence of these specific men'—i.e., of the prophets and apostles.

All along the line, the Bible speaks of the revelation of God in Jesus Christ not only in its opposition to all human beings, to individual human beings, and to humanity in general. Of course it does that, too, and one must say that this opposition is the essential content of the Bible. We have seen earlier that humanity, as it is addressed and claimed by revelation, belongs as such to scripture's content, being taken up in revelation. But now we must go further and say more concretely that the content of the Bible, as understood in this setting, has a definite form, which cannot be separated from it as this content. The Bible as witness of divine revelation comes to every person, all people, and in a measure includes them in itself. Rightly understood, all humanity, whether it is aware of it or not, does actually stand in the Bible, and is therefore itself posited as a witness of divine revelation. But that this is the case is made possible and conditioned by the fact that in the first instance not all but certain specific men stand in the Bible: that is, the men who in face of the unique and contingent revelation had the no less unique and contingent function of being the first witnesses. Because there were and still are those first witnesses, there could and can be second and third witnesses. We cannot speak about Yahweh's covenant with Israel without at once speaking of Moses and the prophets. Similarly in the New Testament, indissolubly bound up with Jesus Christ, there are the figures of his disciples, his followers, his apostles, those who are called by him, the witnesses of his resurrection, those to whom he himself has directly promised and given his Holy Spirit. The church can say anything at all about the event of God and man only because something unique has taken place between God and these specific men, and because in what they wrote, or what was written by them, they confront us as

---

[58] *KD* I/2, p. 538 (ET 486).

living documents of that unique event. The existence of these specific men is the existence of Jesus Christ for us and for all men. It is in this function that they are distinguished from us and from all other men, whom they resemble in everything else. Therefore the specific and explicit self-witness of scripture consists in the fact that, from the standpoint of the form in which its content is offered and alone offered to us, it is the witness of the existence of these specific men.[59]

In support of the concept of apostolic mediation as such,[60] Barth appeals to a range of New Testament texts, including the Gospel passages most commonly cited in this connection (Lk. 10.16; Mt. 10.40; Jn. 20.21). Together, these texts teach us that 'in the relationship between Jesus Christ and the apostles there is ... repeated or reflected in some degree the economy of the incarnation of the Word', so that as the Word uniquely reveals the Father 'there is no hearing or receiving of Christ which does not have the form of a hearing and receiving of his disciples'.[61] Two basic questions necessarily follow at this point: First, who are these disciples whom we must hear and receive? And second, how are they present to us?

The disciples (or apostles—Barth uses the words interchangeably) are, again, those who stood in a unique historical proximity to Jesus. But their access to Jesus, and so their identity as apostles, consists in Jesus' self-presentation to them in the truth and reality of his being. Their recognition of Jesus as the Son of God:

is traced back to election, revelation, calling, separation, new birth—concepts which as it were shatter the immanence of the historical relation from within inasmuch as God is the subject of the action denoted by them, inasmuch as it is God's good-pleasure (eu0doki&a, Mt. 11.16; Gal. 1.15; Eph. 1.9) that as a purely external truth first creates and posits the inner truth as such in the free action denoted by these terms, quite apart from all the undeniable historical relations, in these relations but not through them.[62]

---

[59] *KD* I/2, pp. 538–9 (ET 486); cf. pp. 603–6 (ET 542–4).

[60] Barth is not seriously enticed by the modern Protestant attempt to sidestep any notion of apostolic succession. Against Harnack, he asserts quite simply that the church cannot be holy and catholic without being apostolic; 'one would have to deny the *Christus praesens* to deny in principle the *vicarius Christi*' (*KD* I/1, p. 99 (ET 97)).

[61] *KD* I/2, p. 540 (ET 487); cf. pp. 554–5 (ET 500): 'Holy scripture is marked off as a sign of revelation from the sign of the true humanity of Christ by the fact that because of the uniqueness and therefore the temporal limitation of revelation, because it has terminated in the ascension of Christ, the latter is hidden from us, i.e., it can be seen only as it is attested by scripture and the proclamation of the church and in faith. But since holy scripture is the original form of its attestation, since, unlike the proclamation of the church, it attests revelation in its uniqueness and temporal limitation, it belongs to the first and original sign, the true humanity of Christ. That the Word has become scripture is not one and the same thing as its becoming flesh. But the uniqueness and at the same time general relevance of its becoming flesh necessarily involved its becoming scripture.'

[62] *KD* I/1, p. 153 (ET 148).

The concepts of election, revelation, calling, and so on 'are not to be regarded as later explanations of an event that is properly and intrinsically immanent'.[63] According to the New Testament itself, the apostles are to be regarded strictly as witnesses to an event in which they participate by grace, 'not therefore as thinkers, not as religious personalities or geniuses, not as moral heroes, although they were these things too in the right sense and in varying degrees'.[64] We are given in scripture only 'incidental glimpses of their humanity' (i.e., of their personal dispositions, habits, etc.) as it is pressed into service by the revelation they attest, continually being referred to the apostles' obedience to Christ in the discharge of the commission laid upon them, which is to say we are referred to them only insofar as they witness to Christ in the power of the Spirit. But in this function they are present in scripture as the specific form of the humanity to whom God's revelation in Jesus Christ is first addressed.

> Over against the Lord Jesus, absolutely subordinate to him but distinct from him, there is another element in the reality of his revelation, an apostolate, men commissioned, authorized and empowered [*beauftragte, bevollmächte und befähigte*] by him to witness, men whose human word can be accepted by all kinds of people as proclamation of the 'wonderful works of God'. This is the doing of the Holy Spirit.[65]

In the final analysis, then, the scriptural basis for the scripture principle involves nothing less than the narration of the commissioning, authorizing, and empowering (or the calling, commissioning, and sending forth [*Berufung, Beauftragung und Aussendung*][66]) of these apostles.

The point is well made in David Demson's comparative study of Barth and Hans Frei. Demson's overarching constructive proposal is that a satisfying theological hermeneutics (among other things, one that holds together a deep sense of interpretative self-involvement and a proper emphasis on extra-textual reference) will involve an adequately developed doctrine of inspiration. For our immediate purposes, the book's importance lies in the way Demson carefully works through the concepts of apostolic calling, commissioning, and sending in Barth, rightly noting that for Barth the existence of the apostolate is ingredient in Jesus' identity, specifying him as the Lord who does not will to be alone but who calls these particular men, upholds them through his intercessory death, and who in his resurrection power sends them into the world as his witnesses.[67] Because the

---

[63] *KD* I/1, p. 153 (ET 148).

[64] *KD* I/2, p. 544 (ET 491).

[65] *KD* I/1, p. 477 (ET 455).

[66] *KD* I/2, p. 247 (ET 226).

[67] See Demson, *Frei and Barth*, pp. 5–6, 9. Demson shows in some detail how Barth develops these three aspects of the one movement of grace exegetically in the *Church Dogmatics*, each corresponding to one stage of Jesus' career as it is narrated in the Gospels and Acts: Jesus calls his disciples at the beginning of his public ministry; upholds them by

object of their witness is precisely the Lord who has called, commissioned, and sent them, they themselves form an ineluctable part of the gospel: In witnessing to Jesus they witness to themselves—not only as those whom Jesus came to save, but as those through whom this salvation wills to be known to all, and known in this determinate form. And as the one who has gathered, upheld, and sent the apostles, Jesus wills to gather, uphold, and send all others precisely by including them in the soteriological dynamics of the apostolate—in the identity-forming movement from calling through sending. The apostles are appointed to share in Christ's own work to the extent that they witness to his unique life uniquely given for all. But they do not share in his intercessory or redeeming work, which they can only receive.[68] This is the basis and limit of their apostolic identity, which has not only an 'exemplary validity' (H. Arendt)[69] but a theological capacity to incorporate all those who hear and believe through their words. Because the identity of the saving God is inextricably bound up with these who first heard and saw and believed, we can never move beyond them to a God who relates immediately to us in our individuality or our humanity as such. Nor can we think of them and their witness in abstraction from the God to whom they witness and who wills that our new life

---

his death in Jerusalem, at once exposing their need and enduring their failure; and commissions them at the end of the forty days between the resurrection and ascension.

[68] Demson, *Frei and Barth*, p. 14; cf. p. 26 n. 1, which speaks of 'the apostles' passive inclusion in his intercession and exaltation and ... their active participation in his mission'. Demson draws a number of important hermeneutical conclusions in the course of his discussion: Because the relationship of Jesus and the apostles as narrated in the Gospels is materially basic to and formally normative for our relationship with God, Demson argues, this relationship 'forms a crucial hermeneutical basis for the explication of the New Testament and, therefore, for Scripture as a whole' (22). Specifically, every scriptural text will be explicated in terms of the movement from calling through commissioning to sending—as either leading to or following from the instantiation of this relationship with the original apostles. And every text will be applied by and to the present church correspondingly: 'The applicative sense, in this way, is not so much merely controlled by the explicative sense but ingredient in it' (23). Demson further—and perceptively—notes that because the Gospels are exponents of the movement they narrate, their unity must be described first in theological terms and only then in literary categories (of typology or figuration). Literary devices are of course employed in scripture, but they are 'employed in function of the event of Christ's gathering, upholding, and sending of his own' (47). And because 'this is the unvarying form of Christ's presence, consonant with his identity' (47–8), it follows that a gap in one's christology at this point (a failure to take full account of the specificity of Christ's relationship with the Twelve) will result in a corresponding hermeneutical deficiency, one that in Hans Frei's case works itself out as an overemphasis on general literary categories.

[69] On this phrase in Arendt, see Richard J. Bernstein, 'Judging—the Actor and the Spectator', in *Philosophical Profiles: Essays in a Pragmatic Mode* (Cambridge, 1986), pp. 221–37 (235, 237).

conform to theirs, as we too are called out of darkness, upheld in our weakness, and sent out in a power that is never our own.[70]

Demson relies on material from later volumes of the *Dogmatics* to make this argument, but we have seen that the seeds of it are present in the prolegomena, where Barth clearly wants to claim both that in witnessing to God scripture necessarily witnesses to the objects of his grace, and that according to the New Testament these objects are not in the first place simply individual human beings nor humanity as such but the apostles called, upheld, and sent by Jesus. But the concept of apostolicity, like the trinitarian material we examined above, is developed in the prolegomena only insofar as it allows Barth to articulate, at least in broad terms, the proper dogmatic context of the scripture principle. This means, among other things, that Barth's presentation in Volume One brings together apostolicity and canonicity without any serious consideration of the relevant exegetical issues that he will explore in later volumes. Here Barth simply presumes, for example, the propriety of numbering Paul among the apostles, indeed in many ways as the most significant apostle, without pursuing his later line that according to the New Testament Paul takes Judas' place among 'the Twelve'.[71] In the prolegomena, the stress is placed on the fact that the existence of the apostles, who are to be understood as living for us wholly as witnesses to Christ, gives us every reason to speak in the most serious terms about the mediation of revelation, and provides a key to understanding scripture's place in the economy of salvation. Thus for Barth, Paul's own strong claims regarding his place in this economy are neither scripturally exceptional nor theologically problematic. Rather:

> It was in keeping with the New Testament as a whole when in 2 Cor. 5.18 he described the reconciliation accomplished in Jesus Christ, and the 'gift' of the 'ministry of reconciliation', as two sides of one and the same thing. In the *analogia fidei* there is again a similarity between God and man, between the heavenly and earthly reality. 'We are ambassadors for Christ, as though God did beseech by us: we pray you in Christ's stead, be ye reconciled to God' (2 Cor. 5.20). In this saying we could easily find the whole biblical basis of the scripture principle.[72]

But of course there is a significant step from identifying the 'us' to whom Christ gave the ministry of reconciliation with the apostles to identifying the

---

[70] Cf. in this light *KD* I/1, p. 104 (ET 102): Scripture 'does not seek to be a historical monument but rather a church document, written proclamation'. Scripture and the church's ongoing proclamation 'may thus be set initially under a single genus, scripture as the commencement and present-day preaching as the continuation of one the same event, Jeremiah and Paul at the beginning and the modern preacher of the gospel at the end of one and the same series'.

[71] See *KD* II/2, pp. 529–63 (ET 477–506).

[72] *KD* I/2, p. 540 (ET 488); cf. pp. 572–3 (ET 515–16).

apostles with the New Testament texts, or at least arguing that the apostolic witness is not available to us otherwise than in these texts. And in taking this step—which involves rejecting the Roman Catholic appeal to an unwritten apostolic tradition—Barth makes a series of formal claims about the freedom of the canon *qua* written text.

The relevant argument in §4.2 proceeds thus: Church proclamation is undertaken in recollection of God's past revelation and in expectation of future revelation. Despite Augustine and against modern Roman Catholic theology, scripture does not allow us to understand this recollection along the lines of a Platonic *anamnesis*. The church is not asked to recall an unchanging truth about itself; it is referred to Jesus Christ, the entirely free revelation of God 'who has the church within himself but whom the church does not have within itself'.[73] The sovereignty of Christ over the church is expressed in the fact that the church is confronted by the canon—'a factor which is very like it as a phenomenon, which is temporal as it is, and yet which is different from it and in order superior to it'.[74] And this canon is the written proclamation of the prophets and apostles. The proclamation of the *apostles*, because, as we have seen, they are ingredient in God's revelation in Jesus Christ; their *written* proclamation, because they must live on in their particularity and authority in the church and can do so after their deaths only insofar as they are present in written texts. Here is the parting of the ways with the Roman Catholic conception of apostolic succession.

> The protest of Protestantism in this question of succession is directed solely and simply against the fact that the *Tu est Petrus*, etc., is mechanically transferred over Peter's head to every succeeding Roman bishop as a second, third and hundredth Peter, as if the succession and tradition of the Peter of Matthew 16, to whom flesh and blood had not revealed such things, could be related to any succession but a spiritual one, or as if, being spiritual, it could be *tied* to the secular circumstance of such a list of bishops.... [I]n these circumstances apostolicity necessarily ceases to be a divine gift and human task and becomes an assured human possession that is 'preeminently' understood in a mechanically historical and legal way.... Spiritual succession obviously presupposes that the *successor* is spiritually but not mechanically identical with the *antecessor*, so that the *antecessor* still has elbow-room of his own as distinct from the *successor*. Such elbow-room, however, is not given to Peter in the Roman Catholic system. Here the *antecessor* is taken up and absorbed in the *successor*. What constitutes the apostolicity of proclamation here is the watch at Peter's grave. On this presupposition neither Peter, the apostolate, nor the Holy Spirit is any longer a free power in the church and over against the church. On this presupposition the church is again left to itself and referred to itself and its self-reflection.[75]

---

[73] *KD* I/1, p. 103 (ET 100).

[74] *KD* I/1, p. 103 (ET 101).

[75] *KD* I/1, p. 106 (ET 103–4).

Again, such ecclesiastical presumption is avoided only by strict attention to scripture as text, for here the apostles' words, being fixed in writing, resist absorption. 'On the written nature of the canon, on its character as *scriptura sacra*, hangs [an apostle's] autonomy and independence, and consequently his free power over against the church and thus the living nature of the succession.'[76]

Barth is not unaware of the fact that scripture functions as an authority in the church only as it is actively appropriated. He acknowledges that 'this real, biblical canon is constantly exposed to absorption into the life, thought, and utterance of the church inasmuch as it continually seeks to be understood afresh and hence expounded and interpreted'.[77] But again, what is most interesting here is not Barth's admission that interpretation is unavoidable, but that he does not describe this unavoidability in the usual, general terms—because texts as such are inexhaustibly interpretable or because authors, living or dead, have no right or ability to constrain the interpretations their texts engender or suffer. The Bible as text is exposed to the church (or, perhaps better, continually exposes itself to the church) because God hides himself in his revelation in order to reach people who invariably attempt to absorb the gospel into their own aspirations and projections, who unfailingly seek to impose themselves upon it, and who do so because they are intent on saving themselves.

We recall here that church history is, on Barth's reading, a monotonous series of attempts to domesticate revelation. And so Barth is extremely sensitive to anything that looks like structural or methodological self-justification in the church, not least any attempt to secure church unity or continuity through a prescribed politics of interpretation.

---

[76] *KD* I/1, p. 107 (104); cf. *KD* I/2, p. 561 (ET 505), pp. 647–8 (ET 581–2): 'The fact that the primary sign of revelation, the existence of the prophets and apostles, is for the church book and letter does not rob it of its force as witness.... The *Schriftlichkeit* of this primary sign cannot prevent it from being in the church of every age a real sign, a sign just as powerful and definite as was once the personal existence of the living prophets and apostles to the growing church of their day. But it is its written nature that is also its protection against the chance and self-will to which it would be exposed without it. Its written nature makes it a sign which, however differently it may be seen and understood and, of course, overlooked and misunderstood, is still unalterably there over against all misunderstandings and misinterpretations of it, is still unalterably the same, can always speak for itself, can always be examined and questioned as it is, to control and correct every interpretation. Its written nature guarantees its freedom over against the church and therefore creates for the church freedom over against itself. If there is still the possibility of misunderstanding and error as regards this sign in virtue of its written nature, there is also the possibility of being recalled by it to the truth, the possibility of the reformation of a church which has perhaps been led into misunderstanding and error.'

[77] *KD* I/1, p. 108 (ET 106).

All exposition can become predominantly interposition rather than exposition and to that degree it can fall back into the church's dialogue with itself. Nor will one banish the danger, but only conjure it up properly and make it acute, by making correct exposition dependent on the judgment of a definite and decisive teaching office in the church or on the judgment of a historico-critical scholarship which comports itself with equal infallibility.[78]

That said, Barth also believes the history of the church is a series of events and moments in which God makes himself known as Lord of the church. And Barth finds that these are moments of renewed engagement with scripture—an engagement that cannot be reduced to the discovery of a new reading strategy (or the rediscovery of an old one), although of course when the Bible speaks it is heard in ways that are themselves recognizable and instructive for future descriptions of the church's responsibility towards scripture.[79] Even the most historically fruitful churchly reading practices can only follow the text's self-presentation and cannot be accorded independent significance. Thus it is in recognition of the sheer priority of God's speaking through scripture that Barth insists that:

> the exegesis of the Bible should ... be left open on all sides, not for the sake of free thought, as liberalism would demand, but for the sake of a free Bible. Here as elsewhere the defense against possible violence to the text must be left to the text itself, which in fact has always succeeded in doing something a purely spiritual and oral tradition cannot do, namely, maintaining its own life against the encroachments of individual or total periods and tendencies in the church, victoriously asserting this life in ever new developments, and thus creating recognition for itself as a norm.... Already as a text the canonical text has the character of a free power. All the church need do is just this: After any exegesis propounded in it, even the very best, it has to realize afresh the distinction between text and commentary and let the text speak again without let or hindrance, so that it will experience the lordship of this free power and find in the Bible the partner or counterpart which it must find in it if it is to take the living *successio apostolorum* seriously.[80]

Again, the church cannot guarantee its own adherence even to this demand. The call to leave the Bible truly free is in Barth's understanding a distinctive Protestant contribution to the church, and in making it he is calling the Protestant church back to its Reformation roots. But there can be no true Protestant *sola scriptura* without *sola gratia*, and in confessing the latter the church confesses that it can confess neither on its own initiative. Even the call to leave the Bible to defend itself can be mere performance. But that is no reason not to take this demand seriously as such.

If we read all this in the light of the challenge to the scripture principle outlined above, Barth's argument can be summarized in four points: 1) as the Roman

---

[78] *KD* I/1, pp. 108–9 (ET 106).

[79] Cf. *KD* I/2, p. 577 (ET 519).

[80] *KD* I/1, p. 109 (ET 106–7).

Catholic church rightly insists, the scripture principle must be confirmed exegetically;[81] 2) scripture does in fact explicitly confirm it; 3) it does so by attesting the existence of an apostolate whose existence is ingredient in and at least to some extent formally correlative to the existence of Jesus Christ; and 4) it does so as written text, representing formally what it attests materially—the sovereignty of Jesus Christ over the apostolic church.

Interpretation and Proclamation

Thus far we have found in the prolegomena to the *Church Dogmatics* a series of ways in which Barth speaks of the necessity of scriptural interpretation, and have focused our treatment of them through the doctrines of the incarnation and the apostolicity of the church. We have seen how Barth describes the manner in which God's gracious hiddenness in revelation opens up space for the church to live in the world as a community of witness that receives its orders from the incarnate, crucified, risen, and ascended Christ through the prophetic-apostolic witness of scripture. And we have seen how Barth develops the scripture principle primarily in terms of apostolic appointment and then also in terms of textual determinacy.

We have not yet directly addressed one further aspect of the necessity of scriptural interpretation that we have presupposed and hinted at throughout. And that has to do with the fact that the church's preaching, if it is to be real repetition of the promise of Christ's presence with the church, 'cannot consist in the mere reading of scripture or in repeating and paraphrasing the actual wording of the biblical witness'.

> This is only its presupposition. The concrete encounter with God and man today, whose actuality, of course, can be created only by the Word of God himself, must find a counterpart in the human event of proclamation, i.e., the person called must be ready to make the promise given to the church intelligible in his own words to the men of his own time.[82]

To speak theologically of scriptural interpretation involves speaking of this contemporary proclamation. Interpretation, in other words, involves the movement from reading to representation, a movement in which one takes responsibility for the text as one understands it, and in doing so necessarily moves beyond quotation

---

[81] Cf. *KD* I/2, p. 511 (ET 462): A doctrine of scripture 'cannot claim abstract validity, but its confirmation must always be found in exegesis and therefore in scripture itself'. Note that although Barth will formally agree with the Roman Catholic position on the need to find the scripture principle in scripture itself, he is less concerned about logical coherence than about theological appropriateness. That the scripture principle at least intends to be genuinely *a posteriori* to God's revelation is the primary issue for Barth.

[82] *KD* I/1, pp. 59–60 (ET 59).

to reiteration. Specifically, it means the movement from scriptural reading to preaching as this reflects the gracious concreteness with which God always addresses his creation.

In the language of Barth's 1932–33 homiletics lectures, scriptural interpretation is bound up with the *Originalität* of preaching.[83] That preaching must be 'original' (or 'authentic') means first that preachers are responsible for what they say in the pulpit. The theological grounding for this is found in the doctrines of justification and sanctification, which tell us that 'preachers just as they are, as sinful human creatures, are called upon to expound the text', and which rule out the idea that 'certain thoughts are given to preachers that they otherwise would not have, after the manner of infused grace'.[84]

> Pastors are not to adopt a role. They are not to slip into the clothing of biblical characters. That would be the worst kind of comedy. They are not to be Luthers, churchmen, visionaries, or the like. They are simply to be themselves, and to expound the text as such. Preaching is the responsible word of a person of our own time. Having heard myself, I am called upon to pass on what I have heard. Even as ministers, it matters that these people be what they are. They must not put on a character or a robe. They do not have to play a role. It is you who have been commissioned, you, just as you are, not as a minister, as pastor or theologian, not under any concealment or cover, but you yourself have simply to discharge this commission.[85]

The responsibility of the preacher to be himself in the act of preaching follows from the character of the gospel the preacher is to proclaim. The gospel is comprehensive, so that preaching is necessarily self-involving. To adopt a role would be to deny formally what the preacher must materially convey—that the good news applies to all and just so to me. It is the news of God's grace to sinners, so that preaching can only follow on hearing, receiving the news that one must then proclaim. 'Originality ... does not imply the "free, independent, converted, born-again personality". It applies to those who live by the forgiveness of sins.... Only in this movement through judgment and grace can preaching be truly original.'[86] And it is the news of the God who graciously meets us in history,

---

[83] Barth, *Homiletik. Wesen und Vorbereitung der Predigt* (Zürich, 1970), p. 64; ET *Homiletics*, trans. Geoffrey W. Bromiley and Donald E. Daniels (Louisville, 1991), p. 81.

[84] Barth, *Homiletik*, p. 64 (ET 81). On the meaning and significance of these doctrines in this connection, see the discussion of the *Vorläufigkeit* of preaching (pp. 55–8 (ET 71–5)) that forms (both materially and formally) the pivotal section of the second, constructive part of the lectures. This central section ties together the first four criteria of a sermon (its *Offenbarungsmäßigkeit, Kirchlichkeit, Bekenntnismäßigkeit,* and *Amtsmäßigkeit*), which treat the objective presuppositions of preaching and so reflecting the justification of the preacher, with its final four (*Biblizität, Originalität, Gemeindemäßigkeit,* and *Geistlichkeit*), which characterize preaching as human act, or the preacher's sanctification.

[85] Barth, *Homiletik*, p. 65 (ET 81–2).

[86] Barth, *Homiletik*, p. 66 (ET 82–3).

where and as we are, so that preaching must be simple and fresh—speaking to the congregation without seeking to manipulate or impress them, scripturally responsible but not bound to a well-worn theological system or worldview. Thus Barth can even appeal (with qualified approval) to Tillich's concept of *kairos* in stressing the preacher's attention to the concrete needs and expectations of the congregation. 'Living with their congregations, preachers live out a history with them, and they are constantly agitated by the question: "How is it with us now?"'[87]

Preaching is thus not simply exegesis: 'Exegesis and meditation must become speech to others: address, my own speech.'[88] But it is based on exegesis: To Barth's mind, the fact that the church has truly understood God's revelation as its own being, the apostles as its foundation, and scripture as its canon will show itself in the fact that its preaching is based solely and strictly on scripture. Finally, 'die Predigt ist *Schriftauslegung*'.[89] In a church that understands itself:

> there can be no question at all of preachers declaiming their own systematic theology or expounding what they think they know about their own lives, or human life in general, or society or the state of the world. If they live by justification, by their faith, it is no longer possible for them to offer systematic theology of this kind, or their own knowledge of how things are or how they ought to be, or ideologies by which people think they may live. Humanity does not live by the immanent goodness of things. When we ask what justifies us, we are referred again to our first four points [revelation, the church, its commission, and the call to proclamation]. We stand before holy scripture. It bears witness to *revelation*, it establishes the *church*, it gives the *command*, and through it comes the *vocation*. The act of those who live by justification, then, can be no other than that of understanding and expounding the scriptural word, and to that extent repeating it. To be sure, preachers will always feel the burden of their own systematic theology, but it is one thing to admit this constant threat and another to deny it, one thing to hear and another to reject the claim that even with their own ideas they are set there to expound this book—*that* and nothing else.[90]

All this means that scriptural interpretation is not an option for the preaching church. The two concepts, scripture and preaching, belong together; to the extent that the church ceases to be fundamentally a preaching church (and Barth thinks this true of both the Roman Catholic and modern Protestant churches), it ceases to see that responsible interpretation of scripture (not simply citation of scripture or interpretation of the religious history of Israel and the early Christian communities) is constitutive of its existence in the world.

As we transition to our final chapter, we return again to Barth's starting point: The churches of the Reformation venture to proclaim the gospel in the belief that

---

[87] Barth, *Homiletik*, p. 67 (ET 84–5).

[88] Barth, *Homiletik*, p. 65 (ET 82).

[89] Barth, *Homiletik*, p. 59 (ET 75).

[90] Barth, *Homiletik*, p. 59 (ET 75–6).

'the strictly personal free Word of God ... reaches its goal in the equally personal free hearing of men, the hearing of faith, which for its part, too, can be understood only as grace'.[91] And in doing so they set out on a different course than that taken by the Roman Catholic church or modern Protestantism. The task of a prolegomena to a church dogmatics is, at least in part, to clarify this difference. And in doing so, it must stress the freedom of God's Word over the church, in part by taking up in a new context the Reformation *sola scriptura* insofar as it belongs with the *sola gratia* to the *solus Christus*. But in so doing, it must also insist on the freedom of humanity before God; the ethical question must be raised again precisely because the question of God's freedom has forced itself on the church.

In this chapter, we have begun to see why it is that precisely because Barth takes with characteristic seriousness the freedom of God in and over the church and therefore the sheer graciousness of any encounter between God and humanity in scripture and through the church's proclamation, he needs also to stress that the human activity of proclamation (in all its aspects, including the exegetical work that attends it) is not thereby rendered superfluous, but is given a share in God's own reality, truly grounded in and characterized by grace, and therefore truly necessary.

We have also begun to see how it is that Barth grounds the freedom of the church in the freedom of the Word. Precisely because the Word of God comes to the church as a command which it can avoid only at the cost of compromising its own being in the world, the church is freed from the task of setting its own agenda and maintaining its own relevance. It simply is as it proclaims the gospel which it hears in scripture; and this means that the relationship between the church and scripture is simply a given. As Barth was later to put the point:

> If one were to ask a child why, out of the many women in the world, it calls this one and this one alone its mother, the only possible answer would be for the child to repeat and confirm the proposition after whose ground it was asked: This woman just *is* my mother. That she is, is for this child an entirely unproblematic fact. Just so, all meaningful (i.e., not only apparently but truly indicative) claims regarding the authority and meaning of the Bible denote a fact concerning whose existence there can be no debate, because this fact is grounded in itself and speaks for itself and thus can be explained only by being repeated and confirmed.[92]

More specifically, the church simply assumes, that is, it remembers and anticipates in faith, the material authority of scripture prior to any interpretative work it undertakes. And this means that the church is free from the burden of rendering scripture authoritative, either by defining its canonical shape or by assuming control of its translation and interpretation. Of course the church has and will recognize some texts as canonical and not others, and it takes responsibility

---

[91] *KD* I/1, p. 69 (ET 68).

[92] Barth, *Die Schrift und die Kirche* (Zurich, 1947), p. 3.

for these decisions. Of course in making its confession the church resists certain lines of scriptural interpretation as incompatible with the truth of its own existence. But in doing so the church does not encroach upon the power and clarity of the Word of God in scripture. Rather, the church's ongoing interpretation of scripture assumes scripture's authority at every point—not least its authority to question the church's traditional understanding and contemporary presentation of these texts. And again, because this is the authority of the Word of God, which does not will to be alone but which wills a community of witness in the world, and because this community exists insofar as it is sustained by the one who has promised to be with it precisely in the written witness of his apostles, the authority of scripture does not negate the church's own responsibility. As it stands, in its concrete form as the written word of the prophets and apostles, scripture continually demands renewed interpretative work in the service of proclamation. We will take up the question of how best to describe the shape of this interpretative work in our next, final chapter.

Chapter 4

Hearing and Obeying
the Word of God

In the previous chapter, we emphasized the occasional nature of Barth's dogmatic lectures in Bonn and Basel, suggesting especially that in reading the first volume of the *Church Dogmatics* we do well to attend closely to the ways in which he is concerned to distinguish his own contemporary restatement of the Protestant scripture principle from alternative (modern Protestant and Roman Catholic) accounts of the manner of God's presence to the church, the authority of scripture, and the nature of theology's task. And we chose to describe his doctrine of scripture as at least in part an extended response to the charge that the Protestant scripture principle illegitimately abstracts the scriptural text from the life of the church. We isolated three aspects of this response: First, while acknowledging that the decision to identify these specific texts and not others as canonical is indeed an act of the church, and that scripture nowhere contains a list of texts to be considered canonical, Barth does not concede that this means the scriptures recognized as canonical do not constitute themselves uniquely authoritative in and for the church. Second, Barth argues that in narrating the history of Israel and especially the calling, commissioning, and sending of the apostles, scripture does in fact testify to its own contingency, uniqueness, and normativity, and in this way contains the legitimate basis of the Protestant scripture principle. In this chapter, through a close and perhaps at times laborious reading of several crucial passages in §§19–21, we will see Barth describing the characteristic interpretative freedoms and responsibilities of the Christian church, and will read this material in part as a response to the third aspect of the Roman Catholic objection to the Protestant *sola scriptura*—namely, that scripture nowhere dictates the terms on which it is to be interpreted and applied. More generally, we will attempt to trace the theological motivations and consequences of Barth's decision to describe scriptural interpretation as an act of Christian *obedience*.

In doing so, we will bring together once again and in a somewhat different manner several strands of argument we have already seen to be ingredient in Barth's dogmatic account of the act of scriptural interpretation: the complex engagement with Roman Catholicism and Protestant modernism; the characteristic prioritizing of exegesis over hermeneutical reflection; the irreducibly theological yet undoubtedly also historically and culturally implicated description of the scriptural text, the identity of the interpreter, and the context of interpretation; the sharp delimitation of the church's interpretative work by continual reference to grace and prayer. In all this we will have occasion to ask exactly what sort of work the notion of obedience should perform in a theology of scriptural interpretation, in what directions it pulls us, and how it might be complemented by other terms.

Reading Scripture as Witness

We begin with what Barth calls 'the basic statement' of the doctrine of scripture: 'The Bible is the witness of God's revelation.'[1] The primary function of this statement is to locate scripture in relation to revelation and thus to identify scripture ontologically: As witness, scripture is not identical with revelation, but it exists in strict relation to it. But the formula also has the function, sometimes overlooked, of structuring a theological account of the church's interpretative responsibilities and freedoms. It serves to remind the church that the hermeneutical determinations it invariably brings to scripture are not determinate of scripture's being, which is constituted by its relation to revelation. And it serves to remind the church that all its interpretative work is finally responsive to a reality that precedes, enables, and judges it. When we interpret scripture, Barth insists, 'we enter a concrete, specific situation whose form does not depend at all on us but which is this situation and not another by a necessity that lies in the matter itself'.[2] And this means, among other things, that to speak of scripture as 'witness' is not a way of objectifying a reading strategy to be preferred on other grounds. Again, it is simply a recognition of a reality that precedes us, and an attempt to order our response to it appropriately. 'The doctrine of holy scripture as such involves ... the confession in which the church clarifies that perception which corresponds to a right and necessary posture of obedience to the witness of revelation.'[3] This confession is grounded in the fact that scripture has set before the church the lordship of the triune God. And while it is true that any confession of this fact will involve the reader of scripture acknowledging the proper authority of the tradition (thus §20) and being willing to take personal responsibility for the future of the church (§21), the most important factor is the reality of scripture's presentation of God's revelation, a reality which is not limited by the most loyal adherence to tradition or the deepest existential commitment.[4] Both the church's interpretative

---

[1] *KD* I/2, p. 511 (ET 462).

[2] Barth, *Erklärung des Johannes-Evangeliums*, ed. Walther Fürst (Zürich: TVZ, 1999), p. 4; ET *Witness to the Word. A Commentary on John 1*, trans. Geoffrey W. Bromiley (Grand Rapids: Eerdmans, 1986), p. 3.

[3] *KD* I/2, p. 509 (ET 460); cf. p. 643 (ET 577).

[4] Cf. *KD* I/2, p. 754 (ET 673): 'Scripture is itself spirit and life in the comprehensive and profound sense of these ideas—the Spirit and life of the living God himself, who draws

responsibilities and its freedoms are grounded in the prior reality that the Bible is the witness to God's Word. And as such they are only (but importantly) secondary definitions of the church's obedience, which can only follow the basic confession that there is a Word of God for the church, and that this Word comes to the church in the Bible which witnesses to it.[5]

As the church acknowledges that it has encountered its Lord in scripture, it recognizes the distinction between the Word of God and the words of his servants. This is the limitation in the concept of witness: In the Bible, we hear of the lordship of *God* in *human* words. But we do genuinely hear—in the technical sense still to be discussed—God's Word in these words, so that the Bible 'is simply revelation as it comes to us, mediating and therefore accommodating itself to us— to us who are not ourselves prophets and apostles, and therefore not the immediate and direct recipients of the one revelation, witnesses of the resurrection of Christ'.[6] A real witness—*ein wirkliches Zeugnis*—is not identical with the intended object of its witness, and this limitation is at the heart of the gospel: That which is not God really can exist with and for God as his witness. And a real witness actually does make available the object to which witness is borne, so that the object—and the witness with it—really is recognized as such.

Crucially, neither the speaker nor the hearer can underwrite the real presence of the object of testimony. The speaker can only intend to make the object known; the hearer can only be ready to hear what the speaker intends and therefore to encounter the object intended. The reality of this encounter, and therefore the reality of the event of witness and the reality of the speaker's identity as witness, depends entirely on the object making itself available in this network of communicative intentions and expectations. Concretely, the Bible (and, *mutatis mutandis*, church proclamation) is *real* witness to God's revelation—really presenting God's Word to us and thus 'simply revelation as it comes to us'—only when God activates, ratifies, and fulfills its human words.

> *Ubi et quando visum est Deo*, not intrinsically but in virtue of the divine decision taken ever and anon in the Bible and proclamation as the free God uses them, the Bible and proclamation are God's Word.... For (1) proclamation is real proclamation, i.e., the promise of future revelation, only as the repetition of the biblical witness to past revelation, and (2) the Bible is real witness, i.e., the factual recollection of past

---

near to us in faith and witness, who need not wait until spirit and life are subsequently breathed into the document of his revelation in virtue of the acceptance it finds in the church or the *Verständnis*, *Nachfühlen*, and *Kongenialität* which its readers bring to it, but who with his own Spirit and life always anticipates the reactions of all its readers, who in this book really exercises that government in the church which human church government can only follow by interpreting and applying his Word, by recognizing the mighty acts done by him, by preaching the truth he proclaims, by serving his revealed will.'

[5] See *KD* I/2, p. 511 (ET 462).
[6] *KD* I/2, p. 512 (ET 463).

revelation, only in its relation to this past revelation attested in it. This being so, the freedom of God's grace is the basis and boundary, the presupposition and proviso, of the statements according to which the Bible and proclamation are the Word of God. The decisive content of these statements, the positive statements and the evident negations by which they are surrounded, the relation in which these statements are valid, is their relation to revelation. But revelation is simply the freedom of God's grace. It is naturally not the principle of this freedom. This principle is only the obviously necessary product of human reflection on this freedom. It is rather the event in which the free God causes his free grace to rule and work.[7]

To understand scripture, we have to accept it as it comes to us, as human witness to God's revelation in the event of God's free rule. Scripture comes to us as it must to reach us, in truly human terms; and we in turn must apprehend it in its humanity if we are to apprehend God's revelation in it at all, not attempting to circumvent God's accommodation to our need. 'The Bible is a witness of revelation which is really given and really applies and is really received by us just because it is a written word, and in fact a word written by men like ourselves, which we can read, hear, and understand as such.'[8]

Concretely, to read the Bible as a human book means reading it as a historical book, 'the human speech uttered by specific men at specific times in a specific situation, in a specific language, and with a specific intention'.[9] And (here Barth picks up directly the polemics against the historicizing and psychologizing tendencies in biblical scholarship against which he already reacted so strongly in the *Römerbrief* period) the specific intention of the scriptural authors is to direct the attention of the hearer or reader to a specific object; precisely as a human word, the Bible 'points away from itself ... towards a fact [*Sache*], an object [*Gegenstand*]'.[10]

In his commentarial work, Barth develops this point exegetically in connection with the terms 'witness', 'servant', 'prophet', and, especially, 'apostle'.[11] Insofar as an author of a biblical text is identified as a 'witness' or 'apostle', a 'servant' or 'prophet', the reader's interpretative interests must not

---

[7] *KD* I/1, p. 120 (ET 117); cf. p. 114 (ET 111): 'Indem sie wirklich Offenbarung bezeugt, ist die Bibel, und indem sie wirklich Offenbarung verheißt, ist die Verkündigung Gottes Wort.'

[8] *KD* I/2, p. 513 (ET 463–4).

[9] *KD* I/2, p. 513 (ET 464).

[10] Cf. *KD* I/1, p. 114–15 (ET 111–12): 'If we understand them [the prophets and apostles] as witnesses—and only as such do we genuinely understand them, i.e., as they understand themselves—then their *self*, which in its inner and outer determination and movement constitutes as it were the *matter* of their service, must be decisively understood by us from the standpoint of its form as a reference away from themselves.'

[11] For the term 'witness', see esp. the important introduction to Barth, *Erklärung des Johannes-Evangeliums*, pp. 1–11 (ET 1–9) as well as the treatment there of John 1.14 (pp. 118–19 (ET 95–6)).

linger on the 'personality' or 'individuality' of the author but be directed to the theme which the author intends to communicate.

Negatively, this can mean a reorientation of *Einleitungsfragen* away from historical reconstructions of the original moments of a text's generation, reception, and preservation—reconstructions which Barth often simply finds at best inconclusive and at worst distractions from the text which stands before him. In his 1922–23 lectures on the epistle of James,[12] for example, Barth expresses a real desire for more compelling and precise historical information about the relations between author and audience out of which the text arose and within which it had its original effect. But the main lessons he draws from a brief review of some representative commentaries and works of New Testament introduction is that we simply do not know very much about the historical context out of which the epistle of James emerges, and that we would do well to admit that fact upfront. So he urges his students to avoid excessive curiosity about these historical questions, and suggests simply reading the identity of its author, audience, and generative occasion out of the text before them. Thus in relation to the authorship question, Barth speaks of 'James' strictly as the authorial presence presupposed by the epistle in its present, canonical form. Characteristically, he resists too quickly identifying this James either as an apostle (the son of Alphaeus named in Mt. 10.3) or as an early church leader who misunderstood Paul's gospel (cf. Acts 15; Gal. 2.12),[13] speaking of him rather as a distinct voice in the New Testament—not John, not Paul, not a collector of Hellenistic-Christian platitudes, but a figure in the tradition of Old Testament prophecy, indeed as the Jeremiah of the New Testament, one who calls the church to repentance. This James wants to be recognized in the first instance as a 'servant of God and of the Lord Jesus'. Crucially, a 'servant' (or 'slave') is one with no independent legal standing; he is not a 'personality' who has and takes responsibility for himself. And so he is not a figure in whom we may take independent interest. This means resisting the modern interest in religious personalities; but just so it means taking the text seriously as it stands. In short: Exegesis of the received text takes the place of full-scale historical reconstruction in questions of New Testament introduction. And this means that the designations of authorial identity in the text—in this case 'servant'—serve as basic guides to authorial intention and thus to the sort of interpretative interest the text can appropriately receive.

The same basic point applies when the key descriptive term in the text is 'apostle' rather than 'servant' or 'prophet'. Already in his reading of Romans 1.1 in the second *Römerbrief*, for example, Barth offers a highly compressed account

---

[12] 'Erklärung des Jakobusbriefes' (lectures delivered in Göttingen, winter semester 1922–23). Typescript in Karl Barth-Archiv, Basel, Switzerland.

[13] On this early resistance to synthetic readings of New Testament texts to establish exegetical probabilities, see already Barth's disclaimer about his 'manner of working' in the preface to the second *Römerbrief* (*Römerbrief 1922*, p. vii (ET 3)).

of three basic features of apostolic identity, all of which serve to deflect an abstract interest in Paul as a personality and concentrate attention on his gospel of the coming kingdom of God. First, an apostle is one whose identity is *wholly* determined by God's specific and new act: An apostle cannot retreat from his commission to a more secure, self-posited identity (though he does not therefore cease to be available to other, more generic descriptions). Therefore, second, apostolic identity can be acknowledged only in terms of God's decision: An apostle is not available to himself or to others apart from his commission. And this means, third, that to understand and speak of the author of Romans as an 'apostle' means to understand the whole letter as a communicative event generated by a free divine decision.

> However great and important a man Paul may have been, the essential theme of his mission is not within him but above him.... As an apostle—and only as an apostle—he stands in no organic relationship with human society as it exists in history; seen from the point of view of human society, he can be regarded only as an exception, or rather as an impossibility. Paul's position can be justified only as resting in God, and so only can his words be regarded as at all credible, for they are as incapable of direct apprehension as is God himself.... Paul is authorized to deliver the gospel of God ... the Word which, since it is ever new, must ever be received with renewed fear and trembling.... [I]t is an announcement that counts on men not only taking notice but taking part, not only on human reason but on comprehension, not only on sympathy but on collaboration—an announcement that presupposes faith in God, in God himself, and which creates what it presumes.[14]

The priority of the divine agency in establishing the relational networks in which the text originates and operates means identifying the *readers* as well as the author of the text in terms of God's unique action. In the second *Römerbrief*, Barth passes quite quickly over the description of the letter's recipients as 'beloved of God' and (especially) 'called' of Jesus Christ to be saints. But he does recognize the force of these descriptions, and refers to Paul's audience in terms that are generally associated with the doctrines of election and sanctification: 'The same God who had made Paul the apostle of the Gentiles (1.1) had also pressed the *Roman Christians* into the service of his imminent and coming Kingdom. As those called to holiness, they no longer belong to themselves or to the old world which is passing to corruption. They belong to him who has called them.'[15] By the time Barth delivers his lectures on 1 Peter in the summer of 1938, the doctrinal resonances are far clearer and richer.[16] Here Barth observes that according to 1 Pet. 1.1 both the letter's author ('an apostle of Jesus Christ') and its readers ('those ...

---

[14] *Romerbrief 1922*, pp. 3–4 (ET 27–8).

[15] *Römerbrief 1922*, p. 7 (ET 31).

[16] 'Erklärung des ersten Petrusbriefes' (lectures delivered in Basel, summer semester 1938). Typescript in Karl Barth-Archiv, Basel, Switzerland.

who are chosen') stand under God's election [*Erwählung*]. Thus the letter's readers are what they are on the basis of God's decision—not their own, nor that of the apostle. They are not chosen because they have heard the message; rather they have heard it because they were chosen. Again, according to the text itself, the relationship out of which the letter originates and in which it takes effect is a relationship established by and available exclusively in God. And for this reason the text is most appropriately understood as 'witness'—a text which intends to refer its readers to the God in whose decision alone they can know both themselves and the apostle by whom they are addressed.

That said, in the first volume of the *Church Dogmatics*, Barth's discussion of the term 'witness' tends to remain at a more general level, and he concentrates the issue in a simple but far-reaching formula: As a word of indication, a word that points away from itself to an intended object, scripture is a genuinely human word.

> What human word is there which does not do the same? We do not speak for the sake of speaking, but for the sake of the indication which is to be made by our speaking. We speak for the sake of what we denote or intend by our speaking. To hear [*hören*] a human word spoken to us does not mean only that we have cognition of the word as such. The understanding [*Verständnis*] of it cannot consist merely in discovering on what presuppositions, in what situation, in what linguistic sense and with what intention, in what actual context, and in this sense with what meaning the other has said this or that. And the exposition [*Auslegung*] of his word cannot possibly consist only in the exposition which, as I listen to him, involuntarily or even consciously I try to give of the speaker himself. With all this I have not yet arrived at his word as such. At best, with all this I have prepared to listen, understand, and expound. If I were to confuse this preparation with the listening, understanding, and expounding, and concern myself only with the word as such and the one who speaks it, how I should deceive myself! As far as I am concerned, he would have spoken wholly in vain.[17]

This passage is probably most remarkable for its claim that all human speech is ventured 'for the sake of the indication [*Hinweis*] which is to be made by our speaking', which may sound as though Barth is arguing that all speech acts should be understood as instances of what Searle calls 'a referring occurrence'.[18] Of course any such rough comparisons with speech act theory would be misguided: As Barth uses the terms, 'witness' and 'refer' indicate a relationship and a communicative posture of respect for and subordination to the object of reference, not instances of illocutions (one may 'refer' in Barth's terms, by pleading, promising, invoking, reporting, and so on). And as they apply generally to human speech, the concepts of 'witness' and 'reference' are not codifications of communicative rules discovered through general observation and analysis, but

---

[17] *KD* I/2, pp. 513–14 (ET 464).

[18] See John R. Searle, *Speech Acts. An Essay in the Philosophy of Language* (Cambridge, 1970), p. 77.

terms of eschatological and ethical import derived from the church's engagement with scripture.

That said, the significance of Barth's generalizing of the notion of indication begins to become clearer when we recognize that it is only one of several important moves in this passage. The first of these is the distinction between three constituent aspects of the act of interpretation: the one act of interpretation involves *hearing*, *understanding*, and *expounding* an utterance.[19] And within this distinction, Barth gives hearing a basic priority over understanding and exposition, in this way reflecting the priority and freedom of the subject matter over both speaker and hearer (or author and reader).

> We can speak meaningfully of hearing a human utterance only when it is clear to us in its function of indicating something that is described or intended by the word, and also when this function has become an event confronting us, when therefore by means of the human word we ourselves in some degree perceive the thing described or intended. It is only then that anyone has told me anything and I have heard it from him. We may call other things speaking and hearing, but in the strict sense they are only unsuccessful attempts at speaking and hearing. If a human word spoken to me does not show me anything, or if I myself cannot perceive what the word shows me, we have an unsuccessful attempt of this kind.[20]

To 'hear' an utterance is to encounter the object intended by it, to so encounter it that one is fundamentally implicated by it. A relationship is established by the object of witness, and the hearer can no longer exist as she did before. In hearing an utterance, one is necessarily transformed. And, crucially, this hearing is a necessary condition for understanding and expounding the words through which

---

[19] Note that one should not attempt to map this scheme onto the description of the 'individual practical elements of the process of interpreting scripture' in §21.2, where Barth parses *Erklärung* as observation, reflection, and appropriation [*Beobachtung, Nachdenken, and Aneignung*] (*KD* I/2, p. 810 (ET 722)). The first scheme, we might say, serves to highlight the interpreter's dependence on and receptivity towards the free subject matter of the text; the latter to characterize the active shape of that receptivity. Also note that Barth's terminology here, and throughout §§19–21, is not overly precise. In §21.2, for example, Barth uses *Auslegung* as a synonym for *Beobachtung*; in §19.1, it follows *hören/lessen* and *verstehen*. Again, whereas in §21.2 and elsewhere *Erklärung* serves as a broad term for the one complex act of interpretation (comprising *Auslegung* and *Anwendung* (*KD* I/2, p. 694 (ET 621); cf. pp. 650, 664, 730, 784 (ET 583, 596, 651, 673) and *passim*), Barth occasionally uses it in place of *Auslegung* (so *KD* I/2, pp. 570, 577 (ET 514, 519). The standard English translation is similarly fluid. At the risk of imposing an unwarranted rigidity, in this chapter we will consistently use 'interpretation' for *Erklärung*, 'exposition' for *Auslegung*, and 'application' for *Anwendung*. Other important terms will be clarified as necessary in context.

[20] *KD* I/2, p. 514 (ET 464–5).

one has encountered this object. 'Understanding of a human word presupposes that
the attempt to speak and hear has succeeded.'[21]

If and only if this attempt has succeeded—only if the addressee has become a
true hearer, truly acquainted with the object—can responsible understanding
[*Verstehen*] and exposition [*Auslegen*] begin. Understanding, on this account, is a
'return to the word' through which encounter with and knowledge of the object has
been effected. It is 'an inquiry in which even as I turn afresh to the word and
speaker, I take up a standpoint outside the word and speaker, that is, in that
perception of the thing described or intended in the word which is mediated to me
by my hearing of the word'.[22] In other words, in the venture to understand an
utterance, the words themselves and the urgency with which they are spoken
(including the personal motivations of the speaker as he expresses himself through
the linguistic resources available to him) are problematized, and in this sense
understanding is a genuinely critical activity. We will need to say something about
what this activity entails, and what Barth means when he claims that understanding
an author's words in the light of the object of witness means understanding them as
the author intended. But here the important point is simply that the priority of the
object means that the criterion for understanding cannot be identified with the
interpreter's own personal interests and convictions, however broadly shared or
culturally entrenched. Rather the criterion is strictly the object encountered in the
utterance—an object which remains object even as it is encountered, so that it
cannot be co-opted as a leverage point in a systematic critique of the text. 'A
standpoint outside the word and speaker' is not a standpoint *above* the word and
speaker.

Finally, the exposition that follows upon a true hearing of the word 'cannot
possibly consist in a portrayal of the person who speaks to me'.[23] If speech is

---

[21] *KD* I/2, p. 514 (ET 465); cf. pp. 518–19 (ET 468–9): 'It has to be conceded, of course,
… that there might be a *slip* [*Unglücksfall*] somewhere between the word and the reader,
whether in the attempt to speak or the attempt to hear: that what is said does not appear to
the hearer or reader in its factuality, that it cannot do anything with him, and that he for his
part does not know how to make anything of it. If that is the case, he will, as it were, be left
in the air in relation to the word. He will certainly not be able to understand it, because he
has no place from which he can understand it. And naturally he cannot then expound it.'
More concretely, if one has not heard God's Word in scripture, it simply is the case that
'there can be no question of a legitimate understanding of the Bible by this reader, that for
the time being, i.e., until his relation to what is said in the Bible changes, this reader cannot
be regarded as a serious reader and exegete. There can be no question of his exegesis being
equally justified with one which is based upon the real substance of the Bible, divine
revelation.' See also Barth, *Erklärung des Johannes-Evangeliums*, p. 4 (ET 3): 'Nur dann
hören wir (und erst recht: nur dann verstehen wir) das Evangelium, wenn wir von dieser
Beziehung zwischen ihm und uns, … von vornherein nicht absehen.'

[22] *KD* I/2, p. 514 (ET 465).

[23] *KD* I/2, p. 515 (ET 465).

necessarily an attempt to introduce the addressee to an object that exists for the speaker and evokes this expression, exposition must involve a repetition of the speaker's utterance. Not in the sense that the words are repeated as such; but as an attempt to responsibly restate what the speaker has said about the object encountered and thereby to achieve the same effect (knowledge of the object) intended by the original speaker. True exposition means not stopping short of this attempt, not being satisfied with directing one's attention to the speaker as he is available through a more or less sophisticated reconstruction of his historical and social context, his psychological state, and so on.

Attempts at understanding and exposition that do not follow from a true hearing are at once necessarily futile and ethically problematic, revealing a basic moral defect in the interpreter. Specifically, in the attempt to secure oneself from the object, the interpreter necessarily imposes himself on the speaker, presuming that the speaker is fundamentally uninvolved, a self-posited and self-interested individual whose motivation for communicating with another is to express and so confirm his own identity.

> Did he say something to me only to display himself? I should be guilty of a shameless violence against him if the only result of my encounter with him were that I now knew him or knew him better than before. What a lack of love! Did he not say anything to me at all? Did he not therefore desire that I should see him not in abstracto but in his specific and concrete relationship to the thing described or intended in his word, that I should see him from the standpoint and in the light of this thing? How much wrong is being continually perpetrated, how much isolation and impoverishment forced upon individuals has its only basis in the fact that we do not take seriously a claim which in itself is as clear as the day—the claim which arises whenever one person addresses a word to another.[24]

Insofar as such abstract portrayals of a speaker involve sincere and informed historical investigation, they are not wholly worthless; they may uncover all sorts of historical details or psychological insights which may prove useful in the pursuance of a real understanding and exposition (i.e., one that follows upon a real hearing). The point is that such results must be integrated into a genuinely receptive, objective, and responsible engagement with the speaker and his words.

In this sense, Barth can describe the perception and understanding of the words as such, as well as an description of the speaker himself, as preparation for hearing, understanding, and expounding. But historical investigation can be truly preparatory only if one engages in it in the hope that the object will speak through the text in question and, further, if the object actually does so speak.[25] At that

---

[24] *KD* I/2, p. 515 (ET 465).

[25] At least this would seem to follow from Barth's premises if we attempt to spell out the positive sense of the term 'preparation'. One need not necessarily draw this conclusion if the

point, such historical work moves from being preparatory to being properly responsive, an aspect of the attempt to understand the speaker's words in the light of the object. But—and here the freedom of the subject matter and the open-endedness of interpretation cohere in an eschatological ethics of interpretation—responsible understanding and exposition will, in respecting the otherness of the object and the speaker through whose words the object was mediated, necessarily be themselves ventured in the hope that the object will make itself manifest again to the interpreter and to any others for whom he expounds the text. So while he does feel free to identify instances in which commentaries on texts clearly fail even to attempt to engage the author in terms of his theme (and thus never move beyond the 'preparatory' work of abstract historical investigation and reconstruction), Barth does not believe that in the movement of genuine interpretation one can neatly partition preparatory and responsive historical investigation.[26] Each leads to the other, and both depend upon the free self-giving of the object.

At this point, we can take up more directly Barth's claim that his construing the biblical text as witness follows from it being properly understood as a genuine human word. *All* human words as such, Barth argues, point away from themselves, serving to indicate an object to the addressee, who—if he has truly heard these words—must then seek to understand and expound in the manner described. What is the basis of this claim? Not, Barth insists, 'any general considerations of the nature of human language, etc., and therefore not ... a general anthropology'. Rather, these *Erklärungsgrundsätze* follow from 'the only possible explanation of Holy Scripture'.

> If we ask ourselves, and as readers of Holy Scripture we have to ask ourselves, what is meant by hearing and understanding and expounding when we presuppose that that which is described or intended by the human word is the revelation of God, the answer we have given forces itself upon us. Hearing undoubtedly means perceiving revelation

---

term is used in a loose, polemical sense—historical investigation as preparation for real understanding (whatever that means) rather than as understanding itself.

[26] From Barth's early construal of historical criticism as a 'preparation for understanding', David Paul Henry thinks it possible to characterize Barth's theological exegesis as a two-step process, the first concerned with establishing what is in the text through philological and more general historical investigation, the second (Barth's hermeneutic as such) with bringing God's Word in scripture to expression (*The Early Development of the Hermeneutic of Karl Barth as Evidenced by His Appropriation of Romans 5:12–21* (Macon, 1985), pp. 50–1, 97–8). Admittedly, Henry more than once qualifies this scheme (in some cases, 'Barth's two-step method forms a circle' (54), and in any case 'it is easier to separate the two steps of theological exegesis in theory than in practice' (52)). But even with such qualifications the framework is awkward and obscures the theological dynamics at work in Barth's presentation.

through the human word; understanding, investigating the humanly concrete word in the light of revelation; expounding, clarifying the word in its relation to revelation.[27]

In short: from scripture we learn to read the Bible as a human word, and that means to *hear* what it says as a human word; to *understand* it as a human word in the light of what it says; and to *expound* it as a human word in its relationship to what it says.[28] The church learns this hermeneutic from scripture because of 'the unusual preponderance of what is said in it over the word as such'[29]—i.e., because scripture is the witness to God's grace to sinful humanity, and therefore witness to an utterly unique object which for our salvation maintains its freedom even as it gives itself to be expressed and known in human words.

> For it is characteristic of what is said and intended and denoted in the Bible, again in the sense of those who said it, that if it is to reveal and establish itself at all as substance and object, it must do so of itself. How can it be otherwise, when what is said is God's revelation, the lordship of the triune God in his Word by the Holy Spirit? To what is said—and even as they say it, and the biblical witnesses themselves attest it—there belongs a sovereign freedom in face of both speaker and hearer alike. The fact that it can be said and heard does not mean that it is put at the power and disposal of those who say and hear it. What it does mean is that as it is said and heard by them it can make itself said and heard. It is only by revelation that revelation can be spoken in the Bible and that it can be heard as the real substance of the Bible. If it is to be witness at all, and to be apprehended as such, the biblical witness must itself be attested by what it attests.[30]

And if the biblical witness is unusual in that it has a peculiar relationship to a specific subject matter, it is not *merely* an exception to an otherwise prevailing rule. The church understands from the existence of scripture that human language can be called into service by God's revelation without thereby containing or controlling it; and in this light it also can properly understand the relationship of all other words to the objects of their reference. 'It is not at all that the human word in the Bible has an abnormal significance and function. We see from the Bible what its normal significance and function is.'[31]

But we recognize this normal significance and function of language strictly in light of revelation, and so only in faith and hope. In general, objects of reference are not able to overcome our willful inattentiveness and actually make themselves heard. 'Hearing' in the fullest sense is an event of reconciliation; we hear as our sins are forgiven. But the revelation that comes to us in the human words of the prophets and apostles is the 'law and the promise and the sign of redemption which

---

[27] *KD* I/2, p. 515 (ET 466).

[28] *KD* I/2, p. 516 (ET 466).

[29] *KD* I/2, p. 518 (ET 468).

[30] *KD* I/2, p. 519 (ET 469–70).

[31] *KD* I/2, p. 515 (ET 466).

has been set up in the sphere of all other human words'.[32] Correspondingly, while the act of reading the Bible is not simply identical with reading another text, the insight gained in the former case applies in the latter. Specifically, the reader will bring to the text a genuine *Sachlichkeit*, by which Barth means a self-forgetful interest in what is said for its own sake. If this objectivity is not identical with faith and obedience, it can follow from it and lead towards it.

All along the line, then, God's revelation as it comes to us in the human words of scripture establishes itself as wholly free, at once illuminating our spiritual incapability to hear, understand, and expound the text, and imposing a specific set of obligations upon us.

As *hearers*, we are summoned to an unprecedented *openness*, resisting our ingrained self-assertion:

> Our supposed listening is in fact a strange mixture of hearing and our own speaking, and, in accordance with the usual rule, it is most likely that our own speaking will be the really decisive event. We have to know the mystery of the substance if we are really to meet it, if we are really to be open and ready, really to give ourselves to it, when we are told it, that it may really meet us as the substance.[33]

In the venture to *understand*, we are summoned to an unprecedented *modesty*, as the knowledge of the mystery creates in us 'a peculiar fear and reserve which is not at all usual to us. We will then know that in the face of this subject matter there can be no question of our achieving, as we do in others, the confident approach which masters and subdues the matter'.[34]

And our *exposition*, 'which is the goal of all hearing and understanding', we are summoned to an unprecedented *restraint*. We will no longer, or at least not so confidently, read our own thoughts into the text, presupposing both that we know in advance what it is saying and that we are inherently capable of effectively presenting this truth to others.

Again: The fundamental hermeneutical rule as Barth formulates it in this section of the prolegomena is to read, interpret, and expound the biblical text (and therefore all texts) in the light of what it says. And this means: to read scripture in accordance with what it is, the witness to God's revelation. And as scripture is this witness because it puts before us the lordship of the triune God, we can also say that this means *reading obediently what has been obediently written*, or, simply, reading scripture in the *church*. And in this last claim we can begin to indicate the event in which scripture as witness and scripture as Word of God, the readiness to hear and real hearing, the venture to understand and expound and real proclamation, cohere. Of course Barth insists that this event, as the reality of the

---

[32] *KD* I/2, p. 522 (ET 472).

[33] *KD* I/2, p. 520 (ET 470).

[34] *KD* I/2, p. 520 (ET 470).

encounter between God's revelation and his sinful creation, cannot be systematized (we cannot occupy a location from which to do so, and cannot wish to do so). We can only attempt appropriately to respond to this reality by seeking to understand what we mean when we confess that God really does invite us to exist under his lordship precisely as the church that hears the Word of God in scripture and understands and expounds scripture in the light of this Word.

Obedience and Reality

> The free decision of man, the act and work of man, the life of real men, is revealed in the fulfillment of revelation as the outpouring of the Holy Spirit. But it does not have its character as the life of the children of God from itself, but from the light in which it is placed. No positive—and we must add at once, no negative—description of what man does or does not do can clearly reproduce, in the strict sense, the 'Christian' character of his life, of his doing and not doing. It acquires this character only 'from outside', that is, from God. What is essentially 'Christian' in this life and doing and not doing can only be the declaration: He and not I! He and not we! He, the Lord! He for us! He in our stead! The predominant determination of man by revelation, the basis of the life of the children of God, is the fact that this 'he' avails for them, comforting, exhorting, ordering, and limiting—and all with an unrivalled emphasis, because it is the reality of their own existence which is vindicated in it all…. But it is the hidden reality of their own existence. He, he is this reality. He is not I. He is not we. Only indirectly is he identical with us and we with him. For he is God and we are men. He is in heaven and we are on earth. He lives eternally and we live temporally. There is always this eschatological frontier between him and us. But this means that it is only indirectly and not unequivocally that we can grasp that he and not I, that he and not we, as it is declared in the life and doing and not doing of man, and the effects of its comforting and exhorting and ordering and limiting in our human life. The reality of which we are trying to speak in respect of the life and doing and not doing of man is greater than, indeed utterly different from, anything that we can say about it, because he is this reality.[35]

On the basis of this and similar claims regarding the preponderant reality of God's revelation, it has become strangely commonplace to claim that Barth thinks God *alone* is real, or at least that Barth is one-sidedly occupied with the reality of Jesus Christ, 'as if no other objects mattered'.[36] But if Barth does claim that the reality of human being as it comes into view in a church dogmatics is available to us only as it comes to us in revelation, this does not mean that it does not really come to us at all, and therefore that we cannot reckon with the genuine reality of our life before God. Jesus Christ is the Word made flesh, God's Word for others; and precisely as

---

[35] *KD* I/2, pp. 404–5 (ET 368).

[36] Thus Telford Work, 'Annunciation as Election', *Scottish Journal of Theology* 54 (2001): 285–307 (p. 299).

it is perfect in itself, needing no completion, it includes the many, not nullifying their agency but placing it on its only possible footing. The recognition of the ontological primacy of Jesus Christ does not mean that there is no other being, but that all other being exists in and for him. In the first place, this simply follows from a recognition of the Son's role in creation. But as Jesus Christ in the unity of his being as true God and true man is the Word of God's *new* creation, the reconciliation of a *fallen* humanity, we are not free to speak of our creaturely dependence without also speaking of our need of salvation. We do not truly know ourselves as creatures except as we know ourselves to be the objects of God's mercy in Christ and thus as those who have forfeited their being before God and can only receive it anew through an act of unforeseeable and unmerited grace. In more explicitly trinitarian terms: Our existence before God (including our self-awareness of the derivation of this existence) is wholly dependent upon the grace of God the Father as this comes to us in the incarnation of the Son and the outpouring of the Spirit. And the faith that recognizes this life as a gift of grace will not attempt to abstract the reality of human existence from the grace of the self-giving God. Thus: He is the reality of my life. But also, in making this claim: He is the reality over and above any attribution of reality of which I am capable.[37]

That our lives come to us from God means that we exist under his lordship. And as this lordship is the rule of grace that evokes faith, it is the power by which God effects and sustains *fellowship* with his human creation. This is the theological ground of our distinctiveness as human creatures: God's power as it is directed towards us is 'not the power of a natural catastrophe which annihilates all human response, but rather the power of an appeal, command, and blessing which not only recognizes human response but creates it'.[38]

> The man mastered and compelled is precisely the man whom God loves, who is therefore set upon his own feet and made truly responsible. To recognize and respect authority as a member of the church means to love God in return and therefore to be willing and prepared to assume responsibility—real cooperative responsibility. The Christian is not a stone that is pushed, or a ball that is made to roll. The Christian is the man who through the Word and love of God has been made alive, the real man, able to love God in return, standing erect just because he has been humbled, humbling himself because he has been raised up. Just because in the church there is no mere mastery and

---

[37] On the massively complex issue of human agency in the *Church Dogmatics*, compare John Macken, *The Autonomy Theme in the Church Dogmatics: Karl Barth and His Critics* (Cambridge, 1990) with the more nuanced and sympathetic account developed by John Webster in *Barth's Ethics of Reconciliation* (Cambridge, 1995) and elsewhere. Further, *inter alia*, Paul D. Matheny, *Dogmatics and Ethics. The Theological Realism and Ethics of Karl Barth's Church Dogmatics* (Frankfurt a/M, 1990); Hunsinger, *How to Read Karl Barth*, esp. pp. 185–224.

[38] *KD* I/2, p. 741 (ET 661).

compulsion, there is in it a real mastery and compulsion. Just because there is authority in the church, there is also real freedom.[39]

Objectively, the condition of our existence is God's creative, reconciling Word. And again, if we cannot simply collapse creation into reconciliation, neither can we hope to appeal to our createdness *in abstracto*, for in wanting to know ourselves as creatures apart from Jesus Christ who is ours only in faith—that is, in thankfulness and in hope—we show that we have not known and cannot know ourselves as we truly are.

Subjectively, real human existence is *obedient* existence, where this is understood as human participation in the triune life through the Holy Spirit, not merely as personal inclination or outlook, the disposition of a subject whose existence is already secured on other grounds. Real obedience, and therefore real human existence, is the act of the creature born anew and sustained by the Lord in the act of lordship.

One result of all this is a shift in the anthropological component of a theological hermeneutics. What takes center stage is not a general consideration of the intellectual processes implicated in the act of 'understanding', or a construal of the capacities of texts or of language as such to convey meaning. Rather, the starting point is the reality that God graciously confronts the church in scripture, bringing about the obedience of faith where it could not have been anticipated or deserved. And this means the fundamental exclusion of a subject-centered systematic evaluation (either by way of critique or endorsement) of scripture and the church's doctrines and traditional reading practices.[40] On Barth's terms, there simply is no

---

[39] *KD* I/2, pp. 742–3 (ET 662–3); cf. already *UCR I*, pp. 221–2 (ET 179–80): 'We must not be mere leaves growing on the divine tree or floating in the divine breeze, nor must we be drops in the divine ocean, nor stones rolled down by the divine avalanche, nor wheels driven round by the divine motor. On such views the relation is much too continuous, much too much on the same level. And standing before God is taken with far too little seriousness. If *fellowship* between God and us is to mean anything, it must mean that we in our sphere turn no less to God than God turns to us in our sphere.... There has to be a recognition, an acceptance, an acknowledgment, a respecting, a bowing down. That is why there has to be faith and obedience. That is why expressly there has to be knowledge and action, *not* just a "feeling of absolute dependence".'

[40] Thus Kant can praise the Bible 'as the best and most adequate means of public instruction available for establishing and maintaining indefinitely a state religion that is truly conducive to the soul's improvement' while simultaneously rejecting the doctrines of the trinity, incarnation, resurrection, and so on—in both cases because he assumes the (moral) self-sufficiency of the reading subject, a sufficiency which scripture can in no sense question or disturb: 'Action must be represented as issuing from man's own use of his moral powers, not as an effect [resulting] from the influence of an external, higher cause by whose activity man is passively healed. The interpretation of scriptural texts which, taken literally, seem to contain the latter view must therefore be deliberately directed toward making them

location from which such an evaluation could be undertaken; there is, to use the language from his Leutwil lecture, no third way between faith and unbelief—or, as we might now say, between reading obediently and the impossible abstraction of self-assertion. In any case, for Barth such attempts to comprehend scripture from a hermeneutically prior subjectivity are already ruled out by the simple fact that we are members of the Christian church, and as such we learn that we do and can exist in obedient fellowship with our Lord precisely from scripture itself.

> [W]here the church really is the church, then as the church of Jesus Christ it finds itself in a known and as such continually enacted relationship of obedience to what constitutes its being, ground and essence and therefore to Jesus Christ the Word of God. A relationship of obedience, however, is a relationship in an antithesis, an antithesis in which there is an obvious and genuine above and below.... Now it is in such a relationship of obedience to Jesus Christ that we find the church in the original act of revelation attested by holy scripture, in the confrontation of the apostles with the crucified and risen one, which has its Old Testament prototype in the confrontation of the prophets of Israel with Yahweh. Neither in the Old Testament nor in the New Testament do we find even a trace of the possibility that this relationship of obedience, in which the biblical witnesses become what they were, recipients of revelation, was later dissolved and transformed into one in which these men could confront Yahweh or Jesus Christ as those who had a control of their own over that which was revealed to them.... They are never recipients of revelation in the sense that they appropriate revelation and can then recognize and evaluate it for themselves. They are recipients of revelation in the sense that revelation meets them as the master and they become obedient to it. It is because they are obedient that they are prophets and apostles. It is because they are obedient that they have the Holy Spirit. It is because they are obedient that they are appointed and commissioned to be Christ's witnesses to others, to the nascent church and to the world. The church of Jesus can exist only when it repeats this relationship of obedience.... The church of Jesus Christ stands or falls with the fact that it obeys as the apostles and prophets obeyed their Lord. It stands or falls with the known and at any time actual antithesis of man and revelation, which cannot be reversed, in which the man receives, learns, submits and is controlled, in which he has a Lord and belongs to him wholly and utterly.[41]

In other words, as it is presented to us in the scripture that arises from it, the prophetic-apostolic obedience is normative for our relationship with Jesus Christ. Only as the church's obedience to the risen and ascended Lord corresponds to (or 'repeats') that of the prophets and apostles does it have a share in their relationship to Jesus Christ and thus in the benefits of the life he lived for them. And thus arises in all its force the question posed by the existence of scripture as authority in the church, namely the question—not simply of how appropriately to read historical

consistent with the former view' (*The Conflict of the Faculties*, trans. Mary J. Gregor (Lincoln, 1992), pp. 17, 67, 73, 75).

[41] *KD* I/2, pp. 603–4 (ET 542–3).

texts as such, or even of how to read 'classic' texts, the foundational and identity-forming texts which focus the historically extended arguments of convictional communities and traditions, but—of the *conditions of obedience* for those of us who are not apostles. How is it that we can obediently encounter the Lord who precisely as the ascended one, as the Lord of his own time, is not immediately available to us?

> [T]he relationship of obedience between the prophets and apostles and their Lord is a unique relationship as such. It is as unique as the incarnation of the divine Word, as the outpouring of the Holy Spirit, as the reconciliation of man with God in Christ's death and the revelation of it in his resurrection, as the forty days after Easter between the times.... Therefore the existence of the church does not mean the existence of new prophets and apostles who will receive God's revelation in the same direct way, and will be commissioned and empowered as its witnesses. If the church of Jesus Christ exists only when there is a repetition of this relationship to obedience, then we must say: Either, outside that between-the-times there is no church of Jesus Christ at all.... Or, the promise of the forty days is truly and visibly fulfilled before us as was the Old Testament prophecy in the forty days themselves: 'You shall be my witnesses!' and: 'Lo, I am with you always!' The unique revelation did not take place in vain, nor did that unique relationship of obedience take place in vain. Both of them, the revelation and the obedience of the prophets and apostles, continue to exist: indirectly, but in full, unbroken reality, a copy [*Abbild*] of the revelation in which this is always truly and validly present, and a model [*Urbild*] of the obedience, which even though there are no more prophets and apostles, can and should be seriously repeated in every age. This authentic copy of revelation and this authentic model of obedience to it is therefore the content of the witness of the prophets and apostles in holy scripture.[42]

The concrete existence of scripture itself as written witness—as 'authentic copy of revelation'—is thus the basic condition of the church's obedience. And as 'authentic model of obedience', it is a normative and sufficient guide to the shape of that obedience. Together, these two statements represent yet another way of unpacking the Protestant scripture principle. And together, §20 of the prolegomena, in which Barth treats scripture's determinate authority over the church and the proximate authority of tradition within it, and §21, which covers the primary and generative freedom of scripture and some of the ways in which human agency can be exercised on its terms, serve to explain how this is so.

Thus Barth opens §20 by again asking the question that has been at issue throughout the prolegomena: How is the Word of God in scripture heard in the church (and through the church in the world) and obeyed? In Chapter Two (§§8–18), Barth distinguished between the incarnation of the Word and the outpouring of the Holy Spirit as the objective and subjective effecting of revelation. In seeking to understand how obedience to this revelation is real (and thus how the church is

---

[42] *KD* I/2, pp. 604–5 (ET 543–4).

really the church and the world thereby really the world), Barth again distinguishes between an objective and subjective element, an outer and inner determination of obedience that correspond to the possibility of God existing for humanity and the possibility of humanity existing for God.[43]

> Authority is the external determination under which [obedience] becomes possible for man from God; freedom is the inner determination, the determination under which it is possible for God from man. Either way it is primarily and strictly a matter of the authority and freedom which belongs to holy scripture itself in the church. But either way it is secondly a matter of the authority and freedom of the church as such, subject to holy scripture. Holy scripture is the ground and limit of the church, but for that very reason it constitutes it.[44]

The Conditions of Obedience: Authority

As the objective condition of the church's being-in-obedience, the authority of scripture is the authority of the Word of God to whom alone obedience can truly be rendered. Scripture has, according to the controlling thesis of §20, 'direct, absolute, and material' authority over the church.[45] As such it establishes a genuine if secondary authority in the church—the authority of 'fathers and brothers', of fellow-witnesses past and present to whom one must listen as one sets about interpreting the Word which is directed to the church and just so to its individual members.[46] But it is both materially appropriate and strategically necessary to emphasize first, Barth argues, that scripture as such 'is an authority *in* the church which is also an authority *over* the church', an authority, then, which 'limits the authority of the church, that is, it does not destroy but defines it'.[47]

Once again, in his description of the limiting authority of scripture over the church, Barth draws a sharp distinction between the Reformation position and its Roman Catholic and neo-Protestant alternatives, whose 'declared essence', Barth insists, is the self-governance of the church.

> In the one case the final decision rests with the teaching office of the church which comprises both scripture and tradition and expounds them with unchallenged authority, identifying itself with revelation. In the other it rests with the less tangible but no less infallible authority of the self-consciousness and historical consciousness of man. But

---

[43] Put otherwise: §20, 'Authority in the Church', corresponds with the christological §13, 'God's Freedom for Man'; and §21, 'Freedom in the Church', with the pneumatological §16, 'Man's Freedom for God'.

[44] *KD* I/2, p. 600 (ET 539).

[45] *KD* I/2, p. 598 (ET 538).

[46] *KD* I/2, pp. 638–9 (ET 573–4).

[47] *KD* I/2, p. 639 (ET 574).

either way it rests with the church which then has to obey it. And to the extent that this is the case, the church knows no higher authority than its own.[48]

In response, Barth develops a series of interlocking doctrinal, ethical, and historical arguments why 'the Evangelical confession' is also 'the Evangelical decision',[49] specifically a decision to live in obedience to scripture as the Word of God, and to do so by consciously distinguishing itself at every point from the risen Christ and the scripture through which he rules the church. In short: 'The decision in favor of a church of obedience as opposed to a church of self-government'.[50]

The doctrinal moves involve appeals to the doctrine of creation (or to the doctrine of God the creator (cf. §10)), to the an/enhypostatic christology developed in §15.2, and to the trinitarian material on the coherence of the Spirit and Word in §9 and (especially) §12.

From the doctrine of creation, we learn that, while self-government is 'the great prerogative of God', what is created can aspire to self-rule only at the cost of 'open disobedience'. And this is no less true in the church than elsewhere, for the relationship of the church and the risen Christ corresponds precisely to the relationship of creature and creator, at least in the sense that the dependence of the one on the other (and just so the reality of the relationship between them) is complete in both cases.

> The church would not exist without him, just as the creature would not exist without the creator. It is the same relation as that of the creator and creature which exists between him and his church. In his distinctness from it he is one with it; and in its distinctness from him it is one with him. The relation between Jesus Christ and his church is, therefore, an irreversible relation.[51]

But the dependence of the church on Christ is immediately specified as obedience: 'If it lives as his church and has as such its own authority, it lives in obedience to him, in an obedience which neither openly nor tacitly can ever be self-government.' And the question is raised on behalf of 'the cleverer, and to that extent better, representatives of Catholic and neo-Protestant theology' whether— assuming that thus far Barth has only expressed the common faith of the church in his stress on the absolute material authority of God himself—we cannot reckon with the possibility that the church actually is obedient and so that absolute authority can in fact be predicated of the church. Can we, he asks, rule out *a priori* the possibility that the *magisterium* can actually speak pure divine truth or that one can truly discern the Word in the history one lives and is? And if we cannot, must we not at least entertain the idea that 'the church is itself the tradition of the Word

---

[48] *KD* I/2, pp. 639–40 (ET 575).

[49] *KD* I/2, pp. 641, 643, 651–2 (ET 576, 578, 584–5).

[50] *KD* I/2, p. 640 (ET 575).

[51] *KD* I/2, p. 641 (ET 576).

of God and therefore present revelation and therefore Jesus Christ?' And if so, what prevents us actually making this claim?[52]

Whatever its theological merits, Barth's response is doubtless a clever one:

> We at once reply to this question that the claim is resisted by the very fact that it is made at all. The church whose authority is preserved in the differentiation from divine authority, the church which is obedient to its Lord and in which the Word of God is living and present, will definitely not make that claim. Of course it will be the tradition of the Word of God and therefore present revelation and therefore actually—as the earthly body of the heavenly head—Jesus Christ himself. But this will be true as the act and truth of Jesus Christ in the power and mystery of the Holy Spirit.[53]

The obedient church, further, while it will not understand itself as a simple prolongation of the incarnation, will understand itself in terms derived from the doctrine of the incarnation, from which we learn 'that God and man are so related in Jesus Christ that he exists as man so far and only so far as he exists as God', yet 'in virtue of the *assumptio*, the human nature acquires existence (subsistence) in the existence of God'.[54] Thus one arrives at what one might call an an/enhypostatic ecclesiology:

> [T]he Christian church cannot reflect on its own being, or live by it, without seeing itself confronted by the Lord, who is present to it but as its real Lord, with a real authority which transcends its own authority. Its Lord is Jesus Christ. He has called it into life and he maintains it in life. In him it believes. Him it proclaims. To him it prays. It is related to him as the human nature which he assumed is related to his divinity. It looks up to him, as he is present to it, and it partakes of his Holy Spirit, as the earthly body looks up to its heavenly head. He and he alone, with the Father and the Holy Spirit, can have divine glory and authority in the church.... The glory and authority of the church will then be a predicate of his divine glory and authority, as once in the incarnation of the Word human nature was a predicate of his eternal deity and therefore deity could be beheld in the flesh according to John 1.14. But the glory and authority of God are not then a predicate of the church—as little as the eternal Word was a predicate of the flesh. There can, therefore, be no question of the church claiming to be as such the tradition of

---

[52] *KD* I/2, p. 642 (ET 577). Thus (in one of its less careful moments) *The Catechism of the Catholic Church* (Chicago, 1994) can claim that while the *credo ecclesiam* depends entirely on the articles concerning Jesus Christ and the Holy Spirit (§§748–9), 'Christ and his Church ... together make up the "whole Christ" (*Christus totus*)', so that 'the faith of the holy doctors and the good sense of the believer' are summed up in this reply of St. Joan of Arc to her judges: 'About Jesus Christ and the Church, I simply know they're just one thing, and we shouldn't complicate the matter' (§795).

[53] *KD* I/2, p. 642 (ET 577).

[54] *KD* I/2, p. 178 (ET 163).

the Word, revelation, Jesus Christ himself. The grace directed to the church cannot be transformed into a possession and a glory of the church.[55]

Finally, we note again that for Barth the existence of scripture itself as a 'prior human form of the Word of God'[56] tangibly distinct from the church's ongoing acts of service and worship and witness is a necessary condition of the church's obedience. As scripture formally represents the completeness and uniqueness of the revelation of God in Christ, it reminds the church that the existence of the prophets and apostles as they are present in scripture 'is the concrete form of the existence of Jesus Christ himself in which the church has the foundation of its being'. And, again, for Barth the scripture principle is bound up with the notion of apostolic mediation of revelation, which is in turn bound up with the trinitarian claim that the Spirit is not accessible apart from the Word which became flesh and was beheld precisely by the apostles whose witness is codified in scripture. Thus to the question of why what Barth calls 'the Evangelical decision' necessarily involves a disciplined insistence on the fundamental difference between Christ's authority and that of the church even as it recognizes the reality of God's self-giving, Barth responds:

---

[55] *KD* I/2, p. 640–3 (ET 575–7). We might wish to say: It cannot be so for the same reason that in the doctrine of the incarnation the claim that the humanity exists only in the Word cannot be understood to mean that the divine Word exists only in the humanity of Christ. In this (typically Lutheran) christological reversal, Barth wonders, can there be any real confrontation (and so any real relationship) of flesh and Word in the sense of John 1.14? (*KD* I/2, p. 182 (ET 167)). But of course Barth views the sixteenth- and seventeenth-century struggle between the Lutheran and Reformed churches over the so-called *extra Calvinisticum* as a materially proper and possibly inevitable debate between 'two Evangelical theologies in the one Evangelical church' (*KD* I/2, p. 187 (ET 171)). The Evangelical decision for the scripture principle, on the other hand, involves a struggle for the existence of the church. Whether or not Barth should have drawn the same consequences in each case is another question; here we can simply register the fact that while Barth does sharply distinguish the Reformed deployment of the enhypostasis doctrine from the Lutheran, just as earlier he had distinguished the Reformed scripture principle from the Lutheran hermeneutic of justification by grace through faith alone, in neither case does he think these distinctions as more than denominational, consistently reserving the language of heresy for post-Reformation Catholicism and modernist-pietist neo-Protestantism. Indeed, in the important historical excursus on the scripture principle in *KD* I/2 (pp. 606–37 (ET 544–72)), Barth argues that, while the 'concrete polemical sharpness of the Reformed scripture principle' may indeed be a particularity of the Reformed church, the material decision to accord absolute authority to scripture alone was taken just as clearly by Luther himself, so that 'a Lutheran can no more make even slight concessions in this matter to the Catholic position than a Reformed Protestant' (pp. 608–9 (ET 546–7)).

[56] *KD* I/2, p. 640 (ET 575).

The answer can only be the simple one that this concrete necessity is the fact of holy scripture. It is not self-will that the Evangelical church persists in that differentiation, that it claims to be the school in which Jesus Christ is the master, and the flock in which he and he alone is the shepherd, the kingdom of which he and he alone is the king, that it takes care not to reverse this order in its own interest. The church is not in a position to have an opinion on this question. It cannot choose between this possibility and the opposite one in which it itself is master, shepherd, king. The latter possibility is in fact closed to it. It is closed to it because Jesus Christ is gracious and present in his Word. This is, of course, by the power and life of his Holy Spirit. Yet this Spirit is simply the Spirit of his Word. And his Word, in which he himself is present and gracious to his church—and which must not be replaced by or confused with the word which the church itself has and has to speak—is the word of the biblical prophets and apostles. Therefore his Word always confronts the word of man in the church in the form of a human word, i.e., the prophetic-apostolic word.[57]

The historical considerations that attend these doctrinal moves are familiar enough. In broad terms, the historical argument has both a positive and negative element: Negatively, Barth speaks of church history as the story of 'the apparently irresistible revulsion of obedience to self-government'; positively, he speaks of the 'healthy strangeness' of scripture by which 'it can always find new and from its own standpoint better readers, and obedience in these readers, even in a church which has perhaps to a large extent become self-governing, and by these readers a point of entry to reform and renew the whole church and to bring it back from self-government to obedience'.[58] And both the negative and positive statements follow from the conviction that the sixteenth-century Reformers did in fact see the church effectively renewed by scripture itself precisely as it stands over against its readers in its concrete written form. The churches of the Reformation regarded scripture as a lifeline, 'a gift which had to be received with particular thankfulness from the providence which rules over the church'. And in so receiving it, the church became aware of the seriousness of its tendency towards self-governance, not least as expressed in the church's own methods and structures of intellectual and political adjustment.

And in ethical terms, as the church is confronted by scripture, it must gratefully and joyfully and humbly maintain the *Gehorsamstellung* appropriate to it.

Not in denial of the fact that it is adopted by the living and present Word into unity with him, but in recognition of and gratitude for this exaltation, it will remain in this place, it will always return to it, it will not leave it with the claim that it itself has and is direct and absolute and material authority. In the knowledge of the eternal Jesus Christ and in

---

[57] *KD* I/2, pp. 644–5 (ET 578–9).

[58] *KD* I/2, pp. 645, 650 (ET 579, 583); cf. p. 764 (ET 681): 'Church history is the history of the exegesis of the Word of God and therefore of the ever recurrent menace of doing violence to it. But it is also and still more the history of the criticism which it brings and always will bring to bear on its interpreters.'

fellowship with him it will be modest, knowing that he is in it and it in him in the distinction of the creator from the creature, of the heavenly head from his earthly body. In this place it recollects and expects his blessing. This humility, which in the fullness of what it receives and has constantly turns to the origin and object of faith, is the very essence of the Evangelical as distinct from the Catholic and neo-Protestant decision.[59]

That the church can gratefully, modestly, and humbly confess that God has been pleased to be present to it in the concrete form of the scriptural text means that the church is freed from the burden of self-regulation and freed for the common task of confessing its common faith. This involves, as we have already seen in our treatment of Barth's historical theology lectures, what many would consider a very peculiar assessment of the grounds and limits of communal dialogue. Barth simply does not recognize the continuance of interpretative dialogue as intrinsically healthy. Rather, he thinks interpretative disputes can be constructive only if all involved agree that scripture in its concrete freedom as text stands as judge over against all possible interpretations. Otherwise, he claims, such debates are merely party conflicts. And while such give-and-take in the church may (so long as it is carried out peaceably) appear to be a sign of the health of the community, the church 'does not live in the inner movement of these tensions. In them we see rather the process of decay to which the church is at once subject when it ceases to live by the Word of God, which means holy scripture.... These debates in the church are conducted in the absence of the Lord of the church. But are they then really conducted in the church?'[60]

The church freed from the burden of self-governance is freed from party conflict in order that it might be free for common confession. And this means it is free to exercise genuine authority. Indeed, it is free to exercise a human authority which reflects the authority of God, and which is therefore 'true, original, primal authority, the type of all other authority'.[61] It does so, of course, only as it is obedient and therefore only as it does not seek to exercise anything other than the authority for which it has been freed. But it really does exercise it.

And it does so because the Word which calls the church into being is addressed to the church as such and only then to its individual members. The Word itself creates community by requiring a movement from the individual towards others, specifically the movement of confession. In the concrete hearing of the Word of God, there necessarily is a movement from private to public. Individuals in the church recognize that they have not received the Word for themselves but for others; therefore they freely share the faith which they have received from and by

---

[59] *KD* I/2, p. 643 (ET 578).

[60] *KD* I/2, p. 651 (ET 584).

[61] *KD* I/2, p. 654 (ET 587).

the Word.[62] In so doing, they enter an ongoing dialogue, accepting that their own expression of the faith they have received may need to be corrected or even opposed by the church in the light of the Word of God spoken to the church. Of course the confession of the church is marked by sin and therefore by error; but the primary thing to be said about the church is that it is 'the sphere of the lordship of Christ'—that in the church sins are forgiven. Thus the doctrine of justification is related to a hermeneutic of trust, and both to a proper conception of the church's authority:

> Because my sins are forgiven me, I am bold to believe and, in spite of the sin of which I am conscious, to confess my faith as created in me by the Word of Christ. And if this is the case then in relation to the rest of the church and its confession I cannot possibly begin with mistrust and rejection, just as in relation to our parents, no matter who they are or what they are like, we do not begin with mistrust and rejection or with the assertion that we must obey God rather than man, but with trust and respect and therefore, in the limits appointed to them as men, with obedience. As in and with the confession of the church I hear the infallible Word of Christ in his church and the forgiveness of sins, I have to reckon first and above all with the lordship of Jesus Christ in his church; not with sin and therefore with the possibility of falsehood and error which it involves. And this means that I have not primarily to criticize the confession of those who were before me in the church and are with me in the church. There will always be time and occasion for criticism. My first duty is to love and respect it as the witness of my fathers and brethren. And it is in the superiority posited by this fact that I shall hear it.... This is how the authority of the church arises. It always arises in this way, that in the community of hearing and receiving the Word of God which constitutes the church there is this superiority of the confession of some before others, this honor and love, this hearing of the confession of some by others, before the latter go on to make their own confession.[63]

This mutual accounting of those who have heard the Word of God has as its aim a common proclamation of the Word heard and received. This task of common proclamation 'is the compelling practical ground why the faith of the individual cannot be, as it appears to be, a private matter, why the individual with his faith is responsible, why he is forced to come before the public of the church, why he has to make his faith known to others and submit to their judgment if he is legitimately to play an active part in that general search after a true faith'.[64] In view of this unity in common proclamation, the church undertakes to arrive at a common confession of faith as an intermediate goal. Although Barth says that common proclamation is a 'compelling practical ground' for theological debate in the church, it is not a

---

[62] Barth, like Augustine before him, invokes the parable of the talents in making this point (cf. Mt. 25.14–30); see *KD* I/2, p. 656 (ET 588); Augustine, *On Christian Teaching*, trans. R.P.H. Green (Oxford, 1997), p. 6.

[63] *KD* I/2, pp. 657–8 (ET 590).

[64] *KD* I/2, p. 660 (ET 591).

practical ground without a theological basis. The underlying point is that the gift of God's Word to the church is the command of God to the church—precisely the command to proclaim his Word. The implication is that Christian theology, if not guided by the definite aim of common confession leading to common proclamation, can degenerate into what Barth calls 'mere talk' about God. 'But the church', Barth protests, 'is not a poor theological seminar. Much less is it a religious debating club'.[65]

The authority of the church becomes real—it is an event—when the decision of the church past coincides with the decision of the church today. This coincidence is real in the free act of God. In the freedom of God's Word, a specific confession of the church past becomes a confession that the church must hear today if it is to obey the church's Lord, so that the coincidence of confessions past and present is simply 'the mystery of obedience to the Word of God'. And respecting this mystery means not setting down a definitive list of authorities which must be viewed as possessing this genuine, spiritual authority. But Barth does feel free to identify three historical forms to which the individual in the church must be responsible—viz., the scriptural canon, the church fathers, and the church confessions.[66] The church is obedient to the Word of God in scripture alone; responsible to the church fathers and to the confessions; and neutral with regard to all other voices.

Among these other voices is the historical-critical scholarship practiced in the academy. We have seen Barth repeatedly insisting that its legitimacy is beyond question; the only issue is what role it is accorded in the church's reading practices. Of course as historical-critical exegesis—however it is understood—is not all of a piece, and as the church's native reading practices will vary across space and time, there is no sense in trying to specify in advance exactly how the relationship between them will play out in any given case. But Barth stubbornly resists giving it a controlling place among the authorities to which the church must listen.

> No one has read the Bible only with his own eyes and no one should. The only question is what interpreters we allow and in what order we let them speak. It is a pure superstition that the systematizing of a so-called historico-critical theology has as such a greater affinity to holy scripture itself and has therefore in some sense to be heard before the Apostles' Creed or the Heidelberg Catechism as a more convincing exposition of the biblical witness. What we have there is simply the commentary of a theology, if not a mythology. The only thing is that this commentary has not been affirmed by a church, that so far the theology or mythology has wisely hesitated to claim the character of a real decision.[67]

---

[65] *KD* I/2, p. 660 (ET 592).

[66] See *KD* I/2, pp. 666–73 (ET 597–603) (canon); 673–93 (ET 603–20) (fathers); and 693–740 (ET 620–60) (confessions).

[67] *KD* I/2, p. 728 (ET 649–50).

Recognizing the authority of the church's confession—'the first of commentaries' on scripture and so 'the leader of the chorus or the key witness' in the series of commentaries that we must hear as we expound and apply scripture—means acknowledging the seriousness of the decisions the church has taken in the past and those which it may be required to take presently. Against the Roman Catholic position, Barth argues that church confessions are by definition fallible; but, against the neo-Protestant position, he insists that they are not for that reason simply one set of opinions among many. Implicitly, Barth argues, even the liberal Protestant movement recognizes this, having 'not had the confidence seriously and consistently to lay before the church the challenge even of a confession of the non-confessionalism which it has taught and demanded, of a decision in favor of the lack of decision which alone can save'.[68] And the spiritual gravity of Barth's construal of the relative but just so genuine authority of the church past and present is most evident in the observation with which Barth concludes this section: 'since the Reformation and the time immediately after there has never been a new confession in the Protestant sphere'—excepting, that is, 'the latest developments', by which he means the developments leading up to the Barmen declaration. Barth will not claim too much here, thinking it still too early to see what importance can be attached to Barmen and the Confessing Church movement. But the developments of the 1930s at least reopened for Barth and many others the question of the basis on which the church can claim real authority in the face of the most serious challenge and the most pressing temptation. And Barth's exposition of the authority of scripture in the church—an absolute authority which can call forth real obedience and so genuine authority in the church—can be rightly read only when we remember what was at stake.

The Conditions of Obedience: Freedom

A theology that takes as its starting point the revelation of the triune God strictly as it is attested in scripture will not be distracted by the supposedly basic antithesis of authority and freedom. 'As the Son can be revealed only by the Spirit, and in the Spirit only the Son is revealed, so authority must necessarily be interpreted by freedom and freedom by authority.'[69] In the life of the church under scripture, authority and freedom cohere in obedience, for what matters is not authority as such nor freedom as such but the will of God. And, Barth claims, the tendency to abstract from the will of God in either direction—either towards abstract authority (which Barth identifies as characteristic of Roman Catholicism) or abstract freedom (as in neo-Protestantism)—is a symptom of the confusion of grace and nature, an overly optimistic vision of human nature, and a denial of the free grace

---

[68] *KD* I/2, p. 740 (ET 660).
[69] *KD* I/2, p. 746 (ET 666).

of God. 'An absolute principle of authority and an absolute principle of freedom both derive, do they not, from one and the same root, namely, an optimism which is impossible where the thought and effort of the human heart are recognized to be evil from youth upwards, and the sovereign power of the divine Word is discerned and recognized?'[70]

A proper theological description of the church's true freedom follows the same course as that involved in the proper specification of its authority—i.e., it involves an analysis of the obedient relationship of the prophets and apostles to the self-revealing Lord. In scripture, Barth observes, the prophets and apostles make real decisions; their obedience is an exercise of their freedom in that they really choose to act in this way and not another. But this does not mean that their freedom is unbounded, that they can weigh obedience and disobedience as two equally plausible notions, deliberating from a sovereign standpoint within themselves untouched by the claim of the Word of God. The freedom of the prophets and apostles consists precisely in their obedience, in which they participate in the absolute freedom of the Word of God. Concretely, the freedom of the Word involves the calling, commissioning, and sending of the apostles by Jesus, and the freedom of these disciples involves their response to him—i.e., their obedience to the task enjoined on them by the risen Christ. Just as the existence of the church is an exponent of the authority of the apostolic witness, so the church exists only where there is a repetition of the apostolic freedom. But again, because of the discontinuity of the church's time and the time of Jesus' immediate presence to the apostles, there is no straightforward continuity between the freedom of the prophets and apostles and the freedom of the church. There is no apostolic succession except in the unrepeatable, unanticipated event of the fulfillment of Christ's promise to be with the church as it exists as witness in the world.

> If it is true and has been fulfilled, then in the freedom of their faith and witness the prophets and apostles are copies attesting the freedom of Jesus Christ himself, but at the same time they are prototypes attesting the freedom of all human faith and witness in the church founded by their Word. In their freedom, the church must recognize and honor the freedom of their Lord in which the freedom of its members, as members of his body, is grounded.[71]

Because scripture is the product of the prophets' and apostles' obedience to the one revelation of God in Christ, the freedom of these witnesses is a constitutive aspect of scripture. And here Barth again approaches the question of the possibility and necessity of interpretation we examined in the previous chapter. Whereas there we saw Barth grounding the necessity of interpretation theologically in the divine hiddenness in revelation and in the correspondence between God's concrete

---

[70] *KD* I/2, p. 748 (ET 668).

[71] *KD* I/2, p. 752 (ET 671).

encounter with human beings and the encounter between the one who proclaims God's Word and his audience, here he approaches the question from the point of view of the freedom of the prophets and apostles. Because the testimony of these witnesses is the testimony of free human beings, the authority of scripture does not mean we have to translate their words mechanically into our thought forms. As interpreters, we have to yield to and freely follow the way of prophetic and apostolic witness; we have to encounter the object of their testimony and speak from this object as we have encountered it in their words. And this is possible because scripture enjoys 'a living authenticity; for scripture itself is a really truly living, acting, and speaking subject, which only as such can be truly heard and received by the church in the church'.[72] The concrete and enabling authority of the Word is a matter of the gracious freedom of the Word, and for this reason interpretative authority and freedom in the church, though genuine, can only be conceived and exercised *a posteriori*, as obedience.[73]

In this initial orientation to the discussion of freedom in the church, Barth makes three basic moves. First, he briefly develops the basic point that in confessing that genuine faith and obedience is a reality in the church one necessarily confesses that there is genuine freedom in the church. Freedom in the church means 'man's own choice and decision, determination and resolve', the choosing and deciding of human persons who exist in their acts of self-determination.[74] 'Even obedience is choice and decision, although it is essentially a choice and decision in which the obedient man surrenders his own power to him whom he obeys.'[75] Second, he claims that genuine human freedom in the church is grounded in and limited by the absolute freedom of the Word of God. And third, because he understands scripture to be the product of the prophets' and apostles' free (obedient) witness to the incarnate Word and the instrument by which God rules the church, Barth insists that scripture alone must be heard as the principle of both freedom and authority in the church.

Following these introductory remarks to §21, Barth moves to an explanation and illustration of the freedom of the Word of God, in three parts; he then concludes the paragraph, and thus the doctrine of scripture, with a two-part discussion of freedom under the Word, in which he describes first the Word of God

---

[72] *KD* I/2, p. 753 (ET 672).

[73] More generally, as Alan Torrance rightly stresses, *any* theological indication of the freedom of the Word of God must be *a posteriori*, ventured in faith. On one level, this is simply a matter of logical consistency: an *a priori* assertion of God's freedom would simply be a *de facto* denial of that freedom. Thus Barth's insistence on the formal and material priority of divine freedom, in Torrance's words, must 'repose on an *a posteriori* expression not only of the *facticity* but also of the *nature* of the divine "freedom"' (*Persons in Communion*, p. 50).

[74] *KD* I/2, p. 750 (ET 669).

[75] *KD* I/2, p. 751 (ET 670).

as the foundation of human freedom in the church and then the exercise of this freedom in the church's interpretation and application of scripture.[76]

Barth develops his explanation of the freedom of the Word of God by describing its 'peculiar power'. Scripture, as the witness created by the incarnate Word, has a real, concrete, limiting power in the world. In the time between the resurrection and the *parousia*, scripture as the written Word of God is part of the nexus of creaturely powers in conflict, but its power is 'qualitatively infinitely greater' than those it opposes. This is on the surface quite extraordinary language, inviting both ethical and logical objections: As a logical matter, one can ask the familiar question of how one can assert that there is a genuine conflict between powers that differ qualitatively? And more pressingly, how can one meaningfully claim in view of the uses to which scripture has been put that it has such a power of self-differentiation? For his part, Barth recognizes a tension here but refuses to dissolve it, claiming that it is an eschatological tension that must be respected, and fearing an illegitimate lapse into quietism where it is not. And of course the other possibility—of dissolving the tension by simply identifying scripture as one among many basically equal powers in the world, so that it is in a fundamental sense vulnerable to the vagaries of history—is not a serious option for Barth. But in any case the claim that scripture does in fact engage (really engage) the powers in real sovereignty is not a deduction. It is an exegesis of the promise 'I will be with you', the witnessing church's confession of faith.[77] Here and now, the victory of God over all opposing powers is not obvious. The Word's 'secret but decisive superiority' over all other powers is apprehended only in faith. But it really is apprehended thus. 'The whole truth is that in spite of all appearances to the contrary, holy scripture has more power than all the rest of the world together.'[78]

In faith, the church sees the power of the Word manifest in four ways: the Word defends itself against attack; its resists domestication, distinguishing itself from all (mis)interpretations; it makes alien elements (e.g., various interpretative presuppositions) which it encounters serviceable, assimilating them to its own ends; and it changes its own form and therefore its effect on the world.[79] Together, all this adds up to the basic point that scripture is and continually shows itself to be the true subject of church history, so that the church can know that its history is not 'the history of a self-contained, self-centered church, but a history which on the side of the church and individual members of the church has the character of a *response*, the initiative being always with the Word of God as the first and truly

---

[76] *KD* I/2, pp. 754–79 (ET 673–95) (the freedom of the Word); 779–97 (ET 695–710) (the foundation of freedom in the church); and 797–830 (ET 710–40) (the exercise of freedom in the church).

[77] Cf. *KD* I/2, pp. 767–8 (ET 685).

[78] *KD* I/2, p. 760 (ET 678).

[79] *KD* I/2, pp. 763–7 (ET 680–4).

acting subject'.[80] Again, 'all this is the content of faith in the resurrection of Jesus Christ as the revelation of the controlling beginning and end of the church and the world', so that the theological construal of the power of scripture is unintelligible where language of the effective agency of the risen Christ falls into disrepair.

But as free subject in the power of the resurrected Christ, scripture is free to found, preserve, and rule the church. In founding the church, the Word of God both overrules the sin and sickness which prevents human beings from hearing and obeying and also unifies those who hear, overruling 'the natural diversity of men which has been made disruptive by sin and death'. In preserving the church, scripture draws the church along in its own sovereign movement, evoking the church's prayer and demanding the church's *selbstlosen Aufmerksamkeit*.

> Plainly everything depends on whether the church is in fact what it is supposed to be, that is, the sphere in which man has confidence in the Word alone, and therefore in faith alone, acquiring in this confidence the capacity for that self-forgetful attention which with its will to live, its aggressiveness and wisdom, its conservatism and radicalism, the world as a whole does not have. But the church's being what it is supposed to be depends upon its living in the strength of the Word itself. It depends upon the Word continuing to live in its midst in all its power. It depends, therefore, on the real freedom of the Word for which the church can only pray and be thankful.[81]

The preservation of the church by the sovereign Word also means, because this Word is not available to us apart from the biblical witness of the prophets and apostles, that the church's continuance relies wholly on scripture being read, understood, expounded, and applied [*gelesen, verstanden, ausgelegt, und angewendet*] in the church.

> The criterion whether it is following the Word of God with that self-forgetful attention consists in whether through everything that it says itself, or thinks it has or can receive from scripture, it is able and willing to hear the voice of scripture itself as the final verdict which pronounces true death and true life. The continued life of the church depends, therefore, on whether scripture remains open before its eyes, whether all its conceptions, even the best, remain transparent to its content—so that it can itself confirm and legitimate them, or qualify them, or even completely set them aside.[82]

The church is created and sustained by the Word of God for a purpose, 'the purpose of the divine revelation, and therefore the glory of God and the salvation of humankind'.[83] Concretely, the church exists to testify to the reconciliation and coming redemption of all humankind in Jesus Christ. But it cannot discharge its

---

[80] *KD* I/2, p. 767 (ET 684).

[81] *KD* I/2, p. 773 (ET 690).

[82] *KD* I/2, p. 775 (ET 691).

[83] *KD* I/2, p. 775 (ET 692).

duty simply as it sees fit. The church created and sustained by the Word of God is also *ruled* by the Word, which is to say, it is ruled by scripture. 'To say that Jesus Christ rules the church is equivalent to saying that holy scripture rules the church. The one explains the other, the one can be understood only through the other'.[84]

By this point the hermeneutical consequences of the recognition that scripture is subject rather than object to the church (or, better, it is object as it is subject; it is object on its own terms) will be familiar enough: In the first place we can note the simple fact that the church's interpretative possibilities are basically limited. Because scripture is the organ of the rule of the living Word, whether it speaks or remains silent is a matter of grace and judgment: 'What we call the investigation of holy scripture and its results is not at bottom our efforts and their conclusions, of which we usually think in this connection, but rather the *self-initiating movements of the Word of God himself*.'[85]

> We do not truly appreciate either the light which the church receives from the Bible, or the darkness which enshrouds it from the same source, until we recognize in both, beyond all the human effort and human refusal which is also present, the overruling power of the Word of God itself, either to exalt or to abase. Only then do we realize that we cannot read and understand holy scripture without prayer, that is, without invoking the grace of God. And it is only on the presupposition of prayer that all human effort in this matter, penitence for human failure in this effort, will become serious and effective.[86]

We cannot be too wary of generalizations at this point, but it does seem difficult to overestimate the divergence between this construal of the context and possibilities of scriptural interpretation and those widely assumed in the academy. A clear contrast is perhaps most easily drawn with the interpretative presuppositions embodied in that variously defined set of practices known as historical-critical exegesis, where the stability of the text in itself is assumed as the basic condition of the verifiability of any given interpretation. But the point also applies to those self-consciously postmodern accounts in which the stability of the text is considered to be a factor of readerly persistence.[87] For Barth, the stability of

---

[84] *KD* I/2, p. 776 (ET 693). Note in this connection how Barth develops the character of scripture as witness in terms of Christ's prophetic office: 'The Son of God in his human nature, and therefore as God revealed, allows this revelation of himself, this prophetic office of his, to be continued in the prophetic and apostolic witness to his lordship. In the same way his sovereignty, and therefore the sovereignty of God himself, confronts the church in and through this witness.'

[85] *KD* I/2, p. 766 (ET 684).

[86] *KD* I/2, p. 767 (ET 684).

[87] Cf. Murphy, 'Textual Relativism', p. 270: 'If the texts' ability to perform a definite speech act depends upon the existence of a community with shared convictions and proper dispositions, then textual stability is in large measure a function, not of theories of

the text as text is important, but the verification of any given interpretation is to be understood in theological terms and articulated in part through a theological construal of the history of the church. Scripture itself verifies the appropriateness of the church's reading in any given time and place, and does so either by withdrawing from the church or by giving itself to the church in the manner most appropriate to the church's immediate needs. And for Barth the church's interpretative interests and dispositions are also important, but his stress on penitence and invocation can hardly be understood as identity-shaping practices of the virtuous reader. That prayer attends exegesis at every step involves the recognition that to read scripture is to expose oneself to the most radical disruption and reorientation, to enter a relationship in which the most refined and profound moral commitments are subject to judgment.

Of course this reference to grace and prayer is not a way of avoiding personal responsibility for one's own interpretative work, any more than a proper recognition of the authority of other voices in the church means an abdication of one's own responsibilities. Indeed, having indicated the limits of the church's interpretative work in speaking of the absolute freedom of scripture in the church, Barth immediately goes on to conclude his sketch of the doctrine of scripture by defining freedom in the church under the Word as the willingness and readiness to assume responsibility for the interpretation and application of scripture. And as the freedom of the Word to found, preserve, and govern the church is the grace for which the church must pray, the same applies *a fortiori* to the church's freedom responsibly to expound and interpret scripture. Freedom under the Word is a gift of divine mercy; we are made responsible in being made free. And the characteristic exercise of this freedom—*die Urform aller menschlichen Freiheitsakte*—is prayer. For while, like all other constituent acts of interpretation, prayer is an act of human freedom, it is 'the one free act of man in which he confesses that the initiative lies with the freedom of God rather than with his own freedom'.

> Whatever else can and must happen in the special responsibility laid upon the members of the church for the understanding of scripture, at least there must always happen in it that which actually does happen in prayer: confession and faith, awestruck shrinking and comforted appropriation, in which faith and appropriation are only obedience to the grace which always precedes and which only as such will constantly suggest the confession and shrinking. And it hardly needs be said that it is true everywhere that the judgment whether all this happens rightly does not belong to us, that our freedom is only true freedom when the Holy Spirit intercedes for us to enable us to accomplish what of our own resources we certainly cannot do.[88]

---

interpretation, but of how interpretative communities choose to live' (original emphasis removed).

[88] See *KD* I/2, p. 782 (ET 698).

It is only at this point—after characterizing human freedom in terms of prayer, so that interpretative freedom can never be exercised in opposition to the Word—that Barth considers the form of the church's freedom before scripture. The discussion includes three basic moves: First, Barth characterizes human freedom in the church as taking responsibility for the exposition and application of scripture.[89] Second, Barth develops some ramifications of the claim that the fundamental form of responsible scriptural exegesis is the free subordination of all human concepts to scripture.[90] And third, he offers a description of the individual phases (observation, reflection and appropriation) of the one interpretative act.[91] We will briefly trace each of these moves in turn.

Taking responsibility for the exposition and application of scripture means taking responsibility for the future being of the church, 'and this means in concrete terms that we are responsible participants in the great event by which holy scripture lives and rules in the church and in the world'.[92] This participation is not self-evident; we are involved in both the mystery of the incarnation and in Jesus Christ's exercise of his prophetic office through the witnesses he called and commissioned, and both the original movement of revelation and our participation in it are utterly free acts of grace. But if we cannot manufacture our responsible participation in this mystery, neither can we avoid it. All we can do is obey and attempt to clarify our obedience to ourselves and to others by asking what our responsibility entails.

We can do so only by returning again to the fact that God has been pleased to rule the church and the world in human words, and so in words that must be explained (*erklärt*). As the Word of God, scripture is clear and needs no explanation; this 'objective perspicuity' is not something for which we are responsible, but is the presupposition of our responsibility. But in scripture God's Word assumes the form of human words, and human words are ambiguous—not, as a rule, for the speaker, but always for the hearer. And this is why all human words must be interpreted.

This interpretation [*Erklärung*] involves exposition [*Auslegung*] and application [*Anwendung*]. Exposition means establishing the sense intended by the speaker; application means communicating this intended sense to the hearer, so that the words are understood as intended. In many cases, this interpretation can be performed by the hearer herself; in others the speaker is available to clarify his intentions. A third party (and this is what the preacher and thus also the dogmatic

---

[89] *KD* I/2, pp. 797–801 (ET 710–15).

[90] *KD* I/2, pp. 802–9 (ET 715–22).

[91] See *KD* I/2, pp. 811–15 (ET 722–7) (observation [*Beobachtung, Auslegung, explicatio*]); 815–25 (727–36) (reflection [*Nachdenken, Mitdenken, Mitnehmen, Assimilieren, meditatio*]); 825–30 (ET 736–40) (appropriation [*Aneignung, Mitwissen, applicatio*]).

[92] *KD* I/2, p. 797 (ET 711).

theologian are in relation to the Bible and to the church and world) is not always necessary, even on a human level. Simply as a matter of the normal communicative patterns of daily life there is such a thing as self-interpretation. And again, the clarity of scripture on this level is a presupposition of the interpretative work carried out by the preacher and the theologian.

Scriptural interpretation in the narrower sense—as the responsible involvement of the third party—begins where this clarity ends. Here the interpreter must attempt to illuminate the sense of scripture and communicate to the hearer or reader that and to what extent the *Schriftwort* has a sense for her, too. And in this sense, the responsibility for scriptural interpretation is laid upon every member of the church.[93]

The basic form of this responsible *Schrifterklärung* is the subordination of all human concepts, thoughts, and convictions (or images, ideas, and certainties) to scripture.[94] As sinful creatures, we inevitably obscure God's Word with our concepts; and while we cannot avoid this, we must recognize the basically problematic character of our concepts and surrender them as required (Barth here cites Isa. 40.12ff and 50.7ff.). It is important that as a relational concept subordination cannot mean abandonment. We cannot step outside ourselves and must not try to do so. (God's Word in scripture meets us in the movements of our intellectual life, and to try to purify ourselves completely from our admittedly problematic concepts and convictions would mean attempting to side-step God's saving judgment.)[95] Subordination may entail the abandonment of some concepts, the revision of others, and perhaps the addition of still others. But the main point is that in practice we give scripture axiomatic priority over all our ideas. Scriptural exegesis rests on the assumption that the message which scripture has to give us, even in its apparently most debatable and least assimilable parts, is in all circumstances truer and more important than the best and most necessary things that we ourselves have said or can say.[96]

And the basis of this subordination—'the principal rule of all scriptural interpretation'—is to be inferred from the *content* of scripture.

> The content of the Bible, the object of its witness, is Jesus Christ as the name of the God who deals graciously with man the sinner. To hear and then to understand its witness

---

[93] *KD* I/2, p. 801 (ET 714): 'Die ganze Kirche die Organisation eben dieses Vermittlungsdienstes ist'.

[94] *KD* I/2, p. 802–3 (ET 715–16). To the obvious objection, note at once p. 802 (ET 715): 'Subordination does not stand in opposition to freedom!' For while freedom involves self-determination, it does not necessarily involve superiority or even reciprocity. 'If there is an object in regard to which any other activity is excluded, why should not human activity towards it not consist in man's putting himself under it without simultaneously putting himself over it?' And in fact God's Word in scripture is such an object.

[95] Cf. *KD* I/2, p. 808 (ET 720–1).

[96] *KD* I/2, p. 806 (ET 719).

means: to realize the fact that the relation between God and man is such that God is gracious to man, to man who needs him, who as a sinner is thrown wholly upon God's grace, who cannot earn God's grace, and for whom it is indissolubly connected with God's gracious action towards him, for whom therefore it is decisively one with the name of Jesus Christ as the name of the God who acts graciously towards him. To hear this is to hear the Bible—both as a whole and in each one of its separate parts. Not to hear this means *eo ipso* not to hear the Bible, neither as a whole nor therefore in any of its parts. The Bible says all sorts of things, certainly; but in all this multiplicity and variety, it says in truth only one thing—just this: the name of Jesus Christ, concealed under the name Israel in the Old Testament, revealed under his own name in the New Testament, which therefore can be understood only as it has understood itself, as a commentary on the Old Testament. The Bible becomes clear when it is clear that it says this one thing: that it proclaims the name Jesus Christ and therefore proclaims God in his richness and mercy, and man in his need and helplessness, yet living on what God's mercy has given and will give him. The Bible remains dark to us if we do not hear in it this sovereign name, and if, therefore, we think we perceive God and man in some other relation than the one determined once for all by this name. Interpretation stands in the service of the clarity which the Bible as God's Word makes for itself; and we can properly interpret the Bible, in whole or part, only when we perceive and show that what it says is said from the point of view of that concealed and revealed name of Jesus Christ, and therefore in testimony to the grace of which we as men stand in need, of which as men we are incapable, and of which we are made participants by God. From this is to be inferred the basic principle of the subordination of our ideas, thoughts, and convictions to the testimony of scripture itself.[97]

This sort of language has given rise to the fairly widespread objection that 'Barth reinforces the conservative, biblicistic tendency to polarize submission to the authority of scripture and an allegedly arrogant refusal of that submission engendered by loyalty to one or other of the passing trends of the modern world'.[98] The concern is partly about Barth's rhetoric, which sometimes seems to run ahead of his deepest theological convictions. But it should be clear by now that the issue is finally a material one, having to do with the appropriateness of Barth's soteriological sensibilities. One may well question how far Barth can deploy the language of 'subordination' without trailing off into some abstract cultural defensiveness. But the more fundamental question is whether Barth is right to say that 'our own ideas, thoughts, and convictions as such, as ours' run counter to scripture precisely because as sinners we are infinitely invested in securing ourselves from the gracious judgment that scripture wishes us to hear and understand.

Finally, we arrive at Barth's description of the three moments in the one movement of scriptural interpretation—viz., observation, reflection, and

---

[97] *KD* I/2, p. 807 (ET 720).

[98] Thus Francis Watson, *Text, Truth and World. Biblical Interpretation in Theological Perspective* (Edinburgh, 1994), p. 231.

appropriation. In brief: Observation involves what Barth calls a literary-historical investigation of the text; reflection, the process by which what is said in the text becomes what is thought by the reader (who brings to the texts presuppositions radically opposed to scripture); and appropriation or assimilation, the reader's consent to the scriptural message, including her putting it into practice and passing it along as her own.

Perhaps surprisingly enough, given our present interests, a thorough treatment of this material seems largely unnecessary. For without needlessly downplaying the significance of the material, we can say that there is little in it that is really new. Barth clarifies his understanding of some exegetical mechanics and introduces some technical vocabulary in the course of bringing together the basic themes (historical attentiveness, strict objectivity, and so on) that have informed the entire discussion. But he does not make any unprecedented moves. And this is especially true of the way in which he speaks about the reality and character of human agency as it is exercised in the observation of, reflection upon, and appropriation of the scriptural text. In speaking of observation, Barth stresses that we must be open to the text, willing to encounter something unexpected; in speaking of reflection, that we must deploy our interpretative schemes freely, but freely because provisionally, circumspectly, strategically, and relevantly, always remembering that scripture retains its freedom over our conceptions and that we therefore are free from the tyranny of unjustified presuppositions; and in speaking of appropriation, that because scripture exercises its freedom to rule the church, we need not direct our attention away from it in order to discern the cultural conditions which it must address if we are to make good use of it:

> If the church is the assembly of those who hear the Word of God, in the last resort this necessarily means (for what would the hearing amount to otherwise?) the assembly of those who make use of it. But this, too, can mean only the assembly of those who are ready and willing that the Word of God on its part should make use of them.... [I]nstead of our making use of scripture at every stage, it is scripture itself which uses us—the *usus scripturae* in which *scriptura* is not object but subject, and the hearer and reader is not subject but object.[99]

All this adds up to the claim that '*faith—obedient* faith, but faith, and in the last resort obedient faith alone—is the activity which is demanded of us as members of the church, the exercise of the freedom which is granted to us under the Word'.[100] It is not insignificant that in these concluding pages to his doctrine of scripture, as Barth attempts to lay out some of the ways in which this faith expresses itself as it takes up the concrete task of interpreting scripture in the church, that he understands this one complex act to involve observation, reflection, and

---

[99] *KD* I/2, p. 829 (ET 737–8).
[100] *KD* I/2, p. 830 (ET 740).

appropriation. But the actual form of these proposals is in some ways less important than the fact that they are represented as only some of the ways in which the church can freely and appropriately respond to the gracious speaking of God in scripture, and that they are not intended to be of independent interest otherwise.

Summary

What does it mean to say that for Barth scriptural interpretation is an act of obedience? In the first place, it is to say that interpretation is a relational concept (or, perhaps better, an interpersonal event), one that it involves a determined order of precedence and consequence. Interpretation is not an act of unconstrained creativity, but an act in which the interpreter is fundamentally responsive. It is true that the concrete shape of this response cannot be anticipated. The mystery of God's rule—the sheer miracle of grace in which the church becomes a truly obedient community of witness in the world—precludes any final theoretical answer to the question of what exactly the church's interpretation should look like in any given case. But this is the mystery of obedience, not the sheer novelty of the self-asserting subject.

Put otherwise, our interpretative deliberations can only open up to a reality preceding us. And as this reality is available to us only on its own terms, our response to it must be enabled and ordered by this reality itself. This means that a theological description of the act of scriptural interpretation will not be absorbed into more general considerations of the cognitive processes involved in understanding as such, the social dynamics of textual negotiation, the capabilities of language and of texts to mediate meaning, and so on. Any hermeneutical discussion centered on the inherent capacities of the reading subject and the textual medium are, to Barth's mind, simply inattentive to the prevailing activity of the triune God who brings it about in his own time that this relationship and not another exists between this text and its readers. So on Barth's account, the primary thing to be said about the interpretation of scripture is that it is dependent wholly upon a logically and indeed materially prior hearing that, being coincident with the forgiveness of sins, is to be explicated in soteriological rather than abstractly hermeneutical terms.

Again, any construal of the church's interpretative work must reckon with the reality of the church as the agent of this particular action. And Barth repeatedly insists that we simply cannot adequately speak of this reality without constant reference to the work of the risen Christ who establishes and sustains the church entirely by his own command and promise. The language of obedience in Barth's doctrine of scripture serves to underscore this point: The question is not simply how this particular reading community is to live freely in the world with a set of texts which are in some sense authoritative for it. This question, Barth suggests, assumes that the church simply is a community of this sort, whose existence we can assume or, if pressed, ground self-referentially. But if the church really is what Christ promises it will be and commands it to be—the prophetic-apostolic community of effective witness between the times—then such self-establishment is nothing other than a contradiction of the church's own being, a self-justification which is wholly and quite literally inexplicably foreign to God's reconciling presence in Jesus Christ. And no discussion of the church's interpretative practices, however philosophically sophisticated, politically aware, or historically nuanced, can meaningfully address the reality of the situation where the sheer contingency of the church's existence in the world goes unrecognized. Further, if the most concrete form of this recognition is prayer, the church must also continually give explicit theological account of the truth that it exists as the church only in dependence on the Word that it has heard and expects to hear in scripture.

Thus the grounds of the church's scriptural interpretation are identical with its character and its limits, and we find that while we have taken a somewhat different course in this chapter from that of the previous chapter, we have inevitably arrived at the same place: The church's hearing of the Word and the work of scriptural interpretation that attends it are finally to be understood as realities in the life of the people of the God who wills to be our gracious Lord in the humility of the incarnation, in the glory of the resurrection, and in the outpouring of the Spirit; who has chosen to rule his church through the written witness of the prophets and apostles, in a determinate, canonical text which represents formally his own material sovereignty and objectivity over the church; who has chosen to be present to the world through the church's scripture-based proclamation; and who, while choosing to reserve for himself the prerogative of judging the adequacy of this proclamation, allows his church to live towards this judgment in prayer and in dogmatic self-reflection. Of course there is room here for consideration of the intellectual and social processes that attend the church's reading of scripture, and we have seen some of the ways in which Barth undertakes such considerations. But we have also seen that Barth's account is nowhere directed towards the improvement of the church's self-governance, whether through the church's correlation of its self-understanding with received accounts of the interpretative qualities of our humanity or otherwise. Rather, he undertakes in the service of the church's proclamation a dogmatic description of the church's interpretation of scripture which is everywhere focused on the commanding, liberating act of the triune God before whom the church lives by its faithful obedience.

Conclusion

We began this study by advertising its limitations. Now, at its conclusion, they will be more apparent than ever. But perhaps despite them something of the distinctiveness and suggestiveness of Barth's theology of interpretation has come into view.

Much remains to be done. This is in every sense a preliminary work, opening up lines of inquiry that require far more extensive and nuanced treatment than they have received here. And, of course, the textual basis for research in this field continues to grow: As the complete set of Barth's exegetical lectures from the 1920s and 1930s become available, for example, new light will be cast on the whole complex of questions with which we have been occupied, and new connections will need to be drawn.

Further, renewed attention will need to be paid to the constructive potential of this material. Hints in this direction have been scattered throughout the exposition offered here, and while they have not been worked out systematically, they may at least indicate some ways in which Barth may continue to prove an important resource for contemporary reflection on the theological interpretation of scripture.

We have observed, for example, the priority of exegesis over hermeneutics in Barth. On a general methodological level, this reflects a fairly relaxed sense that human communication is not an unnatural act. More closely: People read, and generally read well. Theorizing follows, as occasion demands, but hermeneutical rules are primarily descriptive, simply reminding us how good readers have read the texts in which we are interested. From this perspective the best way to capture what Barth is up to hermeneutically is to attend to his actual exegesis—to track carefully the moves he makes when commenting on scripture, either in his exegetical lectures or in the excursuses of the *Church Dogmatics*.[1] This is, I think, advice we still need to hear. The tendency towards methodological abstraction remains with us, and Barth's instincts in this regard can at least remind us that this tendency is not an inevitability.

But this emphasis on the relative priority of exegesis and the consequent refusal to allow himself to be caught up in methodological abstractions also reflects

---

[1] This is of course the approach most closely, though not exclusively, associated with Hans Frei and those directly influenced by him. See, for example, McGlasson, *Jesus and Judas*; Cunningham, *What is Theological Exegesis?*; further David Ford, *Barth and God's Story. Biblical Narrative and the Theological Method of Karl Barth in the Church Dogmatics* (Frankfurt, 1985).

Barth's sense that the church's interpretative work (whether we are actually explaining a scriptural text or reflecting on our interpretative practices) is at once grounded and limited by scripture's self-presentation. A theological interpretation of scripture assumes from the start that the Bible speaks for itself, and it does so as it is taken up by God in service of his saving self-communication to sinful humanity. Methodological rigidity at this point would reflect a material theological presumption: To place our confidence in a procedure would be to anticipate the terms on which scripture must come to us. Conversely, where confidence is placed in the God who opens blind eyes and unstops deaf ears, a recognition of the relativity of all our procedural refinements follows. As we have seen, in Barth's case this theological conviction about scripture's freedom and authority in the church issues in a tactical call for a certain conceptual restlessness. But the underlying point is that a recognition of the sheer priority of divine action in scripture (brought to expression in the doctrines of election and justification) invites an active methodological humility.[2]

It will be clear from all this that Barth's account of the freedom of scriptural interpretation from hermeneutical distraction involves a particular understanding of what scripture is. The key term here, present throughout Barth's work and massively developed in the first volume of the *Church Dogmatics*, is 'witness'. Scripture is witness to divine revelation. Used in this sense, 'witness' has for Barth something very like ontological force: Scripture is not in the first instance a 'text' of one sort or another, so that general considerations about the capacities of texts to generate or to constrain meaning straightforwardly apply. In this sense, the question of how scripture is like every other text simply misses the force of Barth's argument. What scripture is is determined not by its evident resemblance to other cultural productions, but by its relationship to God's Word. And in that this Word is entirely free, we cannot presume that scripture is available to us for interpretation—that we stand unproblematically in a relationship to scripture which we can ground and maintain self-referentially. Scripture is, in the most basic sense, only as and where God sees fit to take up human language—the words of the prophets and apostles—into his service. A recognition of this freedom of the Word over the scriptural witness does not mean that the church is free to occupy a space between the words of the Bible and the Word of God, and to leverage a systematic critique of scripture's 'ideology' or 'worldview' from this location; all such mitigations of scriptural authority are entirely foreign to Barth's theology. But it does mean that scripture can never be understood as a product of the church's

---

[2] See in this connection the preface to Barth, *Erklärung des Philipperbriefes* (Zürich, 1947) (ET *The Epistle to the Philippians*): Continuity of interpretative aim, where the aim is to serve the self-presentation of God's Word in scripture, involves a procedural fluidity. A lack of methodological self-consciousness is not necessarily a virtue. But a healthy sense of the limits of method is.

appropriation of just these religiously and culturally implicated texts.[3] Scripture has its being in an event of unanticipated grace—the turning of God to his people—a condescension to which the church can only respond in gratitude, recognizing and indicating but never constituting scripture's reality in the economy of salvation.

This sense of scripture's freedom and authority corresponds to a very particular anthropology of reading. Again, the doctrine of election occupies a high profile in Barth's account: That we are in fact readers of scripture is by no means self-evident; it is a function of God's free decision. To recognize ourselves as those to whom scripture addresses itself involves a confession of the triune God's mercy and patience and wisdom. This God has determined to be present to the world in Jesus Christ and in the witnesses of his choosing. The Spirit of Christ who spoke through the prophets and apostles speaks to us in scripture and thereby establishes and rules the church. This church exists under scripture as a community of witness and service in the world. And as I am united to Christ in the Spirit I too can and must take up the church's witness as my own. In short, as readers of scripture we find ourselves already within the field of God's gracious activity, and we recognize that this is not a space we have created or can create for ourselves (in this sense, too, the context of scriptural interpretation is to be described theologically from beginning to end).

All this clearly involves a theological articulation of our limitations as readers of scripture, not least a denial of those strong claims to readerly self-availability characteristic of more familiar hermeneutical models. Barth simply resists the assumption that we are competent to finally expose and overcome the most significant forms of spiritual distortion that lie at the heart of our misreadings of scripture. All that we perceive as the progressive purification of our interpretative interests and aims finally stands under the judgment that God reserves for himself.[4] God's Word alone is finally capable of overthrowing idols; what he requires of and

---

[3] A theological emphasis not immediately clear in more recent exercises in scriptural pragmatics. See the characteristically clear statement in Stephen E. Fowl, *Engaging Scripture* (Oxford, 1998), p. 3: '[T]o identify oneself as a Christian is, at the same time, to bring oneself into a particular sort of relationship to the Bible in which the Bible functions as a normative standard for faith and practice.' On Barth's terms, such talk—and the readerly competence it presumes—is simply incompatible with any real understanding of scripture as witness or of the church as a community of obedience. See further the exchange between Emmanuel Hirsch and Barth as reported in Barth's circular letter of 26 February 1926, an important point of reference in evaluating attempts to align Barth's position to notions of 'figural reading' (*B–Th II*, pp. 41–3 (ET *Revolutionary Theology in the Making. Barth–Thurneysen Correspondence 1914–25*, trans. James D. Smart (London, 1964), pp. 82–4)).

[4] The point is classically made by Irenaeus (*Against Heresies*, 5.25.1): According to scripture, Antichrist, too, is in the business of ideology critique, 'setting aside idols to persuade that he himself is God'; the concentration of our errors is not their elimination.

invites from us is the prayer that he do so, and the work that attends but does not run ahead of that prayer.

This sense of our limitations as readers—our inability to finally see through our interpretative self-interests and to mitigate their effects—follows strictly from the good news that scripture brings to us: We are not our own precisely because we are bought with a price. We are strangers in the world because God has prepared a city for us. So if we must confess our unavailability to ourselves, that follows from a confession that we are entirely clear to the God who has made and sustained and redeemed us; what remain to us impassable obstacles to a responsible inhabitation of the world do not prevent the creator from making common cause with us. More closely, if we cannot position ourselves in relation to scripture, we can confess that God has and will deal faithfully with his church through his Word, and we can pray that he will do so.

Finally, these theological observations on the nature of scripture and the identity of its readers open up to a characterization of the ethics of reading of general relevance. For Barth, in reading scripture as witness to revelation one learns to listen to others with a new persistence and openness and generosity. The resonances with more recent talk of virtuous reading are worth noting; but so are the distinctive ways in which Barth grounds his talk of interpretative humility and patience and confidence. We have explored some of these here; further reading in Barth—not least in later volumes of the *Church Dogmatics*—would open up more opportunities for constructive engagement with what is by any measure a complex, difficult, and rich theology of interpretation.

Bibliography

Primary Sources

'Concluding Unscientific Postscript on Schleiermacher', trans. George Hunsinger, in *The Theology of Schleiermacher. Lectures at Göttingen, Winter Semester of 1923/24*, ed. Dietrich Ritschl, trans. Geoffrey W. Bromiley (Grand Rapids: Eerdmans, 1982), pp. 261–79.

Credo. Die Hauptprobleme der Dogmatik dargestellt im Anschluß an das Apostolische Glaubensbekenntnis (Zürich: EVZ, 1948); ET *Credo. A Presentation of the Chief Problems of Dogmatics With Reference to the Apostles' Creed*, trans. J. Strathearn McNab (New York: Charles Scribner's Sons, 1936).

Das Wort Gottes und die Theologie. Gesammelte Vorträge (Munich: Christian Kaiser Verlag, 1924); ET *The Word of God and the Word of Man*, trans. Douglas Horton (London: Hodder and Stoughton, 1928).

Der Römerbrief (Erste Fassung) 1919, ed. Hermann Schmidt (Zürich: TVZ, 1985).

Die Christliche Dogmatik im Entwurf: Erster Band. Prolegomena zur christlichen Dogmatik 1927, ed. Gerhard Sauter (Zürich: TVZ, 1982).

Die Kirchliche Dogmatik: I. Band: Die Lehre vom Wort Gottes: 1. Halbband (Zürich: TVZ, 1975); ET *Church Dogmatics: Volume I: The Doctrine of the Word of God: Part One*, ed. G.W. Bromiley and T.F. Torrance, trans. G.W. Bromiley (Edinburgh: T&T Clark, 1975).

Die Kirchliche Dogmatik: I. Band: Die Lehre vom Wort Gottes: 2. Halbband (Zürich: TVZ, 1975); ET *Church Dogmatics: Volume I: The Doctrine of the Word of God: Part Two*, ed. G.W. Bromiley and T.F. Torrance, trans. G.T. Thompson and Harold Knight (Edinburgh: T&T Clark, 1956).

Die Kirchliche Dogmatik: 2. Band: Die Lehre von Gott: 2. Halbband (Zürich: Evangelischer Verlag A.G. Zollikon, 1959); ET *Church Dogmatics: Volume II: The Doctrine of God: Part Two*, ed. G.W. Bromiley and T.F. Torrance, trans. G.W. Bromiley et. al. (Edinburgh: T&T Clark, 1957).

Die protestantische Theologie im 19. Jahrhundert. Ihre Vorgeschichte und ihre Geschichte (Zürich: TVZ, 1947); ET *Protestant Theology in the Nineteenth Century. Its Background and History*, new ed. (London: SCM, 2001); *Protestant Thought: From Rousseau to Ritschl* (New York: Harper & Brothers, 1959).

Der Römerbrief 1922 (Zürich: TVZ, 1984); ET *The Epistle to the Romans*, trans. Edwyn C. Hoskyns (London: Oxford University Press, 1933).

Die Schrift und die Kirche, Theologische Studien 22 (Zurich: EVZ, 1947).

Die Theologie Calvins 1922, ed. Hans Scholl (Zürich: TVZ, 1993); ET *The Theology of John Calvin*, trans. Geoffrey W. Bromiley (Grand Rapids: Eerdmans, 1995).

Die Theologie der reformierten Bekenntnisschriften, ed. Eberhard Busch (Zürich: TVZ, 1998); ET *The Theology of the Reformed Confessions*, trans. Darrell L. Guder and Judith J. Guder (Louisville and London: Westminster John Knox Press, 2002).

Die Theologie Schleiermachers. Vorlesung Göttingen Wintersemester 1923/24, ed. Dietrich Ritschl (Zürich: TVZ, 1978); ET *The Theology of Schleiermacher. Lectures at Göttingen, Winter Semester of 1923/24*, trans. Geoffrey W. Bromiley (Grand Rapids: Eerdmans, 1982).

'Erklärung des Jakobusbriefes', (lectures delivered in Göttingen, winter semester 1922/23). Typescript in Karl Barth-Archiv, Basel, Switzerland.

Erklärung des Johannes-Evangeliums, ed. Walther Fürst (Zürich: TVZ, 1999); ET *Witness to the Word. A Commentary on John 1*, trans. Geoffrey W. Bromiley (Grand Rapids: Eerdmans, 1986).

'Erklärung des ersten Petrusbriefes', (lectures delivered in Basel, summer semester 1938). Typescript in Karl Barth-Archiv, Basel, Switzerland.

Erklärung des Philipperbriefes (Zürich: Evangelischer Verlag, 1947); ET *The Epistle to the Philippians. 40th Anniversary Edition*, trans. James W. Leitch (Louisville: Westminster John Knox Press, 2002).

'Fate and Idea in Theology', in H. Martin Rumscheidt (ed.), *The Way of Theology in Karl Barth: Essays and Comments*, Princeton Monograph Series 8 (Allison Park: Pickwick, 1986), pp. 25–61.

Fides Quarens Intellectum. Anselms Beweis der Existenz Gottes im Zusammenhang seines theologischen Programms, ed. Eberhard Jüngel and Ingolf U. Dalferth (Zürich: TVZ, 1981); ET *Anselm: Fides Quarens Intellectum. Anselm's Proof of the Existence of God in the Context of his Theological Scheme*, trans. Ian W. Robertson (Richmond: John Knox Press, 1960).

'The First Commandment as an Axiom of Theology', in Rumscheidt (ed.), *The Way of Theology in Karl Barth: Essays and Comments*, pp. 63–78.

Homiletik. Wesen und Vorbereitung der Predigt (Zürich: TVZ, 1970); ET *Homiletics*, trans. Geoffrey W. Bromiley and Donald E. Daniels (Louisville: Westminster John Knox Press, 1991).

Karl Barth–Emil Brunner Briefwechsel 1916–1966, ed. Eberhard Busch et. al. (Zürich: TVZ, 2000).

Karl Barth–Eduard Thurneysen Briefwechsel. Band 1: 1913–1921, ed. Eduard Thurneysen (Zürich: TVZ, 1973); *Band 2: 1921–1930*, ed. Eduard Thurneysen (Zürich: TVZ, 1974); *Band 3: 1930–1935*, ed. C. Algner (Zürich: TVZ, 2000).

Karl Barth–Martin Rade. Ein Briefwechsel, ed. Christoph Schwöbel (Gütersloh: Gütersloher Verlagshaus Gerd Mohn, 1981).

Letzte Zeugnisse, ed. Eberhard Busch (Zürich: EVZ, 1969); ET *Final Testimonies*, trans. Geoffrey W. Bromiley (Grand Rapids: Eerdmans, 1977).

Revolutionary Theology in the Making. Barth Thurneysen Correspondence 1914–25, trans. James D. Smart (London: Epworth, 1964).

Unterricht in der Christlichen Religion: Erster Band. Prolegomena, ed. Hannelotte Reiffen (Zürich: TVZ, 1985); *Zweiter Band. Die Lehre von Gott/Die Lehre vom Menschen 1924/1925*, ed. Hinrich Stoevesandt (Zürich: TVZ, 1990); ET *The Göttingen Dogmatics. Instruction in the Christian Religion, Volume I*, trans. Geoffrey W. Bromiley (Grand Rapids: Eerdmans, 1990); *Dritter Band. Die Lehre von der Versöhnung/Die Lehre von der Erlösung 1925/1926*, ed. Hinrich Stoevesandt (Zürich: TVZ, 2003).

Secondary Sources

Andrews, Isolde, *Deconstructing Barth: A Study of the Complementary Methods in Karl Barth and Jacques Derrida*, Studies in the Intercultural History of Christianity, 99 (Frankfurt a/M: Peter Lang, 1996).

Augustine, *On Christian Teaching,* trans. R.P.H. Green (Oxford: Oxford University Press, 1997).

Balthasar, H.U. von, *Karl Barth. Darstellung und Deutung seiner Theologie* (Köln: Verlag Jakob Hegner, 1951); ET *The Theology of Karl Barth. Exposition and Interpretation*, trans. Edward T. Oakes, S.J. (San Francisco: Ignatius Press, 1992).

Becker, Carl L., *The Heavenly City of the Eighteenth-Century Philosophers* (New Haven and London: Yale University Press, 1932).

Berkouwer, G.C., *The Triumph of Grace in the Theology of Karl Barth*, trans. Harry R. Boer (Grand Rapids: Eerdmans, 1956).

Bernstein, Richard J., *Beyond Objectivism and Relativism. Science, Hermeneutics and Praxis* (Philadelphia: University of Pennsylvania Press, 1983).

———, 'Judging—the Actor and the Spectator', in *Philosophical Profiles: Essays in a Pragmatic Mode* (Cambridge: Polity, 1986), pp. 221–37.

Bormann, Claus v., 'Hermeneutik I. Philosophisch-theologisch', in Gerhard Müller, (ed.), *Theologische Realenzyklopädie* (Berlin and New York: Walter de Gruyter, 1986), 15:108–37.

Bourgine, Benoît, *L'Herméneutique Théologique de Karl Barth. Exégèse et dogmatique dans le quatrième volume de la* Kirchliche Dogmatik (Leuven: Leuven University Press, 2003).

Bowie, Andrew, *From Romanticism to Critical Theory. The Philosophy of German Literary Theory* (London: Routledge, 1997).

———, 'Introduction' to Friedrich Schleiermacher, *Hermeneutics and criticism and other writings*, trans. and ed. Andrew Bowie (Cambridge: Cambridge University Press, 1998), pp. vii–xxxii.

Boyd, Ian R., *Dogmatics among the Ruins. German Expressionism and the Enlightenment as Contexts for Karl Barth's Theological Development* (Bern: Peter Lang, 2004).

Brunner, Emil, *Die Mystik und das Wort. Der Gegensatz zwischen moderner Religionsauffassung und christlichen Glauben dargestellt an der Theologie Schleiermachers* (Tübingen: J.C.B. Mohr (Paul Siebeck), 1924).

Bultmann, Rudolf, *History and Eschatology. The Presence of Eternity* (New York: Harper & Brothers, 1957).

Burnett, Richard, *Karl Barth's Theological Exegesis*, WUNT Series 2, 145 (Tübingen: Mohr Siebeck, 2001).

Busch, Eberhard, *Die Anfänge des Theologen Karl Barth in seinen Gottinger Jahren*, Göttinger Universitätsreden 83 (Göttingen: Vandenhoeck & Ruprecht, 1987).

————, *Karl Barth. His life from letters and autobiographical texts*, trans. John Bowden (Philadelphia: Fortress, 1976).

Carlen, Claudia (ed.), *The Papal Encyclicals 1878–1903* (Raleigh: The Pierian Press, 1990).

The Catechism of the Catholic Church (Chicago: Loyola University Press, 1994).

Clark, Gordon H., *Karl Barth's Theological Method* (Philadelphia: The Presbyterian and Reformed Publishing Company, 1963).

Colwell, John E., 'Perspectives on Judas: Barth's Implicit Hermeneutic', in A.N.S. Lane (ed.), *Interpreting the Bible. Historical and theological studies in honour of David F. Wright* (Leicester: Apollos, 1997), pp. 163–79.

Congar, Yves M.-J., *Tradition and Traditions. An historical and a theological essay*, trans. M. Naseby and T. Rainborough (New York: Macmillan, 1967).

Crites, Stephen, 'A Respectful Reply to the Assertorical Theologian', in Stanley Hauerwas and L. Gregory Jones (eds), *Why Narrative? Readings in Narrative Theology* (Grand Rapids: Eerdmans, 1989), pp. 293–302.

Cunningham, Mary Kathleen, *What is Theological Exegesis? Interpretation and Use of Scripture in Barth's Doctrine of Election* (Valley Forge: Trinity Press International, 1995).

Dalferth, Ingolf U., 'Karl Barth's eschatological realism', in S.W. Sykes (ed.), *Karl Barth: Centenary Essays* (Cambridge: Cambridge University Press, 1989), pp. 14–45.

Demson, David, *Hans Frei and Karl Barth. Different Ways of Reading Scripture* (Grand Rapids and Cambridge: Eerdmans, 1997).

Denzinger, Henry, *Enchiridion Symbolorum* (Freiburg: Herder & Co., 1954); ET *The Sources of Catholic Dogma*, trans. Roy J. Deferrari (St. Louis and London: B. Herder Book Co., 1957).

Dilthey, W., *Der Aufbau der Geschichtlichen Welt in den Geisteswissenschaften*, ed. Berhard Groethuysen, *Gesammelte Schriften*, vol. 7 (Stuttgart: B.G. Teubner, 1958).

Dorrien, Gary, *The Remaking of Evangelical Theology* (Louisville: Westminster John Knox Press, 1998).

Dupré, Louis, *Passage to Modernity. An Essay in the Hermeneutics of Nature and Culture* (New Haven and London: Yale University Press, 1993).

Erasmus, Desiderius, *The Praise of Folly*, trans. Clarence H. Miller (New Haven and London: Yale University Press, 1979).

Fish, Stanley, *Is There a Text in This Class? The Authority of Interpretative Communities* (Cambridge, MA and London: Harvard University Press, 1980).

Fisher, Simon, *Revelatory Positivism? Barth's Earliest Theology and the Marburg School* (Oxford: Oxford University Press, 1988).

Ford, David, *Barth and God's Story. Biblical Narrative and the Theological Method of Karl Barth in the Church Dogmatics* (Frankfurt: Peter Lang, 1985).

Frei, Hans, 'Afterward: Eberhard Busch's Biography of Karl Barth', in H. Martin Rumscheidt (ed.), *Karl Barth in Re-View: Posthumous Works Reviewed and Assessed* (Pittsburgh: Pickwick, 1981), pp. 95–116.

———, 'The Doctrine of Revelation in the Thought of Karl Barth, 1909–1922' (unpublished doctoral thesis, Yale University, 1956).

———, *The Eclipse of the Biblical Narrative. A Study in Eighteenth and Nineteenth Century Hermeneutics* (New Haven: Yale University Press, 1974).

Gadamer, Hans-Georg, *Hermeneutik I. Warheit und Methode. Grundzüge einer philosophischen Hermeneutik, Gesammelte Werke, Band 1* (Tübingen: J.C.B. Mohr (Paul Siebeck), 1986); ET *Truth and Method*, ed. Garrett Barden and John Cumming (New York: Seabury Press, 1975).

———, *Hermeneutik II. Warheit und Methode. Ergänzungen, Register, Gesammelte Werke, Band 2* (Tübingen: J.C.B. Mohr (Paul Siebeck), 1986).

Glick, G. Wayne, *The Reality of Christianity. A Study of Adolf von Harnack as Historian and Theologian* (New York: Harper & Row, 1967).

Greive, Wolfgang, *Die Kirche als Ort der Warheit. Das Verständnis der Kirche in der Theologie Karl Barths* (Göttingen: Vandenhoeck & Ruprecht, 1991).

Gunton, Colin, *Enlightenment and Alienation. An Essay towards a Trinitarian Theology* (Grand Rapids: Eerdmans, 1985).

Hart, John W., *Karl Barth vs. Emil Brunner. The Formation and Dissolution of a Theological Alliance, 1916–1936*, Issues in Systematic Theology, 6 (New York: Peter Lang, 2001).

Hauerwas, Stanley, *Unleashing the Scripture. Freeing the Bible from Captivity to America* (Nashville: Abingdon Press, 1993).

Henry, David Paul, *The Early Development of the Hermeneutic of Karl Barth as Evidenced by His Appropriation of Romans 5:12–21* (Macon: Mercer University Press, 1985).

Hunsinger, George, 'Beyond Literalism and Expressivism: Karl Barth's Hermeneutical Realism' in *Disruptive Grace. Studies in the Theology of Karl Barth* (Grand Rapids: Eerdmans, 2000), pp. 210–25.

————, *How to Read Karl Barth: The Shape of his Theology* (New York and Oxford: Oxford University Press, 1991).

————, 'Karl Barth's doctrine of the Holy Spirit', in John Webster (ed.), *The Cambridge Companion to Karl Barth*, pp. 177–94.

Irenaeus, *Against Heresies*, in *The Ante-Nicene Fathers*, ed. Alexander Roberts and James Donaldson, vol. 1 (Grand Rapids: Eerdmans, 1956).

Jeanrond, Werner, 'Karl Barth's Hermeneutics', in *Reckoning with Barth: Essays in Commemoration of the Centenary of Karl Barth's Birth*, ed. Nigel Biggar (London and Oxford: Mowbray, 1988), pp. 80–97.

Jehle, Frank, *Ever against the Stream. The Politics of Karl Barth 1906–1968*, trans. Richard and Martha Burnett (Grand Rapids and Cambridge: Eerdmans, 2002).

Jenson, Robert W., *Systematic Theology. Volume 1: The Triune God* (New York and Oxford: Oxford University Press, 1997).

Jüngel, Eberhard, *Karl Barth. A Theological Legacy*, trans. Garrett E. Paul (Philadelphia: Westminster Press, 1986).

Kant, Immanuel, *The Conflict of the Faculties*, trans. Mary J. Gregor (Lincoln: University of Nebraska Press, 1992).

Kershaw, Ian, *Hitler 1886–1936: Hubris* (London: Penguin Books, 1999).

Kirschstein, Helmut, *Der souveräne Gott und die heilige Schrift. Einführung in die Biblische Hermeneutik Karl Barths* (Aachen: Shaker Verlag, 1998).

Kooi, Cornelius van der, 'Karl Barths zweiter Römerbrief und seine Wirkungen', in M. Beintker, C. Link, and M. Trowitsch (eds), *Karl Barth in Deutschland (1921–1935)* (Zürich: TVZ, 2005), pp. 57–75.

Kupisch, Karl, *Karl Barth in Selbstzeugnissen und Bilddokumenten* (Stuttgart/Kiel: J.F. Steinkopf Verlag, 1996).

Laquer, W., *Weimar: A Cultural History, 1918–33* (New York: Perigree, 1980).

Lauster, Jörg, *Prinzip und Methode. Die Transformation des protestantischen Schriftprinzips durch die historische Kritik von Schleiermacher bis zur Gegenwart* (Tübingen: Mohr Siebeck, 2004).

Leslie, Benjamin C., *Trinitarian Hermeneutics. The Hermeneutical Significance of Karl Barth's Doctrine of the Trinity*, American University Studies Series 7: Theology and Religion 66 (New York: Peter Lang, 1991).

MacIntyre, Alasdair, *Three Rival Versions of Moral Enquiry. Encyclopedia, Genealogy and Tradition* (Notre Dame: University of Notre Dame Press, 1990).

Macken, John, *The Autonomy Theme in the* Church Dogmatics: *Karl Barth and His Critics* (Cambridge: Cambridge University Press, 1990).

Marquard, Odo, 'The Question, To What Question Is Hermeneutics The Answer?', trans. Robert M. Wallace, in Darrel E. Christiensen et. al. (eds), *Contemporary German Philosophy, Volume 4* ([n.p.]: The Pennsylvania State University, 1984), pp. 9–31.

Matheny, Paul D., *Dogmatics and Ethics. The Theological Realism and Ethics of Karl Barth's* Church Dogmatics, Studies in the Intercultural History of Christianity 63 (Frankfurt: Peter Lang, 1990).

McClendon, James, *Ethics: Systematic Theology, Volume I* (Nashville: Abingdon Press, 1986).

———, *Doctrine: Systematic Theology, Volume II* (Nashville: Abingdon Press, 1994).

McCormack, Bruce L., *Karl Barth's Critically Realistic Dialectical Theology. Its Genesis and Development 1909–1921* (Oxford: Oxford University Press, 1995).

———, 'The Significance of Karl Barth's Theological Exegesis of Philippians', in Karl Barth, *The Epistle to the Philippians*, pp. v–xxv.

McDowell, John C., 'Theology as Conversational Event: Karl Barth, the Ending of "Dialogue" and the Beginning of "Conversation"', *Modern Theology* 12 (2003): 483–509.

McGlasson, Paul, *Jesus and Judas: Biblical Exegesis in Barth*, American Academy of Religion Academy Series 72 (Atlanta: Scholars Press, 1991).

Molnar, Paul D., *Divine Freedom and the Doctrine of the Immanent Trinity. In Dialogue with Karl Barth and Contemporary Theology* (London: T&T Clark, 2002).

Montaigne, Michel, 'Apology for Raimond Sebond', in *The Essays of Montaigne*, trans. E.J. Trenchmann (New York: Random House, 1954), pp. 368–525.

Mueller-Vollmer, Kurt (ed.), *The Hermeneutics Reader. Texts of the German Tradition from the Enlightenment to the Present* (New York: Continuum, 1985).

Muller, Richard, *Post-Reformation Reformed Dogmatics. Volume 1: Prolegomena* (Grand Rapids: Baker Book House, 1987).

Murphy, Nancey, 'Textual Relativism, Philosophy of Language, and the baptist Vision', in Stanley Hauerwas, Nancey Murphy, and Mark Nation (eds), *Theology without Foundations: Religious Practice and the Future of Theological Truth* (Nashville: Abingdon Press, 1994), pp. 245–70.

O'Hear, Anthony, ed., Verstehen *and Humane Understanding*, Royal Institute of Philosophy Supplement, 41 (Cambridge: Cambridge University Press, 1996).

Palmer, Richard E., *Hermeneutics. Interpretation Theory in Schleiermacher, Dilthey, Heidegger, and Gadamer* (Evanston: Northwestern University Press, 1969).

Proust, Marcel, *On Reading*, trans. and ed. Jean Autret and William Burford (New York: Macmillan, 1971).

Rahner, Karl, 'Scripture and Tradition', in *Theological Investigations. Volume VI: Concerning Vatican Council II*, trans. Karl-H. and Boniface Kruger (London: Darton, Longman & Todd, 1969), pp. 98–112.

Rickman, H.P. (ed.), *W. Dilthey. Selected Writings* (Cambridge: Cambridge University Press, 1976).

Ricoeur, Paul, 'Hermeneutics and the Critique of Ideology', in Brice R. Wachterhauser (ed.), *Hermeneutics and Modern Philosophy* (Albany: State University of New York Press, 1986), pp. 300–39.

Robinson, James, ed., *The Beginnings of Dialectical Theology*, trans. Keith R. Crimm (Richmond: John Knox Press, 1968).

Rolston, Holmes, *A Conservative Looks to Barth and Brunner* (Nashville: Cokesbury Press, 1933).

Rorty, Richard, 'The priority of democracy to philosophy', in *Objectivity, Relativism, and Truth. Philosophical Papers Volume 1* (Cambridge: Cambridge University Press, 1991), pp. 175–97.

Rumscheidt, H. Martin, *Revelation and Theology. An analysis of the Barth-Harnack correspondence of 1923* (Cambridge: Cambridge University Press, 1972).

Runia, Klaas, *Karl Barth's Doctrine of Holy Scripture* (Grand Rapids: Eerdmans, 1981).

Schleiermacher, Friedrich, *Kurze Darstellung des theologischen Studiums*, 2nd edn, in Dirk Schmid (ed.), *Universitätsschriften, Herakleitos, Kurze Darstellung des theologischen Studiums* (Berlin and New York: Walter de Gruyter, 1998), pp. 316–446.

Schmidt, Martin, 'Karl Barth's Geschichte der evangelischen Theologie im 19. Jahrhundert', *Theologische Literaturzeitung* 11 (1950): 654–64.

Schmitt, Carl, *Der Begriff des Politischen* (Berlin: Duncker und Humblot, 1963); ET *The Concept of the Political*, trans. George Schwab (New Brunswick: Rutgers University Press, 1976).

Schnädelbach, Herbert, *Philosophy in Germany 1831–1933*, trans. Eric Matthews (Cambridge: Cambridge University Press, 1984).

Schwöbel, Christoph, 'Trinitätslehre als Rahmentheorie des Christlichen Glaubens', in Wilfred Härle and Dieter Lührmann (eds), *Marburger Jahrbuch Theologie X. Trinität* (Marburg: N.G. Elwert, 1998): 129–54.

Searle, John R., *Speech Acts. An Essay in the Philosophy of Language* (Cambridge: Cambridge University Press, 1970).

Spieckermann, Ingrid, *Gotteserkenntnis. Ein Beitrag zur Grundfrage der neuen Theologie Karl Barths*, Beiträge zur evangelischen Theologie 97 (Munich: Christian Kaiser Verlag, 1985).

Stout, Jeffrey, *The Flight from Authority: reason, morality and the quest for autonomy* (Notre Dame: University of Notre Dame Press, 1981).

Thiselton, Anthony C., *New Horizons in Hermeneutics* (London: HarperCollins, 1992).

Thorne, Philip R., *Evangelicalism and Karl Barth: his reception and influence in North American Evangelical theology* (Pittsburgh: Pickwick, 1995).

Thurneysen, Eduard, 'Karl Barths Theologie der Frühzeit', in *Antwort. Festschrift Karl Barth* (Zürich: Zollikon-Zürich, 1956), pp. 831–64.

Tice, Terrence N., 'Interviews with Karl Barth and Reflections on His Interpretations of Schleiermacher', in James O. Duke and Robert F. Streetman (eds), *Barth and Schleiermacher: Beyond the Impasse?* (Philadelphia: Fortress Press, 1988).

Tillich, Paul, *Perspectives on 19th and 20th Century Theology*, ed. Carl E. Braaten (New York: Harper & Row, 1967).

Torrance, Alan J., *Persons in Communion. An Essay on Trinitarian Description and Human Participation* (Edinburgh: T&T Clark. 1996).

———, 'The Trinity', in John Webster (ed.), *The Cambridge Companion to Karl Barth*, pp. 72–91.

Toulmin, Stephen, *Cosmopolis: the hidden agenda of modernity* (Chicago: University of Chicago Press, 1992).

Vattimo, Gianni, *Beyond Interpretation. The Meaning of Hermeneutics for Philosophy*, trans. David Webb (Stanford: Stanford University Press, 1997).

Ward, Graham, *Barth, Derrida and the Language of Theology* (Cambridge: Cambridge University Press, 1997).

Watson, Francis, *Text, Truth and World. Biblical Interpretation in Theological Perspective* (Edinburgh: T&T Clark, 1994).

Webb, Stephen H., *Re-Figuring Theology. The Rhetoric of Karl Barth* (Albany: State University of New York Press, 1991).

Webster, John, *Barth's Earlier Theology. Four Studies* (London: T&T Clark, 2005).

———, *Barth's Ethics of Reconciliation* (Cambridge: Cambridge University Press, 1995).

———, *Barth's Moral Theology. Human Action in Barth's Thought* (Grand Rapids: Eerdmans, 1998).

———, (ed.), *The Cambridge Companion to Karl Barth* (Cambridge: Cambridge University Press, 2000).

———, 'The dogmatic location of the canon', *Neue Zeitschrift für Systematische Theologie und Religionsphilosophie* 43 (2001): 17–43.

Wilkins, Burleigh Taylor, *Carl Becker. A Biographical Study in American Intellectual History* (Cambridge, MA: The M.I.T. Press and Harvard University Press, 1961).

Williams, Stephen, *Revelation and Reconciliation. A window on modernity* (Cambridge: Cambridge University Press, 1995).

Wood, Charles M., *The Formation of Christian Understanding: An Essay in Theological Hermeneutics* (Philadelphia: Fortress Press, 1981).

Work, Telford, 'Anunciation as Election', *Scottish Journal of Theology* 54 (2001): 285–307.

Index